Canadian Red Cross
Water Safety Services

Water Safety
Instructor Manual

The Canadian
Red Cross Society

The Canadian
Red Cross Society

Canadian Red Cross
Water Safety Services

Water Safety
Instructor Manual

StayWell

StayWell

Printed in the United States of America

Composition by Mosby Electronic Production
Printing/binding by Plus Communications

StayWell
1100 Grundy Lane
San Bruno, CA 94066

International Standard Book Number -0-8151-1499-0

02 03 04 05 / 9 8 7 6 5 4

Acknowledgments

The Canadian Red Cross Society wishes to acknowledge the efforts of the many volunteers and staff involved in the development of this manual. Their commitment to excellence made this manual possible.

Special thank you to the Leadership Advisory Group: Mary Creighton, Janet Dawson, Caroline Gagnon, Rick Graham, Wayne Little, Rae Anne Montague, Gail Stewart-Mores, Joanne Russell, Ray Williams and Louise Wood. Their vision to create a professional and usable instructing resource guided the development of this manual. Their commitment to this vision and unfailing advice as work progressed were truly appreciated.

For their contribution and review, thank you to: Mike Atkinson, Dr. Bill Belanger, Barney Chanda, Beth Clark, Joan Conn, Sharron Crowley, Jacquie Currie, Shelley Dalke, Josianne Dansereau, Janet Dawson, Virginia Edmonds, Tracey Elke, Cathy Forner, Dan Galazka, Caroline Gilbert, Diane Girard, Chris Grose, Angela Henry, Kim Jones, Josee Lanouette, Cindy Lyon, Dr. Larry Maloney, Karen McDonald, Aileen Nauss, the Nova Scotia Water Safety Services Summer Staff, Shane Oatman, Karen O'Neil, Barbara Miles-O'Neil, Brent Page, Parks and Recreation Ontario, Joanne Russell, Dr. Marielle Tousignant and Tom Hodge, Project Manager, Thomas Recreation, Inc.

A special thank you to our manual authors: Sheryl MacMath, for her initial draft of the manual and continued guidance; Louise Wood, for instilling in it a sense of fun, readability, and user-friendliness; and Brent Page, for polishing the final draft.

The Mosby Lifeline staff includes David Culverwell, Senior Vice President; David Dusthimer, Publisher; Claire Merrick, Executive Editor; Ross Goldberg, Editorial Project Manager; Tom Lochhaas, Developmental Writer; Theresa Fuchs, Manufacturing Manager; Elizabeth Rohne Rudder, Design Manager; Deborah Vogel, Project Manager; Mary Drone, Senior Production Editor; and Chris Robinson and Robyn Edwards, Composition Specialists.

Contents

Congratulations on deciding to become a Water Safety Instructor! Being an instructor is being a leader. And being a Water Safety Instructor is being a leader in the *best* water safety program in the world!

The purpose of this manual is to help you become the *best* instructor possible. You can use the manual in many different ways:

- As a guide to your instructor course
- As a reference book
- For review, after the course is over
- As a place to get new teaching ideas

RED CROSS—HOW IT BEGAN

The Red Cross began on a June morning in 1859, in one man's haunting vision of a battlefield strewn with corpses and wounded men left to die in agony, helpless and unattended under the sorching sun of the Italian Lombardy Plain. In a spirit of brotherhood the founder of Red Cross, Henry Dunant, a Swiss businessman, spent 8 days caring for the wounded, regardless of nationality. He was so moved by the unbelievable misery before him that he vowed to enlighten his contemporaries by writing a book, which would become a sensation: *A Memory of Solferino*. Upset by the inadequacy of the care provided for the victims, Dunant invited nations to establish permanent national societies comprised of volunteer medical personnel to supplement the then inadequate army medical services. He organized an international conference in 1863 to promote the protection of those who care for the wounded (medical, ambulance, and hospital personnel), as well as the wounded themselves. Neutrality was to become the cornerstone of the Red Cross organization—a medical worker caring for a victim is not an enemy, but an inviolable being who should be universally respected.

The International Red Cross and Red Crescent Movement's success is due in great part to its universal network. The International Committee of the Red Cross (ICRC), the League of the Red Cross and Red Crescent Societies (League), and at present over 150 National Red Cross and Red Crescent Societies implement its ideals worldwide.

The Water Safety program is unique. That's because it takes every person's needs, interests, and skills into account. Here's how this manual can help:

- *You, The Aquatic Link* gives you an overview of the program's leadership spirit and your role in delivering it to your students.

- *Instructing* starts with a look at the *big* Water Safety program picture— who it's for, what's in it, and how it's set up. It then *presents* things in the order in which you do them: *before* you instruct, *while* you instruct, and *after* you instruct. It's all there, step-by-step, with lots of examples.

- *The Water Safety Program* presents detailed information on each skill in the program. You get *everything* you need to know (e.g., teaching hints, descriptions of the progressions you'll use to instruct, safety tips, the reasons for including what we've chosen to teach). Similar skills are grouped together, and all the facts necessary to learn each skill appear in easy-to-use, summary format.

- *Instructor Worksheets* presents a skill-by-skill listing of the full Water Safety program by level. It covers *AquaTots*, *AquaQuest*, and *AquaAdults*; and it describes the performance criteria for each skill. These are the standards of the program for the students' learning.

Some important reference material is included at the end of the manual. This material is an expansion of the text, (e.g., descriptions of learner characteristics, stroke charts, guiding principles for healthy child development), and all of it will be used at some point in your instructing career.

The Canadian Red Cross, Water Safety Services, believes that changing attitudes *can* reduce drownings and water-related injuries and make Canadians safer in, on, or around the water.

Our success depends on YOU, the instructor. It's really that simple. YOU are the key to the success of our program and to that of your students and to the creation of an environment in which all Canadians have healthy, positive attitudes toward water safety. **YOU are our "aquatic link."**

It's a big load to shoulder, but we know you're up to it! Your commitment begins now.

RED CROSS WATER SAFETY SERVICES AIM AND GOAL

AIM
To prevent water-related injuries and fatalities

GOAL
To reduce drowning and water-related fatalities by providing Canadians with—
- The awareness and knowledge to recognize and avoid dangerous situations.
- The knowledge and skills required to save lives.
- The basic rescue skills to enable them to save others.
- The knowledge and awareness to recognize hazardous environments and equipment in their communities and to provide solutions.

YOU are part of making this happen!

The Leadership Spirit

Leadership Spirit

- You weave injury prevention throughout all your instructing.
- You are committed to the principle of inclusion.
- You are committed to progressive learning.
- You instruct guided by the seven Fundamental Principles of Red Cross.

YOU
The Aquatic Link

- Canadians who Prepare! Stay Safe! Survive! for their water-related activities
- Canadians with water-safe attitudes
- Canadians who intervene to make their communities water safe

Injury Prevention

Humanity

YOU serve your students, not systems. You protect your students' lives and health and, whenever possible, prevent drowning incidents by teaching water safety messages and skills.

Injury prevention is about changing attitudes.

Changing attitudes is about helping students realize there are choices available to them and then giving them the knowledge, skills, and experience to make a wise choice.

When students are able to make wise choices, they can also intervene with friends and family. This intervention takes the Red Cross water safety messages you're teaching into the community.

When incorporating injury prevention in your lessons, use the following three tips or tricks to guide you:

1. Focus on how water-related incidents are *preventable*.
   - Instruct students that there are very few "accidents" but many injuries. Water-related fatalities and injuries are seldom random, unpredictable results of fate, bad luck, or acts of God.
   - Altering personal, equipment and environmental risk factors does reduce the number of incidents.
2. Explore the question *why*.
   - Rather than telling students what's right and what's wrong, provide them with examples and experiences in which they can explore *why* for themselves.
   - Ask, "what would you do in this situation and why?"
   - It's important to let students discover that they have choices of their own.
3. *Experience* choices.
   - Provide a safe environment for students to actually experience, through simulations, the results of a wise and unwise choice.

Leadership

YOU demonstrate leadership by learning something about yourself and the impact your behaviour has on others for creating a positive learning environment.

Red Cross Water Safety in Canada began in 1944 when Dr. R.W.I. Urquart, Chair of the National Committee on First Aid, spoke about the growing concern over the number of injuries and lives lost around water. Red Cross responded by starting a swimming and water safety program in an effort to reduce fatalities.

Although other organizations were involved in swimming instruction, proponents of water safety believed that Red Cross was the best organization to deliver these services to all Canadians.

Red Cross recognized that, along with developing swimming proficiency, it was equally important to focus on prevention through education. A progressive pupil achievement program was developed in 1946, complete with award recognition and certifications at the Junior, Intermediate, and Senior levels. In 1950 a fourth level, Beginner, was added to bridge the gap between nonswimmer and swimmer.

It was also noted that instructor education and training were keys to reducing water-related injuries and providing the leadership personnel to instruct the program. In 1945 the first Red Cross Water Safety Instructor School certified 13 new instructors at the Charlottetown Yacht Club in Prince Edward Island.

In 1981 the program was completely revised with the launch of an eight-level Learn-to-Swim program, known as the *Colour Levels*. This program emphasised continuous evaluation, participant progress cards, and instructor-based evaluation.

In 1990 work began on the Water Safety program's second full revision. It's result was the AquaTots, AquaQuest, and AquaAdults programs launched in 1996. This program provided a continuum for all Canadians, with an instructional emphasis on injury prevention.

INCLUSION

Inclusion is not just about one person, it's about everyone working together.

- It implies teamwork.
  - *YOU work with your students, their parents, your employer, and other instructors to make learning happen.*
- It implies finding and making a place for everyone:
  - *YOU create a positive environment where every student feels accepted.*

*IMPARTIALITY

YOU care for all students alike. You help students solely in accordance with their needs. You help, regardless of nationality, race, religious beliefs, class, or political positions.

*UNIVERSALITY

YOU respect everyone, and your work knows no bounds. You recognize that everyone is equal and that you share special responsibilities and duties in helping your students, parents, colleagues, and employer.

- It implies providing opportunities that are accessible and appropriate.
  - *YOU challenge your students at a level that is appropriate to their abilities.*
- It implies looking through the eyes of your student.
  - *YOU see what your student sees, hears, needs, wants and feels.*

INCLUSION WEDGE

- Persons with disabilities
- Persons with cultural needs
- Older adults
- Economically disadvantaged
- Gender, religion, race

In the past, we found a crack within the program and "wedged" people in—it was a tight fit! The program had been designed to meet the needs of very healthy people with two legs and arms.

INCLUSION WEB

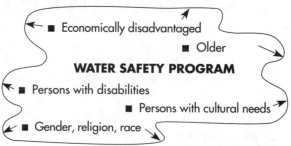

- Economically disadvantaged
- Older
- Persons with disabilities
- Persons with cultural needs
- Gender, religion, race

WATER SAFETY PROGRAM

Today, we design our programs to fit everyone. The program accommodates and shifts.

Remember, the program is only inclusive if YOU have the right "mind set"!

*NEUTRALITY
YOU take initiative, but never sides. All students are able to turn to you with unlimited and total trust. You never play favourites.

PROGRESSIVE LEARNING

Progressive learning is about two things:
- Recognizing *every* student you instruct is *unique*
- Acknowledging that learning is a *journey*, with no real start and no fixed finish.

For each student you instruct, ask yourself how their age, background, natural ability, and personality will affect their learning.

Recognizing that each student is unique means that—
- *YOU understand that people learn at different rates.*
- *YOU understand that a combination of factors, some pre-determined and not easily changed, affect HOW people learn.*
- *YOU plan to allow for these individual factors in every lesson you instruct.*
- *YOU look at learning from the learner's point of view.*

Acknowledging that learning is a journey means that—

> **YOUR STUDENT**
> - A partner in success
> - An active learner
> - Willing to share
> - Helps others feel included
> - Responsible for their own learning and behaviour

- *YOU instruct your students to help them improve, learn, and succeed each and every time they enter the water; to prepare them as the course progresses for a final test rather than notifying them of the test on the last day of a 10-lesson set.*
- *YOU use evaluation to help your students learn; not simply as a judgment tool to "pass" or "fail" them.*

TEACHING
YOU provide accurate program content to reach students in a variety of ways.

EVALUATION
YOU evaluate to assist students in learning and to determine when performance criteria have been met.

- *YOU recognize that participation in one set of lessons (e.g., 10 lessons of 45 minutes each) does not automatically mean all students complete the level. Students learn at a different rates, which, in some cases, will mean that it will take some students more than one set of lessons to complete some levels.*
- *YOU understand that program guidelines regarding recommended class size, class length, and number of lessons are simply guidelines designed to enhance the success of the program and do not guarantee a standard rate of student progress.*

Detailed information on evaluation is found in Chapter 3.

Living the Leadership Spirit

Leadership *makes* the Water Safety program. All the research, messages, and progressions are useless without YOU, the Aquatic Link! You make the program tick!

> CHANGING ATTITUDES
> How do you know when you've changed the water safety attitude of a student? Watch for a change in his or her behaviour in, on, and around the water. That's the key!

Being the aquatic link is a choice. Once you make that choice, you accept certain responsibilities, and you must commit to upholding these responsibilities. Commitment is built by learning what the leadership spirit means to you and applying it in every lesson.

As a Red Cross Water Safety Instructor (WSI), you will influence the lives of your students every time you head into the water to instruct. That's an honour and a responsibility.

Part of this responsibility is knowing that being a WSI means being a leader.

- A leader is committed to his or her students' needs, success, and water-safe attitudes.
- A leader self-reflects on how his or her behaviour affects students.
- A leader willingly adjusts his or her behaviour to ensure the leadership spirit is linked to each and every student.

COMMUNICATION
YOU demonstrate effective interpersonal skills with students, colleagues, employers, and parents.

*INDEPENDENCE
YOU bow to the needs of your students, not to facilities. You are independent. Even though you must abide by the rules and regulations of the site at which you work, you retain your independence and place the needs of your students above all else.

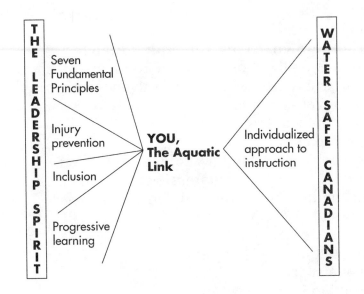

To instruct effectively, and live the spirit, your most powerful tool is the **individualized approach to instructing**. Throughout this manual and throughout this WSI course, you will learn how to use this tool every time you instruct.

The Individualized Approach to Instructing

The *individualized approach to instructing* is about YOUR commitment to the success of *each* and *every* student in your class.

CLASS MANAGEMENT
   YOU ensure active participation of students in a well-managed class.

SAFETY SUPERVISION
   YOU anticipate, prevent, and react to unsafe situations in your classes.

VOLUNTARY SERVICE
YOU work around the clock, but never solely for personal gain. You offer your help voluntarily whenever possible where men and women of action are required.

The success of the class could be determined by having the students successfully swim 1 metre farther, support a front float 10 seconds longer, or learn a reaching assist rescue that may save a life.

When you get right down to it, the individualized approach to instructing is really about creating an inclusive and safe environment where students progressively learn the necessary injury prevention messages and skills to be safe in, on, and around the water.

Let's look at two examples.

Example 1: You're teaching a class how to dive. You take your students through a series of progressions, you use the same spotting techniques for every student, you give the same cues, you provide the same feedback.

Now ask yourself:

- How many students in this class learned?
- Can you say everyone succeeded?
- How was the instructing individualized?

Example 2: You're instructing diving to the same class of six students. You've surveyed your class beforehand and know that one student is terrified of going head-first into the water, one is uncomfortable in deep water, one already knows how to dive proficiently, and one student has a medical condition that prohibits him or her from diving.

While instructing, you have the proficient diver practice standing dives. The student afraid of going head-first practices "dolphin dives." The student uncomfortable in deep water practices rhythmic breathing by the side, while the student with the medical condition begins to practice stride entries. The two remaining students begin their kneeling dive progressions.

As a result of individualizing your approach to this lesson, you have one student who can now do a standing dive, one who can do a stride entry, one who's taken the first few steps to attempting a head first dive, one who has increased his or her comfort level in deep water, and two who have begun their kneeling dives. A front dive was the instructional skill for this lesson, and everyone in the class was successful in some manner.

The second example is the individualized approach to instructing in action!

UNITY
YOU have many talents, but a single idea—to serve the needs of your students.

At first glance it may seem confusing and hard to manage. You need to consider a lot: safety, class management, teaching, evaluation, and feedback, to mention only a few.

As an instructor, you'll need to be competent in the following skills to effectively use the individualized approach to instructing:

- Safety supervision
- Teaching
- Evaluation
- Physical abilities
- Class management
- Communication
- Leadership
- Administration

These are the eight competencies that will be used throughout this course and beyond to measure your performance as a Red Cross WSI.

ADMINISTRATION
YOU prepare, plan, and complete required administrative tasks for the Water Safety program.

PHYSICAL ABILITIES
YOU know and can perform the strokes, skills, and distances of the AquaQuest Program.

THE BIG NUMBERS
Since the establishment of the Red Cross Water Safety program in 1945,

- Over 25 million Canadians have participated in learn-to-swim lessons.
- Approximately 400,000 people have been trained as Water Safety Instructors and Leaders.

In 1993 alone,

- 1.3 million Canadians took Red Cross lessons, and approximately 26,000 people joined the ranks of Instructor.

This chapter brings YOU, the Water Safety Instructor, face-to-face with the *teaching moment* (i.e., that *key* moment when you head out onto deck or across the beach to the waterfront to instruct a class of several unique students).

This chapter links the leadership spirit (injury prevention, inclusion, progressive learning, and the seven Fundamental Principles) with your skills and commitment to the eight instructing competencies to create an *individualized approach to instructing.*

The information in this chapter is organized as follows:

- *"The Big Picture"* gives you an overview of the entire Water Safety program and discusses how content in the program is presented.
- *"BEFORE You Instruct"* covers the things you need to do before a lesson—(e.g., making sure the site is safe and planning the lesson).
- *"WHILE You Instruct"* describes what to do once you're in front of your class—how to communicate, how to get things moving and keep them that way, and how to give effective feedback.
- *"AFTER You Instruct"* describes the evaluation decisions and paperwork that follow each lesson or set of lessons. This section discusses how to decide whether students have met performance criteria and summarizes your administrative responsibilities.

Use this chapter to learn *how* to instruct, Chapter 4 for the specific development of each skill, Chapter 5 for *what* to instruct, and your strategy cards for ideas for instructing specific skills.

The Big Picture

There are three components to the Water Safety program:
- AquaTots
- AquaQuest
- AquaAdults

YOU think optional and flexible to meet the water safety needs of all your students and the communities they live in.

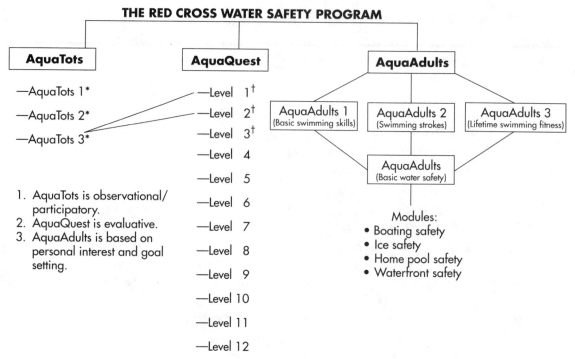

THE RED CROSS WATER SAFETY PROGRAM

AquaTots

—AquaTots 1*

—AquaTots 2*

—AquaTots 3*

1. AquaTots is observational/ participatory.
2. AquaQuest is evaluative.
3. AquaAdults is based on personal interest and goal setting.

AquaQuest

—Level 1†

—Level 2†

—Level 3†

—Level 4

—Level 5

—Level 6

—Level 7

—Level 8

—Level 9

—Level 10

—Level 11

—Level 12

AquaAdults

AquaAdults 1
(Basic swimming skills)

AquaAdults 2
(Swimming strokes)

AquaAdults 3
(Lifetime swimming fitness)

AquaAdults
(Basic water safety)

Modules:
• Boating safety
• Ice safety
• Home pool safety
• Waterfront safety

Content found in AquaTots and AquaAdults is based on content found in AquaQuest.
Detailed performance criteria for all levels are found in Chapter 5.
*Parents/caregivers participate with children.
†Parents/caregivers *may* participate with children.

THE WATER SAFETY PROGRAM STRUCTURE

This section talks about *how* content in all three components of the program (AquaTots, AquaQuest, and AquaAdults) is organized.

There are two main messages:

- Prepare! Stay Safe! Survive!
- Water Safety, Swimming and Safety Scenes

PREPARE! STAY SAFE! SURVIVE!

The main message of the program is Prepare! Stay Safe! Survive!. Here's a summary of what the message refers to:

 Prepare!—everything you do before you head for the water

 Stay Safe!—the things you do during water activities to stay safe

 Survive!—the actions you take to ensure your safety and the safety of others if something does go wrong.

All content in the program is presented in terms of Prepare! Stay Safe! Survive! Refer to Chapter 5 to see how this is done.

WATER SAFETY, SWIMMING, AND SAFETY SCENES

Content in the program is also divided into three areas:

- Water Safety, which has six themes:
  - Stop! Look! Listen!—deals with site safety, supervision, open water, and exposure to heat.
  - Stop! Look! Go Slow!—deals with entries.
  - PFD and Me—deals with the use of personal flotation devices and life jackets.
  - Stay Warm!—deals with ice safety, snowmobiling, hypothermia.
  - Boat Smart!—deals with boating safety.
  - Rescue—deals with self-rescue and the rescue of others.

In addition to these there are four water safety "modules" related to the AquaAdult component: Home Pool Safety, Waterfront Safety, Boating Safety, and Ice Safety.

- Swimming, which has three themes:
  - The Developing Swimmer—deals with beginner progressions
  - Strokes:
    - Front crawl
    - Back crawl
    - Elementary backstroke
    - Breaststroke
    - Sidestroke
    - Butterfly
  - Endurance
- Safety Scenes, which are scenarios that link knowledge and skills from the Water Safety program. They are a sequence of activities in, on, or around the water in which students demonstrate they have the knowledge, skills, and judgment to be water safe and make wise choices. Safety Scenes may include—
  - Entries
  - An endurance component
  - Self-rescue skills
  - Risk activities
  - Strokes and/or water safety skills

Have your safety scenes apply to real-life situations!

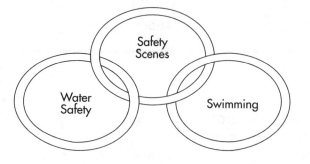

Before You Instruct

This section covers the two key things you need to do BEFORE a lesson:

- Make sure the site is safe.
- Plan your lesson.

Site safety and planning are *crucial* to learning. They make learning exciting for everyone, make your lessons safe, and allow the proper development of skills, which in the end allows your students to learn. On the other hand, *not* doing these things can lead to trouble (e.g., you get lost when you decide to improvise or you may not be ready for an emergency).

ENSURING SITE AND STUDENT SAFETY

Before every lesson, *prepare* for any safety problems or emergencies that could arise. YOUR responsibility is to ensure a safe instructing environment by preventing dangerous situations in lessons, assisting students in difficulty, and coming to the aid of fellow instructors in the event of an emergency. Your preparation should include the following:

- *Assists/aids:* Know where the assists/aids at your site are located, know how to use them, and *always* have one within reach.
- *Equipment:* Know where all teaching equipment (a whistle and assist/aid) and rescue equipment (especially the facility first aid kit and emergency telephone) are located. Check your equipment daily to ensure that all is in order.

- *Procedures:* Know what to expect from the lifeguards and other instructors at your site. Talk to your employer about their established emergency procedures during lessons. These should include:
  - Clearing of the swimming area
  - Supervision of students
  - Rescue and backup
  - Contact of emergency services (if necessary)

  What if you don't feel comfortable in your role during an emergency?
  - Speak to your employer about in-service trainings.
  - Get certified in other areas such as lifesaving and lifeguarding and/or first aid and cardiopulmonary resuscitation.

  Ensure that you become familiar with the emergency procedures of the site you are instructing at and practice these procedures regularly. You should also be aware of the regulations in your province for governing the supervision of aquatic activities. Prepare yourself physically and mentally to deal with emergencies as they may arise.

- *Site:* Know the limitations and danger areas associated with the site you are instructing and warn your students about them. Consider such factors as water quality (temperature, clarity, purity), water depths, underwater hazards, currents, drop-offs, winds, and bottom conditions. YOUR responsibility is to make the instructing environment as safe as possible.

PLANNING YOUR LESSONS

Every lesson is part of a set of lessons, and there are usually 8 to 15 lessons in a set. To cover all the content *and* meet everyone's needs, you need two kinds of plans:
- A plan for the entire set of lessons—these are called **long-term plans**.
- A plan for each lesson in the set—these are called **lesson plans**.

You can't make a good lesson plan if you don't know the plan for the BIG picture, the entire set of lessons. And you can't draw the big picture without knowing something about your lesson plans. There's a lot of give and take between the two kinds of plans. So where do you start, and how do you do it?

LONG-TERM PLANS

The place to start is long-term plans. Two things you need to know BEFORE you make these plans:

- Which skills you are going to instruct throughout the entire set of lessons. This is the time to go to Chapter 5 for a skill-by-skill listing of the full Water Safety program for each level.

- How many lessons there are in the entire set of lessons. This is usually scheduled by your employer. Remember, the completion of a set of lessons does not mean the completion of a level. Many students you instruct will hit stumbling blocks and will need to take a level more than once.

You can learn a lot by looking at other instructor's plans and talking to them. This is *really* helpful when you're just starting out. See the figure on page 19 for one instructor's plan for a set of lessons.

Now you're ready to plan your set of lessons according to the following steps:

1. Refer to skills instructed in the previous level. Always review these and build on them first.

2. Choose which skills to instruct in each lesson, and cover every skill at least three times throughout the set. Group similar skills in the same lesson (e.g., identifying and demonstrating good reaching assists [Level 9]). Start with easier skills and build toward more difficult ones. Use progressions!

3. Write your plan down!

It doesn't matter what your plan *looks like*. You can write it by hand in pencil, or you can output it on a laser printer. You can put lesson numbers across the top or down the side. You can write skill names out in full or use short forms. Just *write it down* so YOU can use it!

Now that you have a long-term plan, you're ready for lesson plans (plans for each individual lesson).

Canadian Red Cross
Water Safety Program

Instructor Worksheet

AquaQuest 5

Instructor: Shelly Wong

Day/Time: Saturday 900-930 am

Session: Winter

Location: Lakeside Pool

N = New
P = Practice

Name and Attendance	Describe when and where to go boating	Preparing to stay warm	Demonstrate how to be a safe boater	Stop! Look! Go Slow! Kneeling dive	Reasons why people choke, stop breathing	Front and side-roll entries	Surface support, 45 seconds	Rhythmic breathing, 15 times, 3 ways	Head-first sculling on back, 5 metres	Back glide and kick, 3 X 15 metres	Front crawl, 3 X 10 metres (one lesson)	Endurance swim, 25 metres	SAFETY SCENES	COMPLETE (C) • INCOMPLETE (I)
Lesson #1	N							N		N	N			
#2	P		N		N		N	P		P	P			
#3		N	P	N	P	N	P	P		P	N			
#4		P	P	P	P	P	P	N	P	P	P	N		
#5		P	P	P	P	P	P	P	N	P	P	P		
#6		P	P	P	P	P	P	P	P	P	P	P		
#7		P	P	P	P	P	P	P		P	P	P		
#8		P	P	P	P	P	P	P		P	P	P		

Water Safety — Prepare / Stay safe / Survive
Swimming — Prepare / Stay Safe / Survive

Next Level

Total Enrolled: ☐ Total Completed: ☐

Recommended Class Size: **1:6-8**

Long-Term Plans

Teaching
- ❑ *I checked the previous level.*
- ❑ *I covered every skill.*
- ❑ *I covered every skill at least three times.*
- ❑ *I started with simple skills and worked on my progressions from there.*
- ❑ *I included water safety and swimming skills in every lesson.*
- ❑ *I included a "screening" on my first day.*

LESSON PLANS

Lesson plans are about students—what they need, want, are interested in, and are able to do. Your plan for the first lesson in a set is mainly an educated guess about what's best, but it *always* includes a *screening*. Screening is a review of the previous level to help you better understand the abilities of your students. It provides you with lots of information about their skill level. As you get to know your class better, you *use* this knowledge to make better, more focused lesson plans.

Before drawing up a lesson plan, you need to do the following:

- List all the skills you're going to instruct in the lesson. You should get this list from your long-term plan.
- Review students' ability levels, background, and interests relative to the level you're instructing. This should take at most 5 minutes per class. "Screen" each student on the performance criteria from the previous level.

Just as with long-term plans, YOU have to be able to use lesson plans, and you can learn *much* from other instructor's plans.

Next, ask yourself these seven questions for every skill in the lesson:

1. Where is each student in the skill progression, and where will he or she finish? (e.g., mouth bubbles vs. complete submersion)? See Chapter 4 for the step-by-step development of each skill.

SCREENING—WHAT IF?

What would you do if on the first day of a Level 7 class you discover a student who is unable to swim 10 metres successfully?
- Speak to the participant, his or her parents, and your supervisor.
- Explain the situation.
- Ask the student to move to a Level 6 class, where he or she will be more likely to succeed.

2. How much time does the skill need? Physical skills, such as strokes need lots of time for students to practice and learn. Things often go faster when you're instructing, so always plan for *more* than your actual lesson time. If the lesson is 30 minutes long, have a plan for 40 minutes.

3. What *teaching method* will help each student get from start to finish? There are different methods to choose from: direct method, discovery method, and games. See page 22 for information on teaching methods, and check your strategy cards for more ideas.

4. What back-up plan do you need in case your teaching method doesn't work? Not every method will work with every student. Remember your individualized approach to instructing? Your plan should include *corrective methods*, other teaching methods to try, and skill modifications. See page 23 for basic information on corrective methods and Chapter 4 for skill-specific examples.

Remember, older adults are not as flexible as children. How far should you manipulate a 65-year-old's legs for a whipkick?

- Be gentle.
- Ask what feels most comfortable.
- Look for alternatives; dolphin kick may work just as well, or better!

5. What *formation* is safest and makes the best use of time? Possibilities include circle, scatter, and wave formations (see page 24).

Consider the following points when choosing a formation:

- The purpose of your formation (e.g., to have students practice a short distance, to have students watch a demonstration, to take attendance)
- The number of students
- The safety of the activity (e.g., will students interfere with each other in diving practice?)

6. What equipment is needed, and where is it?

7. What skills are the main focus of this sample plan? How can your tell?

What your lesson plan *looks like* is up to you. It just has to work for YOU, have the seven key parts, and be *written down*! And yes, ideally they're waterproof!

TIPS FOR SUCCESS
- Include drills and games in every lesson, and make sure there's a *progression* from one lesson to the next.
- *Combine* teaching methods.
- Keep students active and in the water.
- Have many things to look at, hear, and touch.
- Challenge your students: plan activities for varying levels of participation.
- Keep in mind that another instructor should be able to follow your plan if you are absent.

Lesson Plan Form
Name: Shelly Wong
Location: Lakeside Pool
Level: Aqua Quest 5

Time: 9:00 – 9:30 am
Lesson number: 3
Date: Feb. 27

Equipment:	Buoyant Aids PFD's Flutter boards	
Strategy cards: 101, 144, 136, 141		

Time	Progression	Formation
5	Rhythmic Breathing - 10x - call out name - Attendance, with a partner, hopping and changing feet	Circle, shallow
2	Prepare to stay warm - heat loss areas	
5	Review - front glide with kicks, side glides with kick, rolls to the side - front swim ⊕ 2 breaths	Shallow, waves
7	Introduce Kneeling dives	deep, line
2	Surface support - review why people choke	deep scatter
3	Back glides and kicks	
3	Endurance swim - 1/2 way	line, Shallow
2	Safe boater - name equipment	Shallow

Back-up: Pull buoys - back glides

End of lesson notes: A.J.- Flippers for Kick next lesson Josie - completed back glides 1st time Sam - talk to parents about progress

TEACHING METHODS

METHOD	DESCRIPTION	BEST USE
Direct method	• Introduce the students to what they are going to learn. • Explain and demonstrate what you expect. • Let them practice. • Give feedback so they can correct any problems. • Let them practice again.	• Skills with specific steps or procedures (e.g., strokes, front dive, rescue breathing)
Discovery method	• Students learn by doing and figuring out for themselves. • Always a *do* activity, not a discussion. • Learning by observing what others discover • "Everyone try to enter the water without getting your head or face wet."	• Skills with specific *purpose* (e.g., stride entry or front float)
Games method	• Students learn by playing *games with aims* • Scavenger hunt to practice weight transfer	• Practicing skills and building endurance.

METHOD	DESCRIPTION	EXAMPLE
Shaping	• Identify errors in skill performance, and tell students how to correct them.	• If students aren't bringing their arms out of the water on front crawl, show them how to lift their arms out of the water.
Overcorrection	• Students exaggerate a specific aspect of a skill.	• Ask students whose arms are not coming out of the water in back crawl to "touch their arms to their ears."
Physical manipulation	• Alter or control students' physical movement. • Always make sure it's OK with the student.	• Rotate students' shoulders so their arms come out of the water in front crawl.

✓ CHECK-UP

Lesson Plans

Safety Supervision
❑ *I've chosen the safest, most time-efficient formation.*
❑ *I know what equipment is needed and where it is.*
❑ *I checked my class attendance list to see if I have students with allergies, asthma, or other medical conditions.*
❑ *I've included a screening.*

Teaching
❑ *I reviewed students' ability levels.*
❑ *I know where students are in the skill progression and where they'll finish.*
❑ *I broke lesson time into small, manageable chunks.*
❑ *I planned to review existing skills before introducing new ones.*
❑ *I gave every skill a time slot.*
❑ *I've included water safety and swimming content in every lesson.*
❑ *I've chosen a teaching method and checked my strategy cards.*
❑ *I've made a back-up plan.*

TYPE	DESCRIPTION	BEST USES
Wave	• Students take off as a group.	• Effective for the initial learning and practicing of strokes over short distances (10-15 metres) • Allows many students to practice at the same time
Staggered Wave	• Divide students into two or more groups and have each group take off as a wave (about 5 seconds apart).	• Works as effectively as a wave, with more students • Evaluation is easier
Circle	• Students swim in a circle.	• Easy to form and excellent for games • A *loop* is great for continuous endurance swims over a large area (25-50 metres).
Semicircle	• Students are in a semicircle on deck or in the water.	• Effective for stationary activities (e.g., treading water) • Good for practice and demonstrations
Scatter	• Students spread out over a given area.	• Effective for stationary activities (e.g., treading water)

While You Instruct

You have a plan. You know your formations and the skills you're going to instruct. You're so prepped you even know how you're going to instruct them. Now it's time to *do it*.
- Safety first!
- Communicate, communicate, communicate!
- Active and wet!

- Give feedback!
- Adjust as needed!

These things help you take every student's needs, abilities, and safety concerns into account. They help you **individualize** your instructing. These are the elements that make the Water Safety program so special. And making the learning experience special is up to you!

SAFETY FIRST!

Safety is your No. 1 concern when instructing. These safety rules must *always* be followed whenever instructing:

- *Never* leave your class unattended.
- Have a buoyant aid within reach whatever the water depth.
- Always wear a whistle, in case you need to call someone for assistance.
- Establish rules and routines for your students on the first day of lessons. They help participants know what to expect. Keep rules simple and positive. For example, "We always walk on the deck."
- Tell everyone where to meet for the beginning of each class.
- Take attendance at the start of every class* to ascertain how many students are present for that lesson.
- Take head counts throughout the lesson to make sure all students are with you at all times.
- Make sure you can see *everyone all the time.*
  - Stay OUTSIDE formations.
  - Get higher if your class is really spread out.
  - Always be the first to enter the water and the last to get out.
  - NEVER turn your back on a student.
  - ALWAYS put yourself between your class and deeper water.
- Watch out. Are the lanes clear? Is there a bulkhead? What obstacles are there? Are there rocks?
- Enforce and model all rules at all times.
- With formations,
  - Always identify your boundaries.
  - Keep weaker swimmers close to you.
  - Keep energetic kids in the middle so they can't get away.
- Always specify concrete starting and ending points (e.g., lane ropes, docks, land).

> COMMUNICATING
> What will you do if your student is hearing impaired? How will you communicate your rules and those of the facility?
> - Establish eye contact and use gestures.
> - Speak to the parents; they may have a solution.
> - Survey other instructors; one may know sign language.
> - If possible, write things down.
> - Adapt, personalize, invent!

> STOP! LOOK! LISTEN!
> Have your class use the buddy system.

*How long should attendance take? Less time than it takes to read this note!

COMMUNICATE! COMMUNICATE! COMMUNICATE!

Instructing requires good communication. We all communicate with our mouths (verbal) and our bodies (nonverbal or body language). With our mouths we communicate with words, tone of voice, and expressions. With our bodies we communicate with general posture (leaning forward), facial expressions (smiling), and gestures (a thumbs up). When instructing be aware of how you are communicating to your students. Here are a few things to remember:

- Talk *to* people, not *at* them. Treat them as individuals. People are different, and they respond differently to how you praise or criticize them.
- Communicate with students at eye level—it shows respect and confidence.
- When giving instructions,
  - Keep it short and simple.
  - Speak at the level of the student.
  - Be specific.
  - Use key points, not long explanations.
  - Speak assertively.
  - You *don't* have to scream to be heard.
  - Use different cues: seeing (visual), hearing (auditory), and feeling (kinaesthetic). Chapter 4 contains examples of each kind of cue for many of the Water Safety program skills.
  - Make sure students can see *and* hear you. If they're underwater, they can't hear you.
- Keep people's attention by using eye contact and gestures.
- Make sure your body language matches what you're saying. Frowning while saying, "You're really improving" is just plain confusing.

What do you do if someone's trying to get attention? Ignore negative, praise positive, safety first.

> ### EYE CONTACT—NOT ALWAYS
> In some cultures, direct eye contact can mean intimidation. Eye contact is generally avoided in such cultures as a sign of respect.

ACTIVE AND WET!

"I smile, I'm enthusiastic, and I can make a difference."
- Start fast. Get them *in the water*!
- If they're not moving, they're not learning.

What do you do when students are bored? Think fast, think fun, think challenge. Do it now!
- Model what you want. If you stand during your demonstration, don't be surprised if they do too.
- If they're in the water—so are you!

- There's only one good reason to be out of the water when they're in it—you can't see what they're doing.
- If you *have* to get out of the water, don't stay out for long.

GIVE FEEDBACK!

Feedback is information students receive about their performance. It is essential to progressive learning—without it, learning takes longer or just doesn't happen. But before you can give feedback, you need to *see* what students are doing.

The *key* to observing, or seeing what your students are doing, is identifying what specific performance criteria you are looking for in relation to a skill or stroke. For example, when observing a student's front crawl, you are not looking at his or her overall performance of front crawl; rather, you are observing certain, specific criteria such as continuous flutter kick, a bent-arm pull, or horizontal body position.

The more experienced you are in identifying and focusing on specific criteria, the better you'll become at observing the students as they swim past you.

Once you observe what's working and what's not, you can begin to give feedback. There is a myth about feedback—that two types exist: positive and corrective.

Feedback can be something as simple as a wink or an O.K. sign. In fact, there is only one type: constructive. Constructive feedback—
- Communicates that the student is improving.
- Points out an error and offers solutions to correct it.
- Encourages and motivates.

GIVING STROKE FEEDBACK

When giving feedback on strokes, start simple. In the Water Safety program, skills build logically on one another. But skills get complicated fast, and all of a sudden a lot is happening at once. To figure out what's going wrong and what to fix first, you need a *system*. Here's a three-step approach that really works:

1. Check strokes for problems in the following order:
   - Body position
   - Coordination
   - Mechanics
   - Power

   These are the major components of every stroke, and checking and correcting problems in this order works because it fixes the most important thing first. For instance, correcting a problem in body position often fixes other problems in coordination.

2. Once you identify a problem with one component of a stroke, figure out the *source* of the problem. To solve a problem, you need to fix the source. For example, with front crawl, if body position is a problem, the kick is probably the source. This identifies the need to correct the kick first.

3. *After* you've corrected one problem, go through the process again to identify any additional ones.

Imagine going to all the trouble of observing and figuring out what to fix and *not* giving feedback. You might as well not bother with all that work.

PROBLEM SOURCES: STROKE COMPONENTS				
STROKE	**BODY POSITION**	**CO-ORDINATION**	**MECHANICS**	**POWER**
FC, BC Problem sources	Flutter kick—kick not streamlined, knees bent, feet flexed	Lack of shoulder roll	Actions that don't affect body position or coordination	Bent-arm pull
EBS, BS Problem sources	Shoulder and hip placement—bringing knees to chest or using a straight-arm pull	Timing (glide)		Kick
SS Problem sources				Leg action
Fly Problem sources	Bringing hips to the surface of the water	Timing		Kick from hips and bent arm pull

If you are still having problems with a stroke...check out the Task Analysis section in Appendix N.
FC, Front crawl; BC, back crawl; EBS, elementary backstroke; BS, backstroke; SS, sidestroke.

The same goes for *how* you give feedback—if you don't do it right, you might as well not bother. Here's how to get it right:
- Tell your student what's working well.
- Tell your student what needs improvement.
- Tell your student *how* to fix it.
- Keep it *short*, keep it *simple*, and keep it *specific*!

Giving feedback requires practice, practice, practice. Being able to watch several students at a time and determine what feedback to give to

WHO'S DOING IT RIGHT?
"Tish, you're *not* supposed to do a frog kick—get a life! Keep your toes flexed, your knees together and for heaven's sake, EXHALE!"
OR
"Tish, your glide is just the right length. To get more of a whip-kick action, try keeping your knees closer together."

HMM, I WONDER?

each is one of the keys to being an effective instructor. It also reinforces your individualized approach to instructing. One tip to help you succeed in this task is knowing the performance criteria thoroughly—know what you're looking for every time you observe a student!

Make your corrections sooner rather than later. The later you do them, the more your participant has practiced it wrong, and the harder it'll be to fix!

WHAT TO DO AFTER A SINGLE LESSON

- Take a few moments after the completion of a lesson to self-reflect on how things went. It's your opportunity to evaluate the success of your lesson plan as it relates to the progress of your students. Ask yourself:
  - What worked?
  - What didn't work?
  - What would you do again?
  - What would you change and how?
  - Did you take the individual needs of each student into account?

  Be honest and build your observations into your next lesson plan.
- Mark the progress of each student at the conclusion of each lesson. Note which students made progress in their learning and note this progress on your Instructor Worksheets. To ensure that your students have mastered a skill, you should see it performed a minimum of three times. One method of marking their continued evaluation on the worksheets is shown on page 30.

I'M LEARNING ALL THE TIME! WHY AREN'T YOU EVALUATING ALL THE TIME?

When giving feedback,

- Be specific.
- Be positive.
- Direct your feedback at changeable behaviours.
- Be constructive, not destructive.
- Give your feedback sooner not later.

1st Time 2nd Time 3rd Time

PLEASE, LET ME FIX THE FIRST ONE BEFORE YOU TELL ME MORE.

ADJUST AS NEEDED!

Things hardly ever go as you planned. That's why you must take time during every lesson to evaluate how things are going. People don't learn at the same rate or in the same way. When you're observing, you'll see who's not being challenged, who's struggling, and who just isn't getting it. So be ready to adjust and do one or all of the following:

- Use a corrective method to *fix* what's wrong.
- Break down the skill you're having them do. If they're working on a front glide with kick, have them do just a front glide if their body position is wrong.
- If they're not getting it the way you're presenting it, totally change your teaching method. Try something different.

PARENTS

You should expect parents to be eagerly involved in their child's learning. Sometimes a parent's interest may seem to be interference. Many parents' questions usually indicate concern about their child's progress.

Remember ....

- Regular and positive communication will help establish good relations with parents and relieve their anxiety.
- Take time before and after classes to speak with parents.
- Encourage parents to reinforce their child's learning, especially if the child is experiencing difficulties.
- Encourage parents to work through their AquaQuest booklets with their child.

A Parent is Part of The Team!

While You Instruct

Safety Supervision

❑ I have a buoyant aid within reach all the time.
❑ I have a whistle with me at all times in case I need to call for assistance.
❑ I can see everyone all the time.

Class Management

❑ I take attendance and have a meeting place.

Teaching

❑ I incorporate Prepare!...Stay Safe!...Survive!
❑ I keep it simple.
❑ We move and have fun!
❑ I provide at least three in-water demonstrations.
❑ I try to keep my class in the water 95% of the time.
❑ I use at least five different stroke drills/activities.
❑ I adapt teaching strategies to meet individual needs.
❑ I use both water safety and swimming items.

Communication

❑ I talk to people, not at them.
❑ I communicate at eye level.

Evaluation

❑ I provide constructive feedback to each student.
❑ I determine what worked and what didn't and incorporate any lessons learned into future lessons.
❑ I continuously evaluate.

After You Instruct

Now it's time for decisions and paperwork! For every set of lessons you instruct, you need to do the following:

- For every student, decide whether he or she has completed all the performance criteria of the level.
- Give each student the appropriate **recognition award** and **progress memo** to take home.
- Finish your paperwork.

A NOTE ABOUT EVALUATION

An Instructor evaluates to assist the student in learning and to determine when performance criteria have been met.

On page 27 we discussed how you evaluate to assist students in learning (feedback). Here our focus is on determining when performance criteria have been met.

Evaluation of standards consists of two parts, measurement and judgment. Measuring distance, repetitions, or time is relatively easy. You can see Marcel swim front crawl from one side of the pool to the other to complete the 50-metre distance, and you can watch as Leaha does exactly 30 seconds of surface support.

But each item in the Water Safety program has specific performance criteria attached to it, and you are required to measure how Marcel's front crawl "looks" compared to this criteria. This is where the second stage of evaluation, judgment, comes into play. You must decide if Marcel's hand is entering sufficiently in front of his shoulder and whether, during Leaha's surface support, her head stayed well enough above the surface.

One part of the leadership spirit is *progressive learning*—you instruct students to help them improve, not to prepare them for some final performance on the last day of a 10-lesson set. Success in the Water Safety program occurs *every* time your student enters the water. Evaluation must be used to help people learn.

Your attitude is *vital* in making progressive learning a success. Get to know every student in your class and his or her level of ability then weigh your students' success against the performance criteria.

Your final evaluation does *not* happen one hour before the last lesson! You are *always* observing and continuously evaluating.

COMPLETING A LEVEL

Figuring out if students have completed a level is *not* just about whether they can do specific skills. It's about balancing success and performance criteria. It's also about whether students will be *safe* and *successful* in the next level.

If a student is *able* to perform a skill but still needs more practice to meet the performance criteria, he or she has NOT completed the skill. But if a student will *never* be able to perform a skill, you need to make a judgment call. Think about how you'd evaluate these students:

- A man with arthritis trying to do a stroke with whip kick
- A little girl with no left arm who's working on front crawl
- A boy with Down's syndrome who's trying to learn safe snowmobiling practices

Think about the *big picture* for the skill. Is the student achieving the purpose of the skill without compromising his or her or others' safety? The purpose of swimming a stroke is to stay safe in the water. So the man with arthritis *has* completed the skill if he can do back crawl instead, because back crawl will also keep him safe in the water.

Evaluation—Made Simple

1. Ask yourself if your student has met the performance criteria for each item in the level.

   If the answer is YES, then the student has completed the item and can proceed to the next item/level.

   If the answer is NO, then you need to ask yourself:

2. Will more practise enable your student to complete the item?

   If the answer is YES, then the student has not completed the item and repeats the level.

   If the answer is NO, that no matter how much the student practices, he or she will NEVER complete the item, then you need to ask yourself:

3. Will moving the student to the next level jeopardize the student's safety or the safety of other students in the class?

   If the answer is YES, the student may harm himself or herself or others, then the student should NOT be moved forward.

   If the answer is NO, then the item is marked "not applicable," and the student may proceed to the next item/level.

   In cases in which you get to the second or third question, seek advice from other instructors and your supervisor and consult with the parents of the student in question.

   Always think, *safe and successful,* NOT *completing a level.*

Think about what the student can do and whether it's enough for the next level of the program. The little girl won't be able to do 1-2 breathe. But, if her *endurance* is good enough for the next level, she's completed the skill. And the boy with Down's syndrome has completed snowmobiling because he's been *taught* the skill.

If you need help making these kinds of judgments, check with other instructors, your head instructor, or the programmer.

EVALUATING AQUATOTS AND AQUAADULTS
- These two levels are not evaluated.
- The AquaTot levels are observed.
- In the AquaAdult levels you consult with your adult students to set attainable goals toward which you and your student work from lesson to lesson.

For more information on these levels, see Chapter 4.

RECOGNITION AWARDS

The recognition awards for the Water Safety program are as follows:

- **AquaTots**
  - AquaTot booklet—for all students who are *registered* in a lesson set; contains program and water safety information
  - Participation awards—for all students who *have* completed a set of lessons; these awards go in the AquaTot booklets
  - Progress memos—for *all* students; these sheets are for parents/caregivers and contain your specific comments on the student's progress during the set of lessons.

- **AquaQuest**
  - AquaQuest booklet—for all students who are *registered* in a lesson set; contains games, activities, and water safety information
  - Participation stickers and badges—for students who *haven't* completed all the skills in a level by the end of a lesson set; these stickers or badge go in the AquaQuest booklets
  - Completion awards—for students who *have* completed all the skills in a level
  - Progress memos—for *all* students; these sheets are for parents and contain your specific comments on the student's successes and challenges throughout the lesson set

- **AquaAdults**
  - AquaAdult Training Journal booklets

WRITING COMMENTS
- Write/print legibly so parents can read your notes.
- Spell things correctly! If you don't know how to spell something, look it up!
- Be positive and specific. Stress what the student has done first, then mention areas where improvement or further practice is required.
- Sign your name, and, if your signature is illegible, print it too!

OH NO! NOT MORE PAPERWORK!

But it's a snap.
1. Finish filling in your worksheets. Cover all skills for all students, and indicate the number of students enrolled and completed.
2. Hand your worksheets in to your program sponsor.
3. File your long-term plan and your lesson plans away for another day.

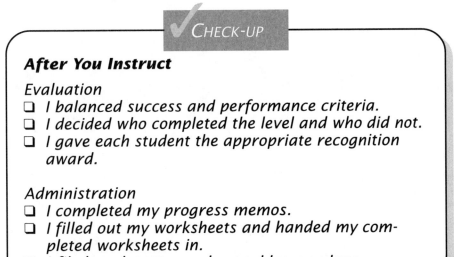

✓ CHECK-UP

After You Instruct

Evaluation
❏ *I balanced success and performance criteria.*
❏ *I decided who completed the level and who did not.*
❏ *I gave each student the appropriate recognition award.*

Administration
❏ *I completed my progress memos.*
❏ *I filled out my worksheets and handed my completed worksheets in.*
❏ *I filed my long-term plan and lesson plans.*

This chapter has three sections:

- *Section 1: AquaTots*—discusses the AquaTot component of the Water Safety program in detail: the aim, how to work with parents/caregivers, medical concerns, and evaluation.
- *Section 2: AquaQuest*—covers everything you need to know about the content (minus specific performance criteria, which are in Chapter 5) and progressions. It has three sections:
  - Water Safety Themes
  - Swimming
  - Safety Scenes

Remember: this section covers content and progressions that are used in the AquaTots and AquaAdults components too!

- *Section 3: AquaAdults*—discusses the AquaAdult component of the Water Safety program in detail: the aim, tips on how to work with adult students, adult learning characteristics, adult learning inventory, and evaluation.

AquaTots

Look out! Here come those laughing, splashing, kicking, bubbling babies—and their water-safe, water-wise parents/caregivers.

When we talk about water and very young children, two strong messages are sent out by Canadian communities:

- There is a need for organized activities and specific recreational times for parents/caregivers and their very young children.
- There is a need for safety education for the parents and caregivers of this age group.

AquaTots aims to reduce child drownings by—

- Teaching safety education to parents/caregivers.
- Providing positive early orientation to water and an introduction to swimming skills for young children.

Red Cross has four specific objectives for AquaTots:

1. To provide activities and information that increase parents' and caregivers' awareness of water risks and hazards for young children
2. To provide activities and information that develop positive water safety attitudes and introduce rescue techniques consistent with Prepare! Stay Safe! Survive!

AGES AND STAGES:
The term infant refers to children up to 1 year of age. Toddlers are from 1 to 4 years of age. Preschoolers include children up to 5 years of age.

LEADING CAUSES OF INJURY DEATH AMONG TODDLERS (1-4 YRS)

BY SEX *Death rate per 100,000 toddlers per year. Canada 1989*

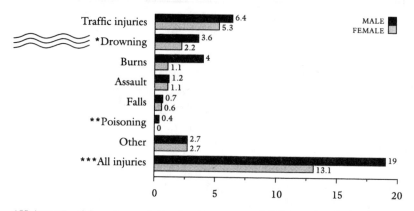

| | MALE ■ |
| | FEMALE □ |

Traffic injuries — 6.4 / 5.3
*Drowning — 3.6 / 2.2
Burns — 4 / 1.1
Assault — 1.2 / 1.1
Falls — 0.7 / 0.6
**Poisoning — 0.4 / 0
Other — 2.7 / 2.7
***All injuries — 19 / 13.1

0   5   10   15   20

*Unintentional drownings excluding boating transport; **Unintentional poisonings;
***All unintentional and intentional injuries. Source: Adapted from Statistics Canada, 1991*

3. To introduce activities and skills appropriate to the learning rates and readiness of young children
4. To provide active challenges that promote individualized development and learning

The AquaTots program is designed for infants, toddlers, and preschoolers, and their parents/caregivers. We want every parent/caregiver and child in our AquaTots program to have fun; to laugh; to play; to learn introductory swimming skills, and to learn how to stay safe in, on, and around the water. We do this with a warm, caring, positive program that promotes learning. We understand the importance of play and how it is a basic tool for learning. We encourage the use of songs, games, and a variety of stimulating equipment and toys to enhance the learning environment.

AquaTots is a three-level program based on the age and the developmental stage of the child:

- AquaTots 1 provides an introduction to discovering water and movement safely.
- AquaTots 2 uses these same introductory experiences and builds on them so that safely moving in water in different ways is the core of the experience.
- AquaTots 3 encourages the child to move, float, and even swim independently.

Infants can enter the AquaTots program as early as 4 months, and they can stay with the program until they are 5 years of age. Children usually move to the AquaQuest program at 3 years of age.

Recommend to your parents/caregivers that infants should be able to hold their heads up independently, usually between 4 and 6 months of age, before they enter AquaTots.

AquaTots 1
4-6 Months to 16 months
(holds head up independently)

↓

AquaTots 2
16 Months to 24 months

↓

AquaTots 3
24 Months and up

↓

Move to AquaQuest
as early as age 3
or stay in AquaTots
until age 5

TEACHING THROUGH PARENTS/CAREGIVERS

In AquaTots you actually teach the parent/caregiver, not the child. The parent/caregiver has the closest relationship with the child during the lessons, not you. This makes it especially important that you communicate key teaching messages to parents/caregivers before they leave your class. Remember, they look up to you as the professional!

There are some things the parent/caregiver needs to know before your lessons start. Parents/caregivers don't arrive at the pool armed with all the right information. It's up to you to answer some of their questions and relieve some of their anxiety. Hopefully, your site offers some type of parent orientation, but if not, you may want to organize one yourself or make up an informative flyer.

Some information to discuss at orientation follows:

- Program philosophy
- What parents/caregivers will learn and what their child will learn
- What to bring
- Health and safety information
- Site rules
- Teaching tips for the class and at home

Try to include a site tour: point out your meeting place and show off the facility!

WHAT DO I BRING?

- Swim suit or swim pants
- Two towels
- A favourite bathtub toy
- Lots of time to change
- A small snack for after the lesson

TO DIAPER OR NOT TO DIAPER

Check with your supervisor or the local health unit to find out if children must wear protective pants to swim at your site. If they do, then suggest swim pants to parents and caregivers. They are a better alternative to diapers that get waterlogged or rubber pants that fill with water and may chafe.

Remember that an orientation is an opportunity to generate excitement about AquaTots, to highlight your instructional approach, and to emphasize the importance of listening and preparing for time around the water.

MEDICAL INFORMATION

Parents and caregivers entering an aquatic program with their child for the first time are understandably anxious about their well-being. They may have misinformation about how safe or effective parent and tot programs are. Explain to them that to ensure that the program would be truly safe and that the child's well-being would be emphasized, Red Cross supported medical research of young children participating in parent and tot programs.

Research considered three questions:

1. Do children who participate in these programs get more colds or infections?
2. Do children who participate in these programs have a significant drop in body temperature?
3. Do children who participate in these programs ingest large amounts of water that could cause significant medical problems?

The answer to these three questions is a resounding NO!

Children participating in parent and tot programs are exposed to no more health risks than in other group activities for children, whether in a daycare facility, a play group, or school. Of course, explain that a child who has an acute infectious disease must not participate in the program.

Children participating in parent and tot programs do not experience a significant drop in body temperature. Still, you and the parent/caregiver should keep these things in mind:

- The water should be well heated for this type of program.
- Children, like adults, have different tolerance levels for the cold, and both you and parents/caregivers should be alert for shivering and blue lips. These signal time to get out of the water, before it becomes an unpleasant experience.

Children participating in parent and tot programs do not ingest large amounts of water, even if they are submerged as part of program activities. However, both parents/caregivers and the instructor must be alert for *unintentional* submersions. All *intentional* submersions must be performed safely, and only when *both* the child and parent/caregiver are relaxed and ready.

Make sure that parents understand that if their child has underlying problems or if they have concerns, they should consult their doctor before participating in AquaTots.

BODY POSITIONS AND HOLDS

Parents do not arrive at a site with a natural sense of how to move in the water or how to hold their child correctly. They need to learn the special techniques for working with their child in water. You will need to explain the physical principles of water (e.g., buoyancy) in terms of the skills you're introducing.

You need to demonstrate and reinforce appropriate body positions and holds for each skill. Emphasize the importance of consistent cues that introduce an activity (eg., 1-2-3 Go, Ready-Swim). And make sure parents/caregivers maintain eye contact with their child at all times.

Supportive holds that parents/ caregivers use in the water are really a child's *training wheels*. Instructors use a *soft touch* working with their students. You need to instill this same *touch* in parents/caregivers as they work with their children.

BASIC PARENT SUPPORT POSITION

Parent/caregiver is low in the water (shoulders underwater) to maintain good eye-to-eye contact with the child on front skills, to maximize buoyancy for the child on back skills, and to keep warm.

FRONT POSITIONS

BASIC FRONT LAYOUT POSITION
1. Parent/caregiver and child are face to face, low in the water.
2. Parent/caregiver supports the child under the arms at the shoulder.
3. Emphasize that they should hold the child like a fragile object!
4. To gain the best horizontal position, parents/caregivers need to extend their arms with the child away from their body.

This technique allows the child to experience the transition of vertical body position on land to that of horizontal in water. Make sure this is a gradual transition.

SIDE-BY-SIDE POSITION
1. This is more advanced position for infants and preferred for toddlers.
2. Parent/caregiver is beside the child (both face the same direction).
3. Parent/caregiver supports the child under the arms by the shoulders from back to front (thumbs are face up at the back of the child's shoulders).

Both of these positions allow the parent/caregiver to tow the child (towboat and barge) *and* gently sweep from side to side so the child can enjoy the water currents passing along the body. Moving water is very relaxing for children.

You must monitor the child's facial position in the water to ensure he or she is not getting a surprise face full of water.

BACK POSITIONS

BACK CRADLE POSITION
1. This position is a very secure-feeling position.
2. The child can be cradled either facing the parent/caregiver and be gently lowered into a back float cradle, or he or she can be cradled in one arm while in a semisitting position with his or her head resting against the parent's or caregiver's shoulder and chest.

Remind parents that they must not only watch their own child, but they must be aware of other class participants around them.

Back Layout Position

1. Parents/caregivers stand behind the child and support him or her by placing their hands under the child's arms at the shoulder.
2. Parents/caregivers should gently lower themselves in the water to shoulder level and touch cheek to cheek, with the child's head supported on the parent's shoulder.
3. Slowly and carefully, the parent/caregiver and child move as one, and the parent/caregiver leans back until the child is in a horizontal supported float with the water level above or below the child's ears.
4. Have parents/caregivers extend their arms to move from a cheek position to a back layout position.

You must monitor the child's facial position in the water to ensure he or she is not getting a surprise face full of water.

Back and Head Support Position

1. This starts with the child holding on to the side or sitting on one of the parent's/caregiver's knees.
2. Parent/caregiver moves from supporting under the arms at the shoulders to placing both hands, fingers spread wide pointing toward the child's feet, under the shoulders. Their hands can provide a stable platform on which the head can rest.
3. Parents/caregivers continue to support with a gentle grasp and slowly stretch their arms out in front while stepping backward.
4. The parent/caregiver encourages the child to look up (small toys held above the child will help).
5. This can be modified to provide more support for the child by having the parent/caregiver extend his or her arms down both sides of the child's body, forming a platform on which the child can lie. Infants enjoy the extra contact this technique provides.

Infants will be more successful at back floating positions, but toddlers will find this a big challenge—they feel as if they're falling backward and may be sensitive to water in their ears. Small toys or balls will help calm the child.

SUBMERSION TECHNIQUES

Submersion is part of the total swimming experience, and young children delight in moving freely underwater. Parents/caregivers should be given the option of *not* submerging a child if they are uncomfortable with this skill. This will help to ease their fears. As they observe the joy and ease with which other children perform submersions, they will often feel more comfortable with this skill.

Submersion is an optional item only in the AquaTots Level 1. Independent submersions initiated by the child are encouraged in Levels 2 and 3.

FACE TO FACE

1. Child is held facing the parent/caregiver in the basic front layout position.
2. Parent/caregiver gives a verbal cue.
3. Parent/caregiver bends at the knees, and the supporting hands are gently lowered until the child is submerged. Parent/caregiver and child must move as a unit.
4. Child is submerged to just under the surface; the forehead and bridge of the nose are angled toward the bottom of the pool. The submersion should last from one to three seconds.
5. Parent/caregiver gently recovers the child to the surface and ends the technique with lots of praise and a hug.

The secret to gentle submersions is to have the supporting hands of the parent/caregiver *melt like chocolate* so that the body weight of the child takes him or her under the surface. This avoids the unpleasant feeling of being pulled, pushed, or dragged underwater. This gentle method also teaches parents/caregivers to *help* the child go underwater rather than leading or pushing the child to submerge.

> **RELAXED AND READY, OR NOT?**
> How do you know if the parent and child are ready for submersion? Check for these cues:
> - Both parent/caregiver and child are relaxed and enjoy the water.
> - Parent/caregiver and child are comfortable getting their faces wet.
> - Parent/caregiver has been taught the proper submersion hold/position.

SIDE-BY-SIDE

1. Parent/caregiver stands beside the child (both face the same direction) and supports the child under the arms at the shoulder from back to front (thumbs are face up at the back of the child's shoulders).
2. Using a verbal cue, the parent/caregiver gently lifts the child slightly, presses on the child's shoulders to angle the forehead and nose toward the bottom, and gently releases his or her grasp to allow the child to submerge.

3. The technique finishes with the parent/caregiver regrasping the child and helping him or her to the surface for lots of praise and hugs.

A more advanced progression has the parent/caregiver moving backwards slowly as the child submerges.

SUBMERSIONS FROM THE POOL EDGE, MAT, PLATFORM, OR SLIDE

1. The entry should be continuous, allowing the body weight of the child to take him or her into the water.
2. Parent's or caregiver's role is to help the child to a safe entry, in the proper face-forward and vertical position, and to recover the child following the submersion.
3. Parent/caregiver and child should move as a unit.
4. Use a cue.
5. Encourage children to kick for propulsion on the recovery.

> **YOU'RE ON!**
> Parents and caregivers need to understand the importance of starting every activity with a cue. Use of a cue signals the child to prepare for an action or an activity. Once a cue is started, the parent or the caregiver MUST follow through with the activity. Parents/caregivers can choose any cue they want (e.g., verbal, taps) as long as they use that same cue consistently.

BEFORE YOUR AQUATOTS LESSON

Getting ready for your AquaTots lesson means that you follow the same steps that you would for any other class—with a few differences!

You still need to make sure the site is *SAFE*, and you still need to *PLAN* your lessons.

SITE AND PARTICIPANT SAFETY

Site safety should encompass the entire aquatic environment, from the dressing rooms to the water. Not only do you need to know about assists, equipment, and procedures, but you must take into account the cleanliness of the deck and dressing rooms, the quality of the water, and its temperature (warm!). Remember, you must anticipate for both the parent/caregiver *and* the child. A child in arms or tugging on a hand causes awkward movements and distracts a parent/caregiver from watching where they are going. Parents and caregivers are also less intimidated by a new environment and may wander into unsafe situations. Make sure you anticipate and prevent!

PLANNING YOUR LESSONS

You need to ask yourself the same questions as when you made your first long-term plan.

- What skills are you going to teach?
- How many lessons are there in the entire set of lessons?

For the AquaTots program you must ask yourself a third question:

- What THEMES are you going to use for each of your lessons?

One of the things that makes AquaTots special is the use of themes to shape the program activities. Since many of the skills that you teach will be repeated often, it is important you make it fun. What better way to do that than to present it in different creative *packages*. And choosing a theme makes your lesson planning easier by giving it a focus.

ONE MORE TIME...
Repetition is an important method to reinforce any skill, but it is especially important at this level and for two reasons. First, younger children, because of their limited motor skills may only progress to a certain point until they reach their next developmental stage. That means you will have to repeat skills until they are ready for the next step in the progression. Second, younger children tend to require more repetition to master a skill.

Lesson Planning with Themes. How do you plan a lesson using themes? It's simple. Just follow these steps:

1. Choose your theme. Start by reviewing the observation criteria for the AquaTots level that you are instructing. Themes like Welcome to...., PFDs, and Safety can all provide focus for a lesson. Or choose themes like The Wet Head Club, A Day at the Circus, or Goin' on a Bear Hunt. Your imagination is the only limiting factor.

2. Choose your skills for that lesson. Check your long-term plan and any evaluation notes you have on class progress.

3. Now choose songs, games, and activities that review your skills and tie in with your theme.

OTHER THEME IDEAS
- Bubble day
- Ball day
- A visit to the zoo, aquarium, or park
- Mini-olympics
- Any special day or holiday
- Happy Birthday
- It floats!
- Boat cruise

When you are planning your lessons for AquaTots, keep these key principles in mind:

- Screen your class, especially parents/caregivers, for their experience and comfort level in the water.
- Focus on *BOTH* the parent/caregiver *and* the child. Remember you are instructing both, and your lesson plan content should reflect this.

- Try to schedule any demonstrations or dry-land activities first, and make sure they are short! Younger children get very cold quickly if they are in and out of the water. If they are on the deck too long, they become a handful for the parent/caregiver to manage.
- Change activities frequently.
- Use lots of different equipment for variety.
- Songs can be used as a signal to start or end a class, to review skills, and to create a positive atmosphere. You don't have to be a songbird, as long as you are enthusiastic.
- Include times for the class to gather in a circle (songs, exploration activities). It helps you control the group, makes it easier to give instructions or demonstrations, and creates a friendly, social atmosphere.

Sample Lesson Plan

Level: AquaTots 2
Lesson no.: 3
Theme: Bears, Bears, Bears...
Lesson objective: Review floats; introduce rollover floats; arm action
Equipment needed: Kickboards, toys, mats, PFDs

Time in Minutes	Activity Description	Formation	Equipment
1 2 3	• Entry into the Pool • Song: Old Brown Bear Had A Cave... (skills review)	Scatter Circle	
4 5 6 7	• Put on and properly fasten a PFD (bears look for the "right" winter coat) • Movement with PFDs • Remove PFDs	Circle	
8 9 10	• Review front and back floats	Circle Scatter	PFDs for adults and children
11 12 13	• Introduce rollover floats (bears rolling over when they sleep) • Practice	Circle	Toys
14 15	• Using buoyant objects for support—practice with kickboards this week; review large mats from last week	Scatter	Kickboards, large mats
16 17 18	• Song: Goin' On a Bear Hunt	Circle Line—follow the leader	
19 20	• Basic kick front and back (assisted)—1 width of each (song: This is the Way Bears Kick Their Feet...)	Line	
21 22 23	• Review shallow water entries—emphasize support positions (bear jump!)	Line	
24 25 26	• Introduce basic arm action on front—child held by parents; reaches for bear berries" (toys, plastic fruit in front...)	Circle	Toys, plastic fruit, etc.
27 28 29 30	• Song: When You're Happy and A Bear... • Safety message and exits	Circle	

WHILE YOU INSTRUCT

You know all the basics to instruct a class from Chapter 3 as needed! You'll soon know where to find all the information you need on themes and progressions (in the next section). All you need now are a few pointers to help "personalize" the program for your students.

Lets start at the beginning

1. Establish the same sort of routines and cues that you would use for any class you instruct. Remember, you're communicating to the parent/caregiver now, and they'll want to know why.

2. Make sure you instruct the class on how to enter and exit the water safely. Parents/caregivers may need to pair with another parent/caregiver. Supervise entries and exits carefully *EVERY* lesson.

3. Sometimes instructors find communicating with parents/caregivers an intimidating experience. That's why you need to remind yourself that YOU are the expert on aquatic learning. Parents and caregivers appreciate goal-oriented statements and clear, concise directions when learning new skills and movements in the water. And once you've mastered the *language of correction*, parents and caregivers will benefit from the learning situation and achieve a higher degree of satisfaction with the task at hand.

> **Communicate!** Here are some useful correction phrases to use when speaking to parents/caregivers:
> - "Try it this way so that...."
> - "I find this method the most effective because..."
> - "In the long run, this method works best because..."
> - "I can see this skill is a challenge for you. Let's see if we can modify it to make it easier.

4. Remember that you set the tone of the class. This is no time to be stiff or self conscious or to worry that you can't carry a tune (no one will even notice). The atmosphere you create through your confidence, knowledge, enthusiasm, and most of all, your sense of fun is infectious. Parents/caregivers and their children will respond by relaxing and enjoying the entire water experience. It will happen if you prepare and put on your best smile!

5. Equipment for AquaTots classes should be as varied as possible. PFDs, floatable mats, kickboards, tot docks, swim bars, water noodles and toys like plastic animals, pails, and balls all add to the water experience. If your site has limited equipment, improvise with items like

plastic jugs, or encourage parents/caregivers to bring their favourite toys or PFDs from home. Always remember to think "Safety First!" when you plan activities with equipment. And always maintain class control and contact when you are using the equipment.

6. Feedback is as important for AquaTots participants as it is for any other level. Direct your feedback at the parent/caregiver, and, when it is age-appropriate, at the child. Always reinforce positive efforts and give parents/caregivers specific feedback. Progressive learning happens at any level, and in this case it happens for both the parent/caregiver and child!

AFTER YOU INSTRUCT

ABOUT EVALUATING AQUATOTS

One of the things that makes the AquaTots program unique is its emphasis on observation, rather than evaluation. All the skill items in each level are designed as an instructional guide for you. Children move to the next level on the basis of their developmental stage, not on their completion of the items. Parents/caregivers are encouraged to observe and applaud their child's progress and experiences but not to focus on achieving a specific goal. Remember that the aim of the course is to provide a positive orientation to the water for young children and to provide safety education to the parents/caregivers. Keep that as your focus, and everyone will have a wonderful time!

AquaQuest

This section covers the following:
- Water Safety Themes
  - Stop! Look! Listen!
  - Stop! Look! Go Slow!
  - PFD and Me
  - Stay Warm!
  - Boat Smart!
  - Rescue
- Swimming
  - Developing Swimmer
  - Strokes
  - Endurance
- Safety Scenes

Four additional water safety modules are used in the AquaAdult component:

- Home pool safety
- Waterfront safety
- Ice safety
- Boating safety

Information on these is found in the next section of this chapter.

📖 Indicates page references to Canadian Red Cross, *Swimming and Water Safety*.

▭ Indicates card references to Canadian Red Cross's *Strategy Cards*.

WATER SAFETY

There are six themes in Water Safety:

- Stop! Look! Listen!
- Stop! Look! Go Slow!
- PFD and Me
- Stay Warm! (ice safety)
- Boat Smart! (boating safety)
- Rescue

Use these pages to find out how each theme in the program *DEVELOPS* progressively.

🦉 Wise Choices

Everytime you see this owl, think about wise choices and how you'll convey this concept to your students. Here are some hints:

- Ask your students "why" (e.g., Why should they always swim with a buddy?).
- Ask your students to find options available to them (e.g., "I could swim alone," or "I could swim with a friend," or "I could swim where the water is supervised.")
- Ask your students to distinguish between "wise" and "unwise" choices.
- Have your students simulate their choice.

Remember:

- Ensure age appropriateness.
- Take it slowly—your students need time to understand each step.

Stop! Look! Listen!

The BIG Picture

- You must first see the big picture before you can make wise choices.
- Every year, many toddlers drown because they weren't supervised.
- When in, on, or around the water, participants are responsible for staying safe.

Teaching Tips

- Focus on games and routines, not lecturing.
- The key concept is being safe in, on, and around the water.
- Use visual and water activities for "Be sure you know" activities.
- Try to simulate environments so participants can experience relevant learning.

THE FACTS

 PREPARE!

- When to swim:
  - During the day, during supervised hours
  - *NOT* in storms, fog, or high winds
  - *NOT* after storms if the water seems to be rising or there is flooding
- At a pool or waterfront, make sure assists are readily available and that there is a working phone. Keep the site address and emergency numbers by the phone. Backyard pools need a fence with a lock, the gate must be kept closed (self-closing and self-latching), and access must be restricted. A well-stocked first aid kit should be on hand, and supervision must be constant (a person can drown in the time it takes to answer the phone).
- Be sun smart: wear a hat with a wide brim or peak; wear sunglasses; wear light clothing to cover as much skin as possible; use sunscreen with a minimum sun protection factor (SPF) of 15, and reapply it frequently (every 3 to 4 hours); use sunscreen on cloudy and hazy days because clouds do not block ultraviolet A (UVA) or ultraviolet B (UVB) rays.

STAY SAFE!

- Swim in supervised areas. Although it's best to swim in an area supervised by a lifeguard, it's not always possible (backyard pool or cottage). In these situations, you need an emergency action plan that includes adult supervision, an emergency signal, safety equipment, and emergency procedures.
- Special note for teens and adults: PFDs are NOT a substitute for supervision by you or a lifeguard.
- Be sun smart: remain in shaded areas; take extra care around the water as the sun's rays are reflected; keep infants under 1 year old out of the sun altogether; drink lots of water or juice to prevent dehydration.

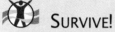 SURVIVE!

- Should you swim to stay warm? NO, because, even though the body produces almost three times as much heat when swimming slowly and steadily or treading water as it does when holding still, this heat and more is lost to exposure to cold water.
- In cold water swimming performance is impaired. You can't swim as far in cold water; but swimming distance in cold water WILL be much less than in warm water, especially if a PFD is not worn.
- Should you ever swim to safety if you find yourself in open water? It's not easy to judge distance, especially under emergency conditions in rough, cold water. It's more than likely that you'll underestimate how far you have to swim; it's best to err on the side of safety. In some cases, shore may be close enough to reach by swimming, despite the faster body cooling rate caused by swimming in cold water. The decision to try to swim should be influenced by your swimming ability, amount of insulation, water temperature, waves, currents, and the chance that a rescuer will come to your aid. If there's a good chance of rescue and you have flotation, stay where you are.

PROGRESSION DESCRIPTIONS

Progression descriptions are listed in the following sections for:
1. Site safety
2. Importance of supervision
3. Show you know
4. Open water
5. Exposure to heat

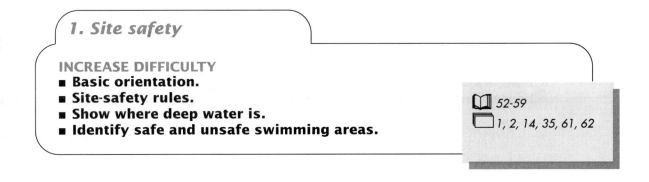

1. Site safety

INCREASE DIFFICULTY
- Basic orientation.
- Site-safety rules.
- Show where deep water is.
- Identify safe and unsafe swimming areas.

📖 52-59
📂 1, 2, 14, 35, 61, 62

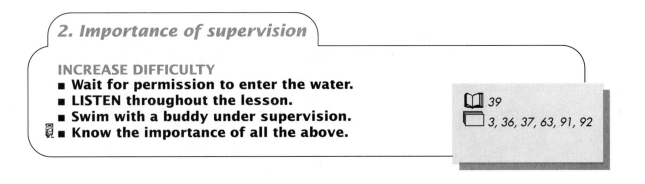

2. Importance of supervision

INCREASE DIFFICULTY
- Wait for permission to enter the water.
- LISTEN throughout the lesson.
- Swim with a buddy under supervision.
- Know the importance of all the above.

📖 39
📂 3, 36, 37, 63, 91, 92

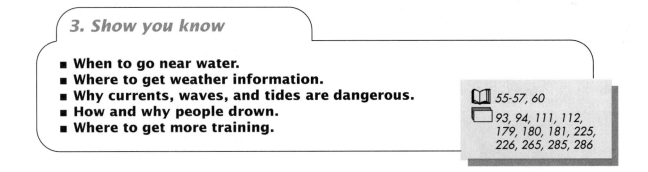

3. Show you know

- When to go near water.
- Where to get weather information.
- Why currents, waves, and tides are dangerous.
- How and why people drown.
- Where to get more training.

📖 55-57, 60
📂 93, 94, 111, 112, 179, 180, 181, 225, 226, 265, 285, 286

4. Open water

INCREASE DIFFICULTY
- Dangers of open water.
- How to Prepare! Stay Safe! Survive!

📖 55-60, 220
📁 182

5. Exposure to heat

- Dangers of heat/sun exposure.
- How to reduce heat/sun risks.

📖 44, 45, 64, 65
📁 241

Stop! Look! Go Slow!

The BIG Picture

- Think about *HOW* you'll enter the water.
- Think about what *CHOICES* you have.

Statistically Speaking

- Diving is the leading sports-related cause of spinal cord injuries. Many diving incidents result in total paralysis from the neck down.
- 95% of diving injuries occur in water 1.5 metres deep or less, in an unsupervised setting with no warning signs.
- Injuries occur from diving into ocean surf, lakes, rivers, quarries, and swimming pools.
- The average diving-related spinal cord injury casualty is male, 17 to 22 years old, with no formal training in diving, who is visiting the location for the first time.
- Over 30% of diving injuries/deaths involve alcohol and/or drug use.
- Statistics show that spinal injuries are rare during supervised dives into water 9 feet (2.7 metres) deep or deeper.
- Authorities continue to disagree about the recommended depth of water needed for safe diving from a deck or from a diving board. Safe diving depth depends in part on the height, weight, and skill level of each person.

Safety Tips

- If you've never seen the participants enter, be sure to SPOT them.
- Feet-first entries must be vertical.
- Ensure that all students know how to return to point of safety after entering the water.

THE FACTS

 PREPARE!

As a Red Cross Water Safety Instructor you are an important role model. You can help prevent spinal cord injuries by setting a good example of where and how to enter the water safely. Diving can be fun in both recreational and sport settings. However, it can lead instantly to serious spinal cord injuries and death. The objectives of teaching basic diving as a skill in the Water Safety program are:

1. To teach students when and where it is safe to dive and to always STOP! LOOK! GO SLOW!; and, *if the site permits,*
2. To teach students how to safely execute a front dive from water level (e.g., deck or dock level).

Executing a safe dive depends on many factors. Things such as the size, skill level, and experience of your students are factors. The conditions and regulations of your instructional site are other factors. Certain sites may not be appropriate for diving, and the skill itself may not be appropriate for all students to perform. It is YOUR responsibility to consider the factors and consult with your supervisor to decide if and where you will teach diving at your site. Use the following safety precautions to help guide your decision.

STAY SAFE!

- Obey "No Diving" signs/markings and diving depth regulations, relevant to your site.
- Check the shape of the pool or waterfront bottom to ensure that the diving area is large enough and deep enough for the intended dive.
- Do not allow diving unless there is ample clearance from the point of entry to the upslope in front of the take-off point (e.g., deck or dock).
- Never dive or teach diving into an above-ground pool or the shallow end of any pool.
- The presence of a diving board does not necessarily mean that it is safe to dive. Pools at homes, motels, and hotels might not be safe for diving.
- Never dive or teach diving in cloudy or murky water.
- In open water, always check first for objects under the surface such as logs, stumps, boulders, and pilings. Be aware of variable or changing depths.
- Teach students to STOP! LOOK! GO SLOW!, entering the water feet first, the first time, to check water depth and hazards.
- The deeper the water, the better.

- Ensure that students are comfortable performing a surface support in deep water.
- Ensure that students are physically and psychologically ready to do the skill. Do not force a student to do a skill. Work on developing comfort and proper technique one step at a time.
- Ensure that students can demonstrate correct hand, arm, and head position before trying to dive and that they can maintain this streamlined safety position during a forceful push and glide in the water.
- Ensure that the deck (or take-off point) is not slippery and that students have their feet placed correctly at the edge.
- Don't let students dive over stationary or hard objects or through innertubes or hoops.
- Supervise every student before, during, and after every dive.

REMEMBER

Always STOP!, LOOK! GO SLOW! when you instruct diving. Consider *ALL* the factors, and work through the series of basic progressions on the basis of the readiness of each student. You play a key role in educating your students and the public about safe diving.

SPOTTING TECHNIQUES FOR DIVING

Provide spotting for students requiring assistance in executing a particular dive technique. You can help from in the water, on the deck, or on the dock.

FROM THE WATER
1. Kneeling dive: Position yourself in the water to the side of the kneeling student. Have the student place his or her hands on your hand, which is just above the water in front of them. Guide them down and away from the edge as they push toward the water. Quickly move your hand away as their head enters the water or, if necessary, travel with the student, continuing to guide the path of the dive.

From the Deck or Dock

1. Kneeling dive: Kneel next to the student with one hand just above his or her head and one hand holding the student's ankle. As the student pushes toward the water, press down on the head. Lift up on the leg, if necessary, to keep the student from doing a belly flop.
2. Stride dive: Stand to the side of the student with one hand around the front of the waist and the other hand on the rear leg, above the knee, to stabilize the body. As the student falls toward the water, lift up on the rear leg and guide the student into the water.
3. Standing dive (for a student having difficulty lifting the legs): Sit at the edge to one side of the student. Place one arm in front of the student midway between the feet and knees, about 12 inches in front of the legs.

In program sites where diving is not taught due to unsafe circumstances, all Progress Memos are marked "Diving not taught at this program site."

Note: *These assists and the basic diving progressions are demonstrated in the "Swimming Skills" video.*

PROGRESSION DESCRIPTIONS

Progression descriptions are listed in the following sections for:
1. Shallow and deep-water entries and exits
2. Kneeling dive
3. Front and side-roll entries
4. Front stride dive
5. Stride entry
6. Front dive

1. Shallow- and deep-water entries and exits

INCREASE DIFFICULTY:

- **Wade in/use ladders.**
- **Slip-ins.**
- **Sit-jumps.**
- **Standing jumps.**

MOVE FROM ASSISTED TO UNASSISTED:

- **Hold onto participant's body.**
- **Hold both hands throughout.**
- **Hold one hand throughout.**
- **Support participant only during recovery.**

📖 *99*

▭ *4-6, 39-41, 65,*
   66, 95

2. Kneeling dive

INCREASE DIFFICULTY:

- **"Dolphin dives" in shallow water—skill takes place in water;
  not an entry.**
- **Dolphin dives while in deep water: using hips to guide body motion.**
- **Somersaults while in deep water: controlled by tucking head and
  bending at hips with legs straight. Kneeling dive into deep water.**

📖 *103*

▭ *133, 134-136*

3. Front- and side-roll entries

INCREASE DIFFICULTY:
- **Somersaults in shallow water.**
- **Somersaults in deep water.**
- **Side rolls from land.**
- **Forward rolls from land.**

CUES

Skill: Forward roll

    Visual– *Bring your bottom over your head.*

    Auditory– *Try to cover your ears with your knees.*

    Kinaesthetic– *Curl yourself into a tight little ball.*

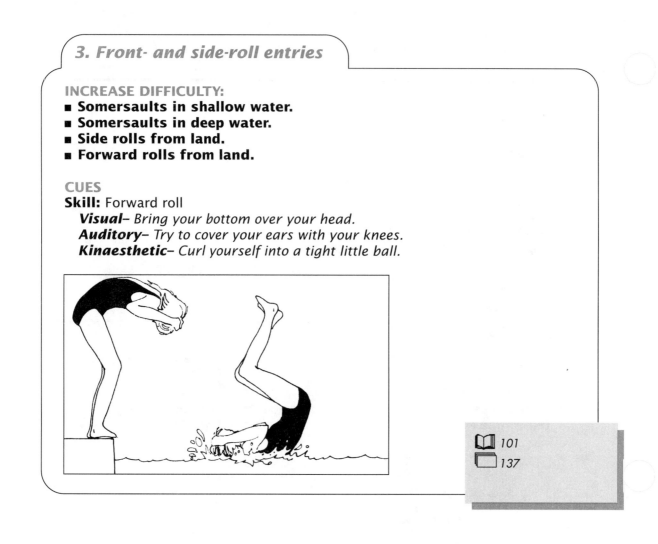

📖 *101*
▭ *137*

4. Front stride dive

INCREASE DIFFICULTY:

- **Sit dive.**
- **Kneel dive (one knee).**
- **Stride dive (one leg extended).**
- **Arms and hands extend above head throughout dive, to protect head, and steer up after entry.**

CUES

Skill: Keep chin tucked in a front dive

 Visual– *Touch your chin to your chest.*

 Kinaesthetic– *"Squeeze" your chin in nice and tight.*

Skill: Maintain pike at entry.

 Visual– *Keep yourself like a "V."*

 Auditory– *Think of dropping forward like a leaky faucet— "drip, drip."*

 Kinaesthetic– *Keep your stomach muscles tight.*

Continued.

CORRECTIVES

Problem: NOT TUCKING THE HEAD IN.
Corrective Method:
  Physical manipulation–Gently push down on their head when students are diving while pushing them out with your other hand.
  Overcorrection–Tuck a bathing cap or cloth under their chin so that students have to keep it in while they dive.
  Shaping–Tell students to keep their chin tucked into their chest at all times.

Problem: DROPPING KNEES FORWARD.
Corrective Method:
  Physical manipulation–Place one hand on their head and the other hand on their quadriceps while they dive.
  Overcorrection–Have students kick back behind them while they dive.
  Shaping–Tell students to try to get their bottom over the top of their head.

Problem: A BELLY FLOP.
Corrective Method:
  Physical manipulation–Using the hand on students' arm, pull them forward and down into the water.
  Overcorrection–Have students practice a forward roll into the water.
  Shaping–Have students keep their eyes on the bottom for the entire dive.

Problem: OPENING ARMS AFTER ENTRY, resulting in a nonstreamlined body position.
  Physical manipulation–Have students lock their thumbs together as they dive.
  Overcorrection–Give students something to hold in their hands as they dive.
  Shaping–Have students hold their hands together as tightly as they can.

102-103
133-136, 159

5. Stride entry

IMPORTANT FACTS

- **Feet first.**
- **Lean forward—it helps prevent up-down movement.**
- **Hands come together to force water down.**
- **Legs need to be wide open—it spreads the body out.**

REMEMBER:

- **There's NO SUCH THING as standard form! Some do the splits, and others jump in like a football player ready to tackle.**
- **This is a perfect chance to try the "discovery" method.**

CUE

Skill: Stride entry

Visual–Step forward off the plank.

Auditory–Slap your hands together in front of you.

Kinaesthetic–Stretch your leg forward as wide as possible until your hamstrings have a slight pull.

📖 99
▭ 183

INCREASE DIFFICULTY

- **Dive with a jump.**
- **Aim farther and farther from the edge.**
- **Dive just below the surface.**

CORRECTIVE

Problem: Diving too deep on shallow dive.

Corrective Method:

Physical manipulation–Hold students' arms up at a level nearly parallel to the water surface, and keep their hands aiming in that direction throughout the beginning of the dive.

Overcorrection–Place your hand parallel to the water surface, about 5 cm off the water and 30 cm in front of students; have them dive where your hand was.

Shaping–Have students reach forward as they dive into the water (make sure they tuck their chin in just before entering the water).

104
267, 268

PFD and Me

The BIG Picture

- Wearing a PFD is a wise choice.
- If PFDs are comfortable and people are used to them, they're more likely to wear them.
- Many people who drown weren't wearing an approved flotation device or were wearing it improperly.

Teaching Tips

- If you expect participants to wear their PFDs properly, you must too!
- All buckles and ties must be fastened properly *BEFORE* entry.
- PFDs that fit properly allow complete movement but *DON'T* rise above the ears.
- Wearing PFDs or life jackets does not replace supervision.

THE FACTS

☑ PREPARE!

- PFDs and life jackets can keep you afloat, can protect you from cold water, and may save your life.
- PFDs provide adequate flotation within prescribed limitations (see approval statement following), are acceptable on all pleasure craft, come in many sizes according to chest size or weight, come in over 120 styles, are adjustable and versatile, allow freedom of movement, and offer varying amounts of protection from the cold. PFDs *CANNOT* turn you over in the water.

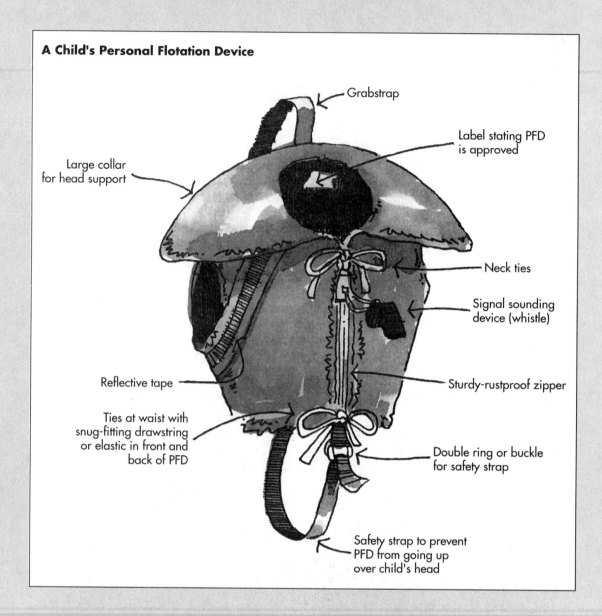

A Child's Personal Flotation Device

Grabstrap

Label stating PFD is approved

Large collar for head support

Neck ties

Signal sounding device (whistle)

Reflective tape

Sturdy-rustproof zipper

Ties at waist with snug-fitting drawstring or elastic in front and back of PFD

Double ring or buckle for safety strap

Safety strap to prevent PFD from going up over child's head

- The Department of Transport (DOT) approves PFDs and life jackets. The approved colours are orange, yellow/gold, and red (for ease of identification in search-and-rescue operations). Always check the label—it's either silk-screened or sewn into the PFD or life jacket. The label identifies it as a PFD or a lifejacket, says whether it's approved, indicates the size and weight of the person that it was made for, and describes how to care for it.
- PFDs and life jackets must fit to be effective:
  - Is your PFD/life jacket comfortable?
  - Is your PFD/life jacket snug?
  - Are all the zippers, buckles, and snaps fastened?
  - Does your PFD/life jacket come up over your nose when you pull it at the shoulders (it shouldn't if it fits properly)?

STAY SAFE!

- Check PFDs and life jackets regularly for discolouration or fading; check for tears; check the texture/quality of flotation material; and check zippers, buckles, and straps.
- If you're in trouble, stay calm, call for help, roll on your back, relax, and wait for help.

Survive!

- The Heat Escape Lessening Posture or Position (HELP) technique involves holding the inner sides of the arms over the sides of the chest, and pressing the insulation foam material of the PFD to the body. The forearms can be placed across the central chest to help hold the PFD foam against the body in this region. The thighs are held together to reduce inner-thigh heat loss. Raising the thighs forward to about perpendicular to the trunk partially closes off the groin region, with its slightly higher rate of heat loss.
- The Huddle Position can be performed by two or more people huddling together (while awaiting rescue). People in the group should face one another, press their own legs together, press their chests together (behind the insulating PFDs), and interlock arms (with one arm under the other person's). Although this may allow more heat loss than the curl-up, individual HELP position, the Huddle Position is better if the PFD, wave conditions, and swimming experience make it hard to maintain a stable individual position or if small children are immersed (they can be placed in the middle of the Huddle).
- Using HELP (or Huddle) while wearing a PFD can help someone survive up to one-third longer in cold water.
- If a boat capsizes, passengers should stay with the boat—it will probably float and support them. In cold water, climbing onto the overturned hull will help reduce heat loss; PFDs will also provide insulation.

PROGRESSION DESCRIPTIONS

Progression descriptions are listed in the following sections for:
1. Orientation and movement
2. Knowledge
3. Cold water, HELP

1. Orientation and movement

INCREASE DIFFICULTY—SHALLOW TO DEEP WATER:
- **Put PFD on properly with assistance.**
- **Put PFD on properly without assistance.**
- **Move in water in PFD.**
- **Float in water in PFD.**
- **Change directions in PFD.**
- **Do different entries while wearing PFD.**

45-49
7, 8, 43, 44, 68, 69

2. Knowledge

INCREASE DIFFICULTY:
- **Identify when to wear a PFD.**
- **Choose an appropriate PFD.**
- **Describe how to properly care for PFDs.**

45-49
67, 113, 114

3. Cold water, HELP

HELP:
- **Protects major heat-loss areas.**
- **Head stays out of water.**
- **Must be stable and controlled.**

HUDDLE:
- **Done in groups.**
- **Provides warmth from combined body heat.**
- **Provides sense of security.**

62
207, 208

Stay Warm!

The BIG Picture

- Being prepared does *NOT* decrease the fun!
- Learn to notice *SMALL* details—it makes for wise choices.
- Risks are different in different environments.
- Adapt and personalize!

Safety Tips

- Any simulation of hypothermia or ice conditions must be strictly supervised *AT ALL TIMES*.
- Discourage careless behavior.

Teaching Tips

- Focus on movement; classes should be active, rather than lectures or question and answer sessions.
- Even if it's summer, relate things to outdoor activities in other seasons.
- Develop fun activities to emphasize serious messages.
- Set an example—practice what you preach!
- Encourage participants to tell their own stories and talk about injury prevention. Use local maps. Adults can talk about spring/fall camping and fishing trips.
- Remember, hypothermia can even occur on hot summer days if going into cool or cold water.

The Facts

☑ Prepare!

- Proper clothing for ice-related activities includes the following:
  - Warm clothing worn in layers (keeps warm air in and cold air out)
  - Helmet (to protect from head injuries)
  - Wool hat (over 50% of body heat is lost through the head and neck during cold-air exposure)
  - Mittens (rather than gloves, since fingers generate body heat when together in the mitt)
  - Wool socks (wool is best for holding warm air next to the body and for insulation even when wet; wool keeps wetness away from the skin, so you don't get as cold as fast; new synthetics such as polypropylene are also effective).
- Basic safety equipment for ice activity includes the following:
  - First aid kit
  - Blanket
  - Reaching assists such as a ladder/pole, a rope with a weighted floatable end, life jacket, long tree branch
  - Matches in waterproof container (for adults)
- The following precautions should be taken with snowmobiles:
  - *Thick* ice is needed for support, because snowmobiles are *heavy*.
  - Wear a PFD-floater coat.
  - Snowmobile with a buddy.
  - Follow the shoreline.
  - Have the necessary rescue equipment, and leave at least 15 metres between snowmobiles, so that one may respond in an emergency.
- Ice forms on fresh water when the surface temperature falls to 0° C, or at lower temperatures if impurities are present, as in salt water. The date of the annual freeze-up, the rate of ice growth, and ice quality depend on factors such as air temperature, solar radiation, wind speed, snow cover, wave action, currents, and the size and depth of the water body. Generally, small lakes and slow-moving streams freeze over earlier than large lakes or fast-moving streams.
- There are two types of ice:
  1. Clear ice—formed by the freezing of water
  2. Snow ice—formed when water-saturated snow freezes on top of ice
- The colour of ice indicates its strength and quality. Clear blue ice is generally the strongest; white opaque ice has a high air content, and its strength depends on the density—the lower the density, the weaker the ice. High-density white ice has a strength close to that of clear blue ice. Grey ice generally indicates the presence of water as a result of thawing and is unsafe.
- Hypothermia is caused by exposure to cold or cold stress in either air or water. Heat loss from the head is particularly important in air hypothermia. Hypothermia can occur in any season, even summer.

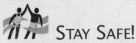 STAY SAFE!

- The National Research Council indicates that "to initially determine effective ice thickness, the rule of thumb is 1 inch of clear blue ice for every thousand pounds." However, "ice that is less than 6 inches (15 cm) thick should not be used because natural variations reduce the uniformity of thickness."
- Many communities have departments or organizations that are responsible for measuring and reporting ice thickness. These communities usually have an ice-thickness hotline with recorded information about specific ice conditions. Otherwise, it is the responsibility of those who plan to use or supervise its use to determine its safety. The Canadian Red Cross Society recommends the following safety zones for ice activities:
  - 15 cm of uniform thickness skating, walking, or skiing by small groups
  - 20 cm for larger groups, such as skating parties
  - 25 cm for snowmobiles or all-terrain vehicles
- Many factors can affect ice safety. Ice may not be safe if any of the following are present:
  - Springs or fast-moving water
  - Dark patches
  - Wind and wave action
  - Decomposing material in the water
  - Waterfowl and schooling fish
  - Water bubblers (devices designed to keep water near boat docks from freezing thick)
  - Discharge from industrial sites
  - Objects protruding through the ice such as tree stumps or rocks
  - One body of water follows into another
  - Currents
  - Snow cover
  - Wet cracks
- Being thick enough in one section does *not* mean ice thickness is safe all over. Avoid ice that has recently frozen, thawed, and then frozen again.

SURVIVE!

- You need to call EMS immediately if someone is suffering from hypothermia.
- Treatment for hypothermia is as follows.
  - Treat gently.
  - Remove from cold stress.
  - Get to shelter.
  - Get warm.

- In immersion hypothermia, the arms and legs cool most rapidly, but long-term survival depends mostly on trying to minimize heat loss from the trunk (including all of the back, the central chest, and abdomen) and any immersed portions of the neck. Although the head is potentially a high heat-loss area, it is usually less important than the rest of the body because it is most often out of the heat-robbing cold water *when a good PFD is worn*.
- When trying to get as much of the body out of the water and onto an object that might float, think trunk, neck, and head first; arms and legs last.
- These variables affect how quickly one progresses into immersion hypothermia:
  - Water temperature: cooling increases with lower temperatures.
  - Body size: larger size (greater body weight) slows the cooling rate.
  - Body fat: greater skin fatness dramatically slows the cooling rate.
  - The amount of body out of the water: the greater the amount of body out of the water, the slower cooling will be.
  - Behaviour in the water: swimming or other voluntary movements will increase the cooling rate in cold water.
  - Wave action: greater wave action increases cooling
  - Clothing worn: regular clothing has very little potential for slowing the cooling rate when immersed in water, but several layers of typical winter clothing or rain gear can slow cooling
  - The type of PFD worn: some types of PFDs can increase survival time
  - Intoxication or illness: any drug dose (including alcohol) or illness that is strong enough to significantly blunt consciousness is likely to blunt the body's defences against the cold

PROGRESSION DESCRIPTIONS

Progression descriptions are listed in the following sections for:
1. Show how to stay warm
2. Exposure to cold
3. Prepare for ice activities
4. Ice rescues

1. Show how to stay warm

STUDENTS:
- Dress warmly.
- Use towels.
- DRY YOUR HAIR!
- Use PFDs for warmth.
- Keep your head dry and covered!

WHAT TO WEAR:
- Wear appropriate clothing.
- Use layering method.
- Watch for danger of wet clothes—you get colder faster.

📖 69
📑 9, 45, 143

2. Exposure to cold

DEFINE AND DESCRIBE HYPOTHERMIA:
- Definition: Drop in inside body temperature
- Signs and symptoms: Shivering, numbness, and lack of coordination

IDENTIFY/SHOW HOW TO PROTECT MAJOR HEAT-LOSS AREAS:
- Know major heat-loss areas
- Keep the head above water
- Protect the trunk of the body

📖 60-64, 75
📑 144, 187

3. Prepare for ice activities

ICE -SAFETY ZONES:
- **Check ice thickness.**
- **Know signs that ice isn't safe: running water, darker colour.**
- **Check for signs**

PREPARING FOR ICE ACTIVITIES:
- **How to prepare for ice activity: clothing, rescue equipment, buddy.**
- **Causes of ice incidents.**
- **Safety precautions for snowmobiling.**

📖 *71*
▭ *161, 162, 269, 270*

4. Ice rescues

ICE RESCUES
- **Stimulate a self-rescue from a fall through ice.**
- **Identify ice rescue equipment.**
- **Stimulate an ice rescue from safe zone.**

📖 *72-74*
▭ *227*

Boat Smart!

The BIG Picture

- Preparing properly is a wise choice.
- Preparation will lead to prevention.

Safety Tips

- For a controlled capsize, the student should *EXPECT* the entry.
- Think about how to plan your capsize—is it safe for students? Can you control the class while one or two students are demonstrating the capsize?

Teaching Tips

- If you need to simulate a boat, try using the deck's edge, inner tubes, etc.
- No matter what you use, don't overcrowd.
- When describing where to go boating, be specific, use local maps, talk to local boaters, go to areas participants are familiar with, and emphasize local conditions and hazards.
- AquaAdults: Check your Adult Learning Inventory; you may have experienced boaters in your class—use them!

THE FACTS

✅ PREPARE!

- In addition to the equipment required by law (a PFD or life jacket for each person, a bailer, two oars with oar locks or two paddles, an effective sound signaling device such as a whistle, and an approved fire extinguisher for motorboats), consider taking a first aid kit, an extra paddle, an anchor, an extra line, a tool kit and spare parts for the boat, charts and compass, a radio for listening to radio reports, and extra throwable safety equipment. Also take food and water and matches in a waterproof container.
- Dress in warm layers for boating.
- Prepare and file a Float Plan that outlines—
  - Date and boater's names.
  - Point of departure.
  - Your destination.
  - When you plan to arrive at your destination.
  - When you expect to return to your point of departure.
  - Planned stopping points on route.
  - Weather forecast for the day.
  - A map of your intended route.

STAY SAFE!

- Check your equipment often for wear or damage.
- Don't overload—check the capacity plate on the boat. If a boat looks overloaded, it usually is.
- Safe entry into and exits from a boat include wearing nonskid deck shoes; watching for waves or wakes that may throw you off balance; alerting those already on board that you are about to board; having another person hold and help stabilize the boat while you board; being careful not to step on equipment; keeping your weight (centre of gravity) low to the bottom of the boat to keep the boat stable.
- When boarding from a dock, step as close to the centre of the boat as you can. Reach down and grasp the side of the boat as you shift your weight to the foot in the boat. Then bring the trailing foot aboard.
- To enter a boat from the beach, ensure the boat is floating and not partly resting on the bottom. Step over the bow or the stern while grasping the sides with both hands. Shift your weight to the foot in the boat. Keep your weight close to the bottom of the boat as you bring your trailing foot aboard.

- Being a safe passenger includes moving slowly; staying low; holding onto something secure when entering, exiting, and moving in the boat; following the instructions of the boat's operator; not consuming alcohol or other drugs.
- If weather and water conditions get dangerous, everyone should check that his or her PFD is properly secured and then take the most direct and safest route to shore.

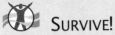 SURVIVE!

- In some situations, boat passengers may have to get down low, move to the centre of the boat, and call for help.
- It is essential not to panic if you get into a difficult situation.
- If a boat capsizes, passengers should stay with the boat—it will probably float and support them. In cold water, climbing onto the overturned hull will help reduce heat loss; PFDs will also provide insulation.
- Rescuers can find you more easily if you stay with and on top of the boat while signaling for help. It's useful to practice straddling your body over the hull of the boat, grasping onto your partner's elbows if possible, and signaling for help.

PROGRESSION DESCRIPTIONS

Progression descriptions are listed in the following sections for:
1. Prepare for safe boating
2. Stay safe while boating
3. Causes of boating incidents
4. Controlled capsize

1. Prepare for safe boating

WHAT TO KNOW AND DO:
- Identify equipment necessary for safe boating.
- Identify when and where it's safe to go boating.
- Make a float plan.

231, 234, 237, 238

115, 139, 140, 185, 186

2. Stay safe while boating

- Be a safe passenger.

231-238

141, 298, 315

3. Causes of boating incidents

- Identifies causes of boating incidents.

240, 241

209

4. Controlled capsize

- Warn students about what might happen.
- Discuss what to do when a boat capsizes, specifically how to reduce exposure to cold.
- The student's controlled capsize should be expected.

244-246

243

Rescue

The BIG Picture

- The focus is *always* on staying safe for the rescue of others; on surviving for self-rescue.
- Stay calm in self-rescue situations.
- *Always* choose rescue techniques that put you in the least possible danger.

Safety Tips

- Throw *carefully*—you don't want to hit the person you're rescuing!
- Monitor the safe use of buoyant objects with young or weak swimmers.
- Formations and control are important when practicing rescues and self-rescue skills.

Teaching Tips

- Work toward calmness and confidence.
- Once the rescue steps are known, vary environmental conditions (e.g., pond, lake, stream, pool)—it adds to the challenge.
- When using buoyant objects for support, let participants try lots of different ones to find out what works best for them. Have them rate their choices from "best" to "worst."
- For adults demonstrating the wade-in rescue, remind them to focus on their own safety first!

THE FACTS . . .

 **PREPARE!**

- Many drownings occur within a few feet of safety. That's why having rescue equipment easily accessible and knowing how to use it is so important.
- Different people may need assistance: weak or tired swimmers, nonswimmers, injured swimmers, and unconscious persons.
- An airway can become obstructed by such things as food or gum, foreign objects, plastic bags, toys, and the tongue.
- You can improvise with rescue equipment: use towels, blankets, umbrellas, coolers, tires, chairs, etc. But it's best to *be prepared*, with the right rescue equipment easily accessible at all times.

STAY SAFE!

- Buoyant objects can be fun, but you can't rely on them for safety— they may deflate suddenly or be carried away beyond your reach, luring you into danger when you try to retrieve them.
- Do NOT endanger yourself in any rescue attempt.
- When performing an assist, you must be in a safe position. You should be firmly braced or secured.

SURVIVE!

- If you're in trouble, stay calm, call for help, roll on your back, relax, and wait for help.
- In some situations, a buoyant throwing assist without a line can be used to support a person in the water until help arrives (or a better rescue aid is located).

PROGRESSION DESCRIPTIONS

Progression descriptions are listed in the following sections for:
1. Survival skills
2. Rescue of others—water
3. Rescue of others—dryland

1. Survival skills

SELF-RESCUE SKILLS:

- Identify buoyant objects.
- Use buoyant objects for support—control and comfort are essential, even in bad conditions.
- Change direction and return to edge—shallow and deep water.
- Surface support—as long as the head is out, it doesn't MATTER how it's done—focus on being relaxed and comfortable.
- Feet-first surface dive.
- Head-first surface dive.
- Surface dives with underwater swims.

📖 105-107, 121-122

📖 71, 72, 97-99, 117-119, 146, 166, 191, 213, 232, 245, 246, 248, 271, 272, 275, 276, 287, 289

2. Rescue of others—water

- Recognize and stimulate types of distressed swimmers.
- Identify good throwing assists.
- Demonstrate a throwing assist (without a line).
- Throwing assist with a line.
- Identify good reaching assists.
- Demonstrate a reaching assist.

📖 252-264

📖 163, 164, 211, 229, 230, 288

3. Rescue of others—dryland

- Survey the scene.
- Show when and how to get help.
- Show how to contact EMS.
- Describe why someone might choke and/or stop breathing.
- Show universal sign for choking.
- Show choking rescue, partial blockage.
- Recognize unconscious person and check airway.
- Demonstrate rescue breathing for an adult.
- Demonstrate choking rescue, complete blockage.
- Demonstrate rescue breathing for a child.
- Describe rescue breathing complications.

AQUA ADULT:

- Rescue breathing for an infant

📖 274-281

📖 120, 145, 165, 189, 190, 212, 231, 247, 273-275

SWIMMING

The Swimming component of the Water Safety program covers:

- The developing swimmer
  - Shallow-water orientation
  - Submersion
  - Front float
  - Front glide/front glide with kick
  - Back float
  - Back glide/back glide with kick
  - Sculling
  - Side glide
  - Deep-water orientation
- Six strokes:
  - Front crawl
  - Back crawl
  - Elementary backstroke
  - Breaststroke
  - Sidestroke
  - Butterfly
- Endurance

Use this section to find out how swimming skills in the program *develop* progressively.

THE DEVELOPING SWIMMER

Developing swimmer skills help students prepare for safe activities in, on, and around the water.

One of the most satisfying and fulfilling experiences in aquatics is teaching someone who was previously frightened of water how to swim. The expression of joy, wonder, and pride on the face of a beginning swimmer who has done something that once terrified him or her—that look is your reward.

Instructing the beginning swimmer presents you with special challenges. A friendly, nonthreatening environment where the participant can play and experiment in his or her new, unfamiliar surroundings is *key*.

Your role is to act as a friend, helper, and facilitator.

OVERCOMING FEARS...

Learning to swim is a terrifying experience for some students. Fear of the water may stem from many sources, and you may hear things like:

"I almost drowned once..."

"My sister told me when I go under the water I'll..."

"Last night on the news I saw two boaters who had..."

"I've never tried this before..."

"Will I die? I can't breathe underwater."

How will YOU react to these situations? What can YOU say to alleviate these fears?

Listen, build on what a student *can* do, use small steps, build self-confidence, and develop trust.

PROGRESSION DESCRIPTIONS

Progression descriptions are listed in the following sections for:
1. Shallow water orientation
2. Submersion
3. Front float
4. Front glide/kick
5. Back float
6. Back glide/kick
7. Sculling
8. Side glide
9. Deep-water orientation

1. Shallow water orientation

MOVE WATER IN FOUR DIFFERENT WAYS:

- **Comfortable**
- **Willing to experiment**
- **Introduction to action/reaction**

CUES

Skill: Making water move

   Visual—Make big waves.

   Auditory—Make the water rumble.

   Kinaesthetic—Feel the water push against your hand like a wall.

MOVE *THROUGH* WATER IN TWO WAYS:

- **Comfortable**
- **Willing to experiment**
- **Stable**
- **What makes it easier to move through water? (streamlining)**

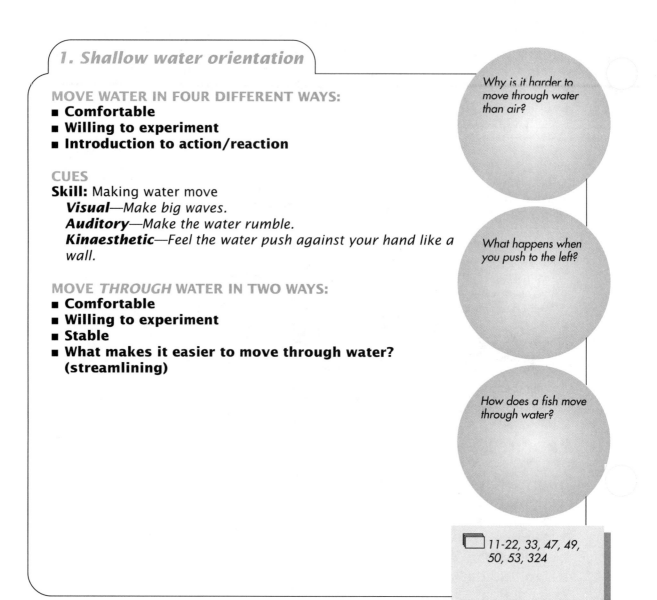

Why is it harder to move through water than air?

What happens when you push to the left?

How does a fish move through water?

11-22, 33, 47, 49, 50, 53, 324

EXHALE THROUGH MOUTH AND NOSE:
- **Comfortable.**
- **No hyperventilation.**

CORRECTIVE
Problem: LEMON FACE, tense facial muscles.
Corrective Method:
  Physical manipulation—Have students rub their face with their hands to create a relaxed face every time they bring their face out of the water.
  Overcorrection—Students stretch their face as wide and as big as possible every time they bring their head out of the water.
  Shaping—Get students to relax their face, as if it is being pulled toward the bottom of the pool.

SUBMERGE FACE:
- **Relaxed.**
- **Exhales continuously.**

CUES
Skill: Exhaling underwater
  Visual—Make big bubbles.
  Auditory—Make the water burp.
  Kinaesthetic—Feel your lips vibrate.

Why is it important to be relaxed when breathing?

CORRECTIVE
Problem: NOT EXHALING UNDERWATER.
Corrective Method:
  Physical manipulation—Practice blowing bubbles into hands underwater.
  Overcorrection—Practice "Shark Burps"—letting out air underwater all at once.
  Shaping—Remind student at the surface to breathe in only.

SUBMERGE HEAD:
- **Top of head, including ears and hair, goes under.**
- **Student opens eyes.**
- **Student submerges on request—no hesitating.**

Try submerging your head while blowing nose bubbles. Stop moving and blowing bubbles while still underwater. No water will go in your nose. Why not?

Continued.

Submersion—cont'd.

RHYTHMIC BREATHING:
- **Exhales underwater, inhales above water.**
- **Continuous and rhythmic.**
- **Relaxed and rhythmic.**
- **No hesitation at surface.**

CUES
Skill: Rhythmic breathing
Visual—*Become a human jack-in-the-box.*
Auditory—*"Pop goes the weasel."*
Kinaesthetic—*Make yourself feel as if you're going up and down in an elevator.*

CORRECTIVE
Problem: NOT INHALING ABOVE THE WATER.
Corrective Method:
Physical manipulation—*When students come up out of the water, hold onto their waist until they've taken a breath in.*
Overcorrection—*Have students try to do their rhythmic breathing very slowly, taking at least 3 seconds above and below the water.*
Shaping—*Have students practice inhaling air until their lungs feel very full.*

Problem: BREATHING QUICKLY AND ERRATICALLY, resulting in coughing and lack of breath control.
Corrective Method:
Physical manipulation—*Hold students' hands and have them breathe rhythmically with you.*
Overcorrection—*Students count to three every time they enter the water to exhale and every time they bring their head out to breathe.*
Shaping—*Students practice sighing underwater and then come up for a relaxed breath with their shoulders down and relaxed.*

RHYTHMIC BREATHING IN DIFFERENT POSITIONS:
- **Comfortable.**
- **Adaptable.**
- **Different positions (e.g., up and down, side to side, with buoyant aid, deep to shallow).**

📖 *114*
🗀 *23-27, 51-56, 73, 76, 101, 121, 147, 167*

3. Front Float

FRONT-FLOAT RECOVERY:
- **May use buoyant aid (not a PFD).**
- **Head in, feet off the ground, along surface.**
- **For recovery: bend knees, push down with hands, lift head up and back.**
- **Comfortable and quick.**
- **If needed, support should be under armpits at water level.**
- **If cannot touch bottom, bend, push, lift, and reach for edge, hand, or aid.**
- **AquaAdults: recovery is *key*, know how to recover before floating.**

MUSHROOM FLOAT:
- **Head completely submerged, feet just lifted off bottom.**
- **Comfortable and relaxed.**
- **Can do it with head and body getting lower and lower in the water.**
- **If needed, support should be under armpits at water level.**

STARFISH FLOAT:
- **Shoulders under water, spread out, lean forward, face in; *then* recover.**
- **Hold float longer before recovering *or* crouch down as low as possible in water.**
- **Stretch out and then recover.**
- **Increase amount of time before recovering.**
- **Practice different floating positions.**
- **Roll-over floats (front to back).**
- **If needed, support should be under armpits at water level.**

CUES
Skill: Front float
> **Visual**—*Look like a "starfish."*
> **Auditory**—*"Pop" out like a piece of popcorn.*
> **Kinaesthetic**—*Stretch your arms and legs wide.*

WEIGHT TRANSFER:

CORRECTIVE
Problem: GRIPPING YOU OR THE SIDES OF THE POOL OR DOCK.
Corrective Method:
> **Physical manipulation**—*Try to always hold onto students' hands rather than having them hold onto you; also try to keep their arms open wide.*
> **Overcorrection**—*Keep students away from any edges or sides; keep them low in the water—pretending that the water is their cushion.*
> **Shaping**—*Encourage students to have their shoulders in the water, their arms open wide and moving at all times; keep in mind that moving up and down may be easier than moving side to side.*

When I lift my head, my feet really sink. I guess I should keep my head in! This has a lot to do with my centre of buoyancy and centre of gravity.

Sometimes it takes a while to get stabilized in the water. But if I relax, I'll soon stabilize.

Why is a starfish float easier than a pencil float? Because your body weight is "spread-out."

What would you do with students who sink when they try to front float? Tell them to relax, stretch, and look at the bottom.

115-116
19, 20, 28, 31, 57, 77-79, 81-83, 101, 122, 123

4. Front Glide

FRONT GLIDE (TORPEDO):

- **Head in first, arms in front.**
- **Push gently off bottom or side.**
- **Increase power of push.**
- **Vary arm positions (e.g., both arms in front, one arm at a time).**
- **Roll-over glides (front to back).**
- **Add flutter kick to glides and roll-overs.**

If it's easier to go through the water when I'm like a pencil, where do my arms need to be?

CUES

Skill: Streamlined front glide
  Visual—Become a torpedo.
  Auditory—Blast off like a rocket.
  Kinaesthetic—Stretch your tummy muscles.

CORRECTIVE

Problem: PIKED BODY POSITION, resulting in very little forward movement.
Corrective Method:
  Physical manipulation—Pull students' arms and ask them to stretch.
  Overcorrection—Have students try to position themselves like a great big arch in the water.
  Shaping—Have students stretch themselves like a rubber band from one end of the pool to the other.

Problem: BUNCHING UP INTO A BALL WHEN GLIDING
Corrective Method:
  Physical manipulation—Have student hold onto an edge and ask them to extend their legs back until their toes touch your hands.
  Overcorrection—Hold students up out of the water by their hands until they feel a stretch in their tummy; they then need to create that same feeling themselves.
  Shaping—Have students stretch their body out along the surface of the water.

118
29, 30, 58, 59, 80-86, 102, 103, 106, 107

5. Back Float

MOVING BACKWARD:
- **Shoulders submerged.**
- **Head back until ears are in.**
- **Walking backward.**

CORRECTIVE
Problem: TUCKING THE CHIN DOWN DURING BACK FLOAT, resulting in a piked body position and sinking.
Corrective Method:
Physical manipulation—Use only one hand to gently bring their chin back; don't support them any other way.
Overcorrection—Have students look back at the wall behind them.
Shaping—Have students look up at the ceiling and let their feet drop low in the water.

BACK-FLOAT RECOVERY:
- **May use buoyant aid (not PFD).**
- **In a back-float position, along surface.**
- **For recovery: knees up, push down with hands, chin to chest.**

BACK-FLOAT:
- **Walking backward, tummy up, feet *down*.**
- **Stretch tummy.**
- **Feet will gradually rise.**
- **Increase amount of time before recovering.**
- **Roll-over float (back to front).**

CUES
Skill: Keeping chin back for back float or glide
Visual—Pretend you have a banana in your throat.
Auditory—Try to yodel while on your back.
Kinaesthetic—Tilt your chin back until your neck is stretched tight.

CORRECTIVE
Problem: Students PIKE THEIR BODY, usually by lifting their feet to the surface.
Corrective Method:
Physical manipulation—While ensuring that their shoulders remain at the surface, push down on students' feet as you ask them to get their belly button to the top.
Overcorrection—Have students try to get their belly button to touch the sky and their feet to touch the ground.
Shaping—Have students lower their feet while keeping their tummy up.

116
19, 57, 79-83

6. Back glide

- **Head back, shoulders and arms in.**
- **Baby push off bottom or side.**
- **Increase power of push.**
- **Vary arm positions (e.g., beside, on tummy, overhead).**
- **Roll-over glide (back to front).**
- **Add flutter kick to glides and roll-overs.**

This is easier than floating! The water rushing under my body really pushes my feet up. I guess moving in the water can be a bonus!

📖 119
▭ 58, 82-87, 106, 107, 127

7. Sculling

- **Explore how to manipulate and move water with lower arms and hands (standing, floating, using buoyant aid).**
- **Start in shallow water and move to chest and deep water.**
- **Head first on back.**
- **Feet first on back.**
- **Head first on front.**

To go feet-first, I need to push the water toward my head. That's action and reaction at work. So how do I need to position my hands so that they push the water toward my head?

📖 120
▭ 32, 125, 126, 148-150, 168, 193, 194, 233

8. Side glides

- May use buoyant aid.
- Head on shoulder, ear resting on leading arm.
- Trailing arm resting on hip.
- Ability to perform on both sides.
- Add flutter kick.

📖 117-119
📁 106, 107, 124

9. Chest and deep water orientation

- Entry in chest/deep water: ladder, slip-in, front standing jump.
- Explore flotation and movement.
- Exits safely.

📁 73-75, 108

 ## STROKES

Efficient strokes help students enjoy swimming and can ensure they stay safe should they find themselves unexpectedly in deep water.

> **Drills...**
> Your strategy cards contain a series of "tried and true" stroke drills to assist you in instructing strokes. Make sure you refer to them when preparing your lesson plans and especially when you teach.
>
> **Stroke Posters...**
> If your site has a set of Red Cross Stroke Posters, haul them out and use them to help you instruct!
>
> **Short Distance Principle...**
> - "Practice Perfect" not practice makes perfect.
> - Success increases when introductions and initial practicing happens over short distances.
> - Three-times rule: strokes have to be seen done correctly three times in one lesson.
>
> **Swimming Skills Video...**
> Do you have access to a VCR/TV? Why not spend 5 minutes before your class heads to the water and show them strokes in action. Use the Red Cross Swimming Skills video to your advantage!
>
> **Injuries!**
> Make sure you teach proper stroke techniques and drills at all times. If any student feels pain while swimming or practicing, STOP the activity immediately.
>
> **Remember...**
> No two swimmers perform a stroke exactly the same way!
>
> **Stroke Charts...**
> Stroke charts with detailed performance criteria for each level are found in Appendix I.

Learn the following stroke terms:

Body roll—the rotation of the body around the mid-line, an imaginary line that runs down the centre of a swimmer's body.

Power phase—the part of a stroke when the arm or leg is moving the body.

Glide—the part of the stroke after the power phase when the body keeps moving without any effort.

Recovery—the stage of a stroke when the arms or legs relax and return to the starting position.

Catch—the part of a stroke when the swimmer's hand first engages or "catches" the water and begins to move the body forward.

Front Crawl   The front crawl, sometimes called freestyle, is for most people the fastest stroke. Many people learn this stroke first.

PROGRESSION DESCRIPTIONS

Progression descriptions are listed in the following sections for:
1. Front/side glide
2. Front/side glide with kick
3. Arm action/roll-overs
4. Continuous rolls with kick/pyramid swims
5. 1, 2 Roll to breathe
6. Arms—recovery
7. Arms—power

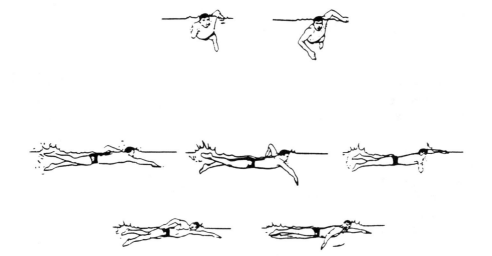

1. Front/side glides

USE TO PRACTICE BODY POSITION

FRONT GLIDE:
- **Along surface.**
- **Stretched body position.**
- **Can hold until comes to a complete stop.**

SIDE GLIDE:
- **Top shoulder back.**
- **Leading arm at surface.**
- **Lower arm along body, underwater.**
- **No sculling.**
- **Continually breathing.**
- **Ability to glide on both sides.**

I go so much farther if I stretch. Imagine going through a small hole in a brick wall.

It's that centre of buoyancy and gravity thing again. When I'm on my side, am I the most stable?

📖 *115-117*
📁 *84, 105-107*

2. Front/side glides with kick

USE TO PRACTICE BODY POSITION
- **Kick provides propulsion and stability.**
- **Stretch legs.**
- **Small and fast kicks.**
- **Loose ankles.**
- **Narrow kick.**
- **Relaxed, straight legs.**
- **Kick originates at hips.**
- **Push water down with toes.**
- **Continuous.**
- **Good propulsion = more buoyancy = less resistance.**

Kicking's great! I move forward by pushing the water backward. The law of action and reaction at work.

CUES
Skill: Small, fast kicks
   ***Visual**—Kick your legs as if they're the wings of a bee.*
   ***Kinaesthetic**—Feel your thighs gently brush each other.*

Skill: Kicks with straight legs
   ***Visual**—Straighten your legs like sticks. Pretend your legs are in casts.*
   ***Kinaesthetic**—Stretch the muscles in your legs like an elastic band.*

Continued.

Front/side glides with kick—cont'd.

Skill: Shoulder back for side glide with kick
  Visual—Place your shoulder behind your ear.
  Kinaesthetic—Pinch your shoulders together.

CORRECTIVE
Problem: KICKING LEGS OUT TO THE SIDES ONE AT A TIME.
Corrective Method:
  Physical manipulation—Use your hands or flutterboards on either side of students' legs to keep them close together, providing room for vertical movement only.
  Overcorrection—Have students do their flutter kick, and have their big toes touch each other over and over again.
  Shaping—Have students keep their legs close together while they're kicking.

Problem: NONCONTINUOUS KICK, resulting in a lack of propulsion.
Corrective Method:
  Physical manipulation—While students' front is supported, hold onto their ankles and maintain their kick.
  Overcorrection—Have students kick twice as fast, continuously.
  Shaping—Have students kick to a count.

Problem: BENDING KNEES TOO MUCH (90-DEGREE ANGLE).
Corrective Method:
  Physical manipulation—Use flippers.
  Overcorrection—Have students imagine having soldier legs.
  Shaping—Have students try to keep their legs straight while they kick.

Problem: FLEXING FEET WHILE KICKING, resulting in very little foward motion (possibly even moving backward); legs are usually quite straight.
Corrective Method:
  Physical manipulation—Place students in flippers.
  Overcorrection—Have students try to curl their toes in under their feet while they kick.
  Shaping—Have students try to push the water with their toes up or to the side.

Problem: NOT KICKING FROM THE HIPS, resulting in a hip sway or side-to-side movement.
Corrective Method:
  Physical manipulation—Use flippers.
  Shaping—Practice swimming through a hula hoop to increase streamlining and minimize knee bend.

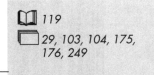
119
29, 103, 104, 175, 176, 249

3. Arm action/roll-overs

USE TO PRACTICE COORDINATION

I need to get my arms out of the water. I create less drag that way than pushing them back through water. But when I reach too high, I sink. Hmmm...

ARM ACTION:
- **Out-of-water recovery.**
- **Alternating arm action.**
- **Reduce splashing.**

ROLL-OVERS WITH GLIDE/KICK, INDIVIDUALLY:
- **Front to back (shoulder out first).**
- **Back to front (face in first).**
- **Side to front.**
- **Front to side.**

CUES
Skill: Using shoulders during roll-over
  Visual—Roll like a log. Flip like a pancake.
  Auditory—"Flip, flop."
  Kinaesthetic—Lead with the shoulder.
Skill: Out-of-water recovery for front crawl
  Visual—Reach for the sky or ceiling.
  Auditory—Try to swim as quietly as possible.
  Kinaesthetic—Reach as high as you can until you can feel a pull through the front of your shoulder.

CORRECTIVE
Problem: UNDERWATER RECOVERY.
Corrective Method:
  Physical manipulation—While holding onto students' arms just above the elbows, rotate their arms in complete circles.
  Overcorrection—Have students reach for the ceiling, sky, or your hand while swimming.
  Shaping—Have students create rainbows above the water with each recovery.

131-134
31, 129, 151

4. Continuous rolls/pyramid swims

USE TO PRACTICE COORDINATION

CONTINUOUS ROLLS WITH KICK:
- **On side, one arm up, one arm down.**
- **Roll from side to front, front to side, continuously.**
- **Shoulder controls movement.**
- **Exhale underwater, inhale above water.**

CORRECTIVE
Problem: KICK STOPS WHEN student BREATHES, resulting in a stop-and-start motion, a lowered body position, and sculling.
Corrective Method:
   Physical manipulation—Hold students while they breathe, until they are kicking.
   Overcorrection—Have students create extremely large splashes with their kick whenever they breathe.
   Shaping—Break down the skill to simply rolling from front to side to front with a focus on maintaining a continuous kick.

Problem: NOT ROLLING SHOULDERS ENOUGH ON FRONT CRAWL, resulting in sculling on their sides, breathing to the front, and a wide arm entry.
Corrective Method:
   Physical manipulation—Every time students move to breathe, push their shoulder back with your hand.
   Overcorrection—Have students roll onto their back to breathe while their arms remain in alternate positions.
   Shaping—Have students roll to breathe until they can see above the water.

PYRAMID SWIM:
- **Start on side, position as above.**
- **Breathe, roll onto front, switch one arm, roll to other side to breathe.**
- **Shoulder controls movement.**
- **Do *slowly*.**

Is it easier to walk on your tip-toes or to use your whole foot? Your whole foot, of course. Same applies to swimming. The greater the area you push with, the greater the propulsion.

📖 135
🗂 151-153

5. 1, 2 Roll to breathe

USE TO PRACTICE COORDINATION AND BREATHING/TIMING

- **Breathe, roll until face is underwater, do three arm rotations, roll to other side to breathe on third arm pull.**
- **OK to pause on side to breathe.**
- **Reduce breathing time until there's no pause.**
- **Goggles help sensitive eyes.**

CUES
Skill: 1, 2, 3 breathe
   Auditory—"Pepsi, Coke, Seven Up."

CORRECTIVE
Problem: LIFTING HEAD TO BREATHE ON FRONT CRAWL.
Corrective Method:
   Physical manipulation—When students breathe, touch their cheek as a reminder to breathe to the side.
   Overcorrection—Have students hold a cap or piece of cloth under their chin while they swim.
   Shaping—Have students look at their shoulder as they breathe.

Problem: PAUSING TO BREATHE IN FRONT CRAWL.
Corrective Method:
   Physical manipulation—Walk beside students while they swim, tap their shoulder when they breathe to remind them to go under.
   Overcorrection—Have students breathe for a count of "0."
   Shaping—Have students reduce the amount of time it takes them to breathe.

📖 137
▭ 169, 170, 250

6. Arms—recovery

HANDS ENTER FORWARD OF HEAD:
■ **Get a good catch.**

CORRECTIVE
Problem: ARM ENTRY CROSSES OVER.
Corrective Method:
Physical manipulation—Walk in front of students as they swim toward you; as their hands enter the water, gently push them out to the side.
Overcorrection—Have students' hands enter at 9:00 and 3:00.
Shaping—Have students reach out to the sides when they swim.

Problem: ARM ENTRY IS WIDE.
Corrective Method:
Physical manipulation—Have students swim through a hula hoop.
Overcorrection—Have students try to have their arms cross over.
Shaping—Have students start reaching in closer to their head when they swim.

Problem: ARM DOES NOT ENTER THE WATER FORWARD OF THE HEAD.
Corrective Method:
Physical manipulation—As students swim toward you, gently pull their wrists out in front of them.
Overcorrection—Have students reach across the pool as they swim.
Shaping—Have students reach for your hand in front of them; they must touch your hand before starting their pull.

Problem: UNDERWATER CROSSOVER OF THE ARMS IN FRONT CRAWL.
Corrective Method:
Physical manipulation—As students swim and their body turns side-to-side, hold onto their ankles to exaggerate their side to side movement.
Overcorrection—Have students imagine they're swimming over the world and therefore need to pull way out to their side.
Shaping—Have students focus on having a bent-arm pull that doesn't cross over their midline.

> What happens if I cross over my hands on entry? I go this way and that way in a zig-zag or wiggly fashion. Hmmm—not very streamlined.

Continued.

Arms—recovery—cont'd.

HANDS ENTER IN LINE WITH SHOULDERS:
- **No crossovers or wide entries.**
- **For streamlining.**

CUES

Skill: Arm entry in line with shoulder for front crawl
   Visual—Draw a line from your shoulder to the wall or shore.
   Auditory—Slap the water in front of your shoulder.
   Kinaesthetic—Touch your arm to your ear as you recover.

Skill: Bent arm recovery for front crawl
   Visual—Create a triangle as you bring your arms forward.
   Auditory—"Creak" your arms forward like a rusty hinge.
   Kinaesthetic—Lift your elbow high, until you feel a pull in your triceps.

RELAXED ARM RECOVERY
- **Bent arm, loose wrists.**
- **Elbow higher than hand.**

131-134
195, 215, 218

7. Arms—power

BENT-ARM PULL IN S PATTERN:
- **Early catch at beginning of the pull.**
- **Scoop and pull past hips.**

CUES

Skill: High elbow pull for front crawl

   Visual—Pretend you're reaching over the top of a barrel.

   Auditory—"Snap" your hand down from your elbow at the beginning of your pull.

   Kinaesthetic—Reach forward so that you can feel a stretch.

CORRECTIVE

Problem: CATCH-UP.

Corrective Method:

   Physical manipulation—Position yourself to the side of students, hold their hands at opposite positions, and rotate slowly.

   Overcorrection—Have students use a board or ring and swim with a forward catch-up (hands meet at the top of the stroke).

   Shaping—Have students pause every time both arms are in opposition, parallel to the bottom; then move both arms together. Speed up action until there is no pause.

Problem: SHORT PULL, resulting in very little movement and some sculling.

Corrective Method:

   Physical manipulation—Have students stand up and rub their thumbs against their thighs with arms straight; when they swim, they should try to have their thumbs hit those same spots.

   Overcorrection—Have students try to reach for their knees when they swim.

   Shaping—Have students hit their thigh when they swim.

HANDS PULL PAST HIPS:
- **Stroke efficiency.**

> A strong and long pull is key!

> Whew! I'm glad they finally taught me to use a bent arm pull! It seems to make me less tense and tired.

📖 *132*
📂 *171, 172, 260, 277, 291*

Back crawl   Back crawl is one of the four competitive strokes and the only one performed on the back. It is the fastest stroke on the back and is often called the backstroke.

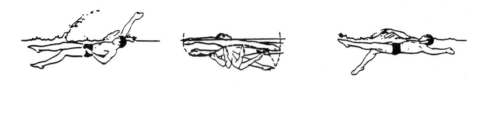

PROGRESSION DESCRIPTIONS

Progression descriptions are listed in the following sections for:
1. Back glide/kick
2. Shoulder roll/arm action
3. Arms—recovery
4. Arms—power

1. Back Glide/Kick

USE TO PRACTICE BODY POSITION

BACK GLIDE:
- Streamlined body position.

BACK GLIDE WITH KICK:
- Provide added propulsion.
- Continuous.
- Small and fast.
- Relaxed, straight legs.
- Relaxed, pointed toes, breaking surface; knees stay under.
- Kick originates at hips.
- Push water up with toes.
- Varying arm positions—by side, hands on top of stomach, arms out of water (from elbow to hands), arms stretched overhead (along water surface).
- Fins help a relaxed kick.

CUES

Skill: Small, fast kicks
> *Visual*—Kick your legs as if they're the wings of a bee.
> *Kinaesthetic*—Feel your thighs gently brush each other.

Skill: Kicks with straight legs
> *Visual*—Straighten your legs like sticks. Pretend your legs are in casts.
> *Kinaesthetic*—Stretch the muscles in your legs like an elastic band.

To get proplusion from my back kick, I need to kick UP. Why?

119
154, 155, 175, 177

2. Shoulder Roll/Arm Action

USE TO PRACTICE COORDINATION

SHOULDER ROLL
- **Back glide with kick, arms by side.**
- **Roll one shoulder out (45-degree angle), then the other.**
- **Body position maintained.**
- **Head stays still, neck in line with spine.**

ARM ACTION
- **Shoulder comes out, followed by arm.**
- **Out-of-water recovery.**
- **Alternating arm action.**
- **Breathing relaxed.**

CORRECTIVE
Problem: UNDERWATER RECOVERY.

Corrective Method

Physical manipulation—Holding onto students' arms just above the elbows, rotate their arms above water on recovery.

Overcorrection—Have students reach for the ceiling, sky, or your hand while swimming.

Shaping—Have students create rainbows above the water with each recovery.

📖 *167-170*
📁 *156, 173*

3. Arms—Recovery
Relaxed Straight Arm Recovery

HANDS ENTER AT 11:00 AND 1:00
- **Increases streamlining.**
- **No crossover or wide entries.**

I see little waves (eddies) around my body when I don't enter in the right place, and these eddies slow me down. I wonder— is that good?

CUES
Skill: Straight arm recovery for back crawl
   Visual—Watch your elbow to make sure it's straight above your body.
   Auditory—"Snap" your elbow straight.
   Kinaesthetic—Reach for the sky or ceiling until you feel a stretch.

CORRECTIVE
Problem: ARM ENTRY CROSSES OVER.
Corrective Method
   Physical manipulation—Walk in front of students as they swim toward you; as their hands enter the water, gently push them out to the side.
   Overcorrection—Have students' hands enter at 9:00 and 3:00.
   Shaping—Have students start reaching out to the sides more when they swim.

Problem: ARM ENTRY IS WIDE.
Corrective Method
   Physical manipulation—Have students swim through a hula hoop.
   Overcorrection—Have students try to have their arms cross over.
   Shaping—Have students reach in closer to their head when they swim.

167-170
197, 217, 218

4. Arms—Power

HANDS ENTER AT 11:00 AND 1:00 WITH AN EARLY CATCH

■ **Grab the water as soon as hands enter.**

ELBOW POINTS TO BOTTOM THROUGHOUT BENT-ARM PULL:

■ **Greater force from a lever.**

HANDS PULL PAST THIGH:

■ **Effective propulsion.**

HAND ACCELERATES THROUGH PULL:

■ **Increase in power.**

CORRECTIVE

Problem: REAR CATCH-UP.
Corrective Method
   Physical manipulation—Position yourself to the side of students, hold their hands at opposite positions, and rotate slowly.
   Overcorrection—Have students use a board or ring and swim with a forward catch-up (hands meet at the top of the stroke).
   Shaping—Have students pause every time both arms are in opposition, parallel to the bottom; then move both arms together. Speed up action until there is no pause.

Problem: SHORT PULL, resulting in very little movement and some sculling.
Corrective Method
   Physical manipulation—Have students stand up and rub their thumbs against their thighs with arms straight; when they swim, they should try to have their thumbs hit those same spots.
   Overcorrection—Have students try to reach for their knees when they swim.
   Shaping—Have students hit their thigh when they swim.

Is it easier to lift yourself onto a counter with bent or straight elbows? How does that apply here? It's the Law of Levers in action.

📖 167-170

📖 174, 251, 260, 279, 293

Elementary backstroke The elementary backstroke is used for recreation, for survival swimming, and for exercising muscle groups not used in other strokes. It can be used to recover from strenuous effort while still making slow but effective progress through the water.

A

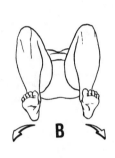

B

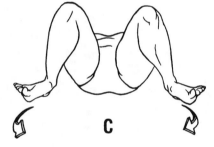

C

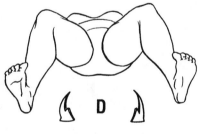

D

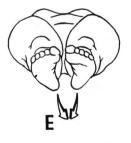

E

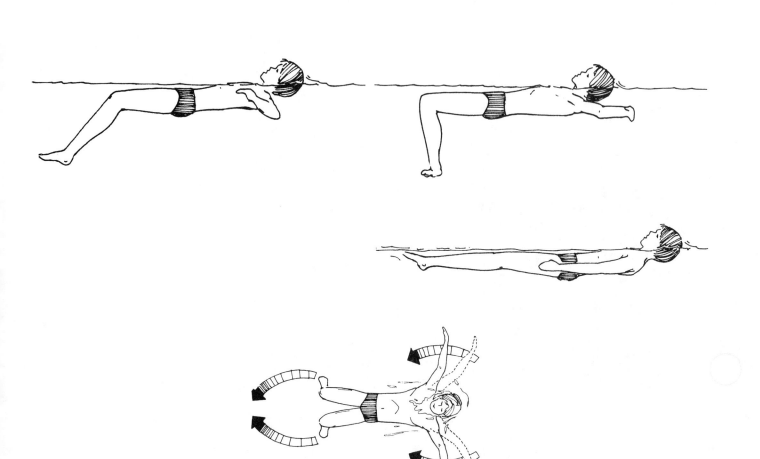

PROGRESSION DESCRIPTIONS

Progression descriptions are listed in the following sections for:
1. Back glide
2. Adding a whip kick
3. Kick and glide/arm action
4. Coordination
5. Power

1. Back Glide

BACK GLIDE
- **Streamlined body position.**
- **Face stays *out of water*.**
- **Hands at side.**

📖 *119*
📖 *154, 155*

2. Whip Kick

ADD A WHIP KICK:
- **Knees slightly wider than hips.**
- **Bend *down from knees* until ankles touch bum.**
- **Flex ankles, keep knees inside ankles, and rotate feet out to the side.**
- **Push water out and around with feet in a circle until the legs are straight again along the surface.**
- **Kick is symmetric.**
- **Do first with no power (stationary).**
- **Increase push near the end of the kick.**
- **Glide after each kick.**

Skill: Kick in the whipkick
    ***Visual**—Imagine you're kicking your legs around a ball.*
    ***Auditory**—"Snap" your legs back together.*
    ***Kinaesthetic**—Try to feel the water push against the inside of your legs and feet.*

CORRECTIVE
Problem: FROG KICK.
Corrective Method
    ***Physical manipulation**—Place your hands on either side of your students' knees during the kick.*
    ***Overcorrection**—Do very small kicks with knees touching.*
    ***Shaping**—Practice making sure the ankles are always wider than the knees.*

Continued.

Problem: POINTING TOES.
Corrective Method
   Physical manipulation—Hold onto their feet to ensure students push against your hands with the inside of their feet.
   Overcorrection—Have students practice whip kick vertically in the deep end; they may need a pull buoy to keep them in place.
   Shaping—Have students stretch their toes to the ceiling throughout their kick.

Problem: BRINGING KNEES TO CHEST rather than ankles to bottom.
Corrective Method
   Physical manipulation—While students do their whip kick, place one hand on the small of their back and the other on their knees; when they kick, don't allow the knees to come forward.
   Overcorrection—Have students try to touch the small of their back with their ankles every time they kick.
   Shaping—Have students touch their ankles to their bottom every time they kick.

Problem: KICKING STRAIGHT OUT TO THE SIDES, resulting in little or no power.
Corrective Method
   Physical manipulation—Place your hands on either side of your students' knees.
   Overcorrection—Have students touch their ankles together at the end of their kick.
   Shaping—Have students focus on the finish of the kick.

143, 146
199, 200, 202, 203, 235

3. Kick and Glide/Arm Action

I can really move without working hard as long as I glide.

USE TO PRACTICE COORDINATION
KICK AND GLIDE
- **Follow each kick with glide.**
- **Stretch body at end of kick.**

ARM ACTION:
- **Coordinated with whip kick.**
- **Reach toward your head, push toward your toes.**

CORRECTIVE
Problem: NO GLIDE.
Corrective Method
    Physical manipulation—Have students reach for your hands on each glide. Glide ends when they reach your hands.
    Overcorrection—Have students count to five at the end of their push.
    Shaping—Have students stretch themselves as long as they can after the push phase.

144-145
219

4. Coordination

- Arms and knees stay just below the surface.
- Arm and leg recovery is slow.
- Breathes in on recovery, and exhales during propulsion.
- Knees and shoulders should be flat.

📖 *144, 145*

5. Power

- Arms and legs accelerate during propulsive phase.
- Increase push throughout kick and pull.
- Extended body position.

CUES

Skill: Streamlined push in the elementary backstroke
   Visual—Stretch yourself out like an elastic band.
   Auditory—Stretch and push to send yourself "sliding" through the water.
   Kinaesthetic—Stretch your tummy muscles.

CORRECTIVE

Problem: ARMS FINISHING AFTER LEGS.
Corrective Method
   Physical manipulation—While holding their wrists, control the arm movements of students while they do their kick (vertically or horizontally).
   Overcorrection—Have students start their pull before starting their kick.
   Shaping—Have students think of themselves as a puppet whose legs and arms push and kick at the same time.

 📖 *144*
🖿 *260*

Breaststroke   The breaststroke is the oldest known swimming stroke. For many centuries it was the first stroke swimmers learned. It is one of the four competitive strokes but is also very popular for leisure swimming because you can keep your head up to see around you and breathe easily, and because you can rest momentarily between strokes.

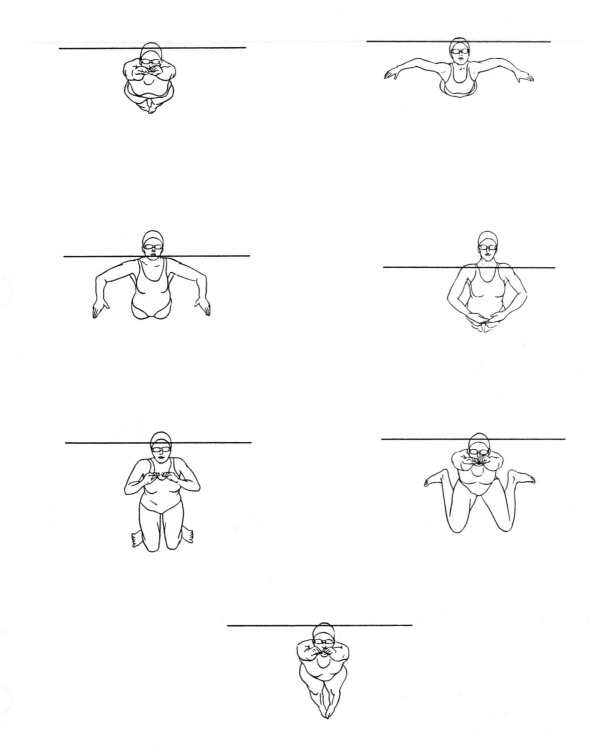

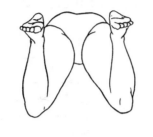

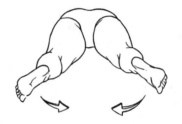

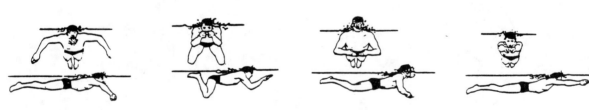

PROGRESSION DESCRIPTIONS

Progression descriptions are listed in the following sections for:

1. Front glide
2. Whip kick
3. Pull, breathe, kick, glide
4. Mechanics
5. Power

1. Front Glide

USE TO PRACTICE BODY POSITION
FRONT GLIDE

- **Horizontal along the surface *or* body position slanted (legs lower).**
- **Spine straight, with neck in line.**
- **Face in the water.**

📖 119
📕 84

2. Whip kick

WHIP KICK AND GLIDE (FACE IN)

- **Knees stay inside ankles at all times and shoulder-width apart.**
- **Pull heels toward buttocks.**
- **Flex ankles, keep knees inside ankles, and rotate feet out to the side.**
- **Bring feet around in a circle until legs are straight again along the surface.**
- **Kick is symmetric.**
- **Follow kick with a glide.**
- **Start to accelerate throughout kick.**

If I bring my feet all the way up to my bum, I get a longer and stronger kick—proplusion again. But recover slowly now—resistance is at work.

CUES
Skill: Kick in the whipkick
   Visual—Imagine you're kicking your legs around a ball.
   Auditory—"Snap" your legs back together.
   Kinaesthetic—Try to feel the water push against the inside of your legs and feet.

CORRECTIVE
Problem: KICKING STRAIGHT OUT TO THE SIDES.
Corrective Method
   Physical manipulation—Place your hands on either side of your students' knees.
   Overcorrection—Have students touch their ankles together at the end of their kick.
   Shaping—Have students focus on the finish of the kick.

📖 153
📕 201-203

3. Pull, Breathe, Kick, Glide

USE TO PRACTICE COORDINATION AND TIMING
BREATHE, FACE IN, KICK, GLIDE:
- **Arms in front, along surface.**
- **Lift head up to breathe.**
- **Face goes in as kick starts.**
- **Follow kick with a 3-second glide.**

PULL, BREATHE, FACE IN, GLIDE:
- **Arms in front, along surface.**
- **Use a small, simultaneous, symmetric bent-arm pull to bring both arms down.**
- **Lift head to breathe as soon as hands separate.**
- **Face goes in as hands stretch forward together.**
- **3-second glide follows pull.**

PULL, BREATHE, KICK, GLIDE, 1, 2, 3:
- **Start breath as soon as pull begins.**
- **As face enters, start kick.**
- **Follow with a 3-second glide.**

CUES
Skill: Small bent arm pull for breaststroke
  Visual—Drop your hands down.
  Auditory—Slap your hands together at the end of the pull.
  Kinaesthetic—Leave your elbows high during the pull.

CORRECTIVE
Problem: BREATHING LATE.
Corrective Method
  Physical manipulation—Stand in front of your students and have them reach for your hand. Have their fingers remain in your hand until they have taken a breath.
  Overcorrection—Have students perform a very small pull with a very short breath.
  Shaping—Have students lift their head to breathe as soon as their hands open.

> If I glide too long, I seem to sink. But if I don't glide enough, I feel like a teeter-totter. The key is to find a balance.

Continued.

Pull, Breathe, kick, glide—*cont'd.*

Problem: KICKING AND PULLING AT THE SAME TIME.
Corrective Method
    Physical manipulation—Hold onto students' legs until their pull is complete; then let go.
    Overcorrection—Have students count to three after their pull, then count to three after their kick.
    Shaping—Have students say to themselves as they swim: "Pull to breathe, kick to glide."

Problem: STRAIGHT ARM PULL.
Corrective Method
    Physical manipulation—While holding their elbows, assist student with the proper arm movments.
    Overcorrection—Have students practice a very small pull that stays in front of their head at all times.
    Shaping—Have students bend their elbows when they pull.

Problem: NO GLIDE.
Corrective Method
    Physical manipulation—Have student reach for your hands on each glide. Glide ends when they reach your hands.
    Overcorrection—Have students count to five at the end of their propulsion.
    Shaping—Have students stretch themselves as long as they can after the propulsive phase.

Problem: LOW BENT-ARM PULL.
Corrective Method
    Physical manipulation—Hold students' elbows at surface.
    Overcorrection—Have students practice sculling with their hands in front of their head with their elbows at the surface and never any lower.
    Shaping—Have students imagine reaching over and around a barrel that's in front of them while they're swimming.

154-156
221, 222, 235

4. Mechanics

- **Body stays at or near surface.**
- **Hands stay forward of shoulders—to reduce negative movements on recovery.**
- **Streamlining and full extension occurs *after* kick.**
- **Breathing is relaxed.**

See me go when I stretch and am streamlined.

📖 *153*

🗂 *237*

5. Power

- **Hands and legs accelerate through propulsive phases.**
- **Inhale during insweep of pull and exhale during recovery.**

Long and strong pull again!

CORRECTIVE

Problem: High bent-arm pull with no force, resulting in little power.

Corrective Method

Physical manipulation—Hold onto students' ankles AND put a mat under their body that extends in front of their head; as students' arms pull, hold their ankles so that they have to work against you.

Overcorrection—Have students practice sculling in front of their head or swimming with their fists.

Shaping—Have students imagine pushing against the wall as they kick to increase their power.

📖 *149-150*

🗂 *260, 261*

Sidestroke   In the sidestroke the body position reduces frontal resistance and lets the face and one ear stay out of the water. Propulsion comes mainly from the kick. The sidestroke is easy to learn because the breathing is simple. Because the sidestroke is a resting stroke and uses less energy than other strokes, the swimmer can use it for long distances without tiring.

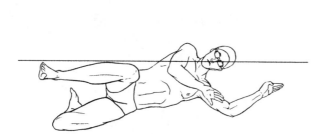

PROGRESSION DESCRIPTIONS

Progression descriptions are listed in the following sections for:
1. Side glide
2. Kick and glide
3. Arm action
4. Mechanics
5. Power

1. Side Glide

USE TO PRACTICE BODY POSITION
SIDE GLIDE:

- **Top shoulder back.**
- **Leading arm at surface.**
- **Lower arm along body, underwater.**
- **No sculling.**
- **Continuous breathing.**

CUES

Skill: Shoulder back for side glide with kick
  Visual–Place your shoulder behind your ear.
  Kinaesthetic–Pinch your shoulders together.

Imagine you're a piece of thread going through the eye of a needle. Glide in a streamlined position—don't fray!

117
105, 106

2. Kick and Glide

USE TO PRACTICE COORDINATION
KICK AND GLIDE:
- **Arms stay in Superman position (one arm up, one arm down).**
- **Bring both legs up together, bending at hips and knees.**
- **Extend one leg forward, one back.**
- **Kick them together (scissor).**
- **Finish with a glide.**

CUES
Skill: Scissor kick
> *Visual*–Stretch your legs wide enough to see one of your feet in front of you.
> *Kinaesthetic*–Stretch your legs as far apart as possible.

CORRECTIVE
Problem: WHIP KICK ON SIDE.
Corrective Method:
> *Physical manipulation*–Have students hold onto an edge or board as you manipulate their legs from their ankles.
> *Overcorrection*–Place boards along the water surface over the top of students' legs while they kick.
> *Shaping*–Have students practice reaching their legs as far forward and backward as possible while kicking.

Problem: NARROW SCISSOR KICK.
Corrective Method:
> *Physical manipulation*–As students perform their kick recovery, stand in front of or behind them, and have them make sure their foot has extended to you.
> *Shaping*–Have students watch their kick as they bring their legs up together and scissor.

161-164
253

ARM ACTION:

- **In a side-glide position, with no leg movement.**
- **Lead arm is extended; trailing arm is on hip.**
- **Leading arm pulls down to chest while trailing arm recovers from hip.**
- **Leading arm recovers to stretched position, and trailing arm pushes down to hip. Finish with a glide.**

CUES

Skill: Arm pull for sidestroke

Visual–Pull your arms in and grasp your heart.

Auditory–Hold a whoopee cushion that explodes with sound when squeezed.

Kinaesthetic–Pull your arms in tight, as if you're cold.

CORRECTIVE

Problem: HANDS MEET IN FRONT OF CHEST OR TOP OF HEAD.

Corrective Method:

Physical Manipulation–Hold onto your student's wrists to guide their arms.

Overcorrection–If their hands meet at their chest, have them try to meet in front of their head, and vice versa.

Shaping–Have students' hands meet in front of their chin.

COORDINATE ARM AND LEG ACTION:

- **Everything comes in together and goes out at once.**
- **Finish with a glide in side glide position.**

📖 *163*
📑 *254*

4. Mechanics

- Kick and arm action are streamlined, with slow recoveries.
- Inhale while legs recover, exhale during power phase.

293

5. Power

- Kick and arm action provide propulsion.
- Accelerate kick and arm through power phase.

260

Butterfly   The butterfly is most often seen as the most difficult of the four competitive strokes. Thus many swimmers, even those good at other strokes, do not try to learn it. But even beginning swimmers can learn the butterfly stroke by practicing timing and technique. The key is relaxing and using your whole body in a flowing motion.

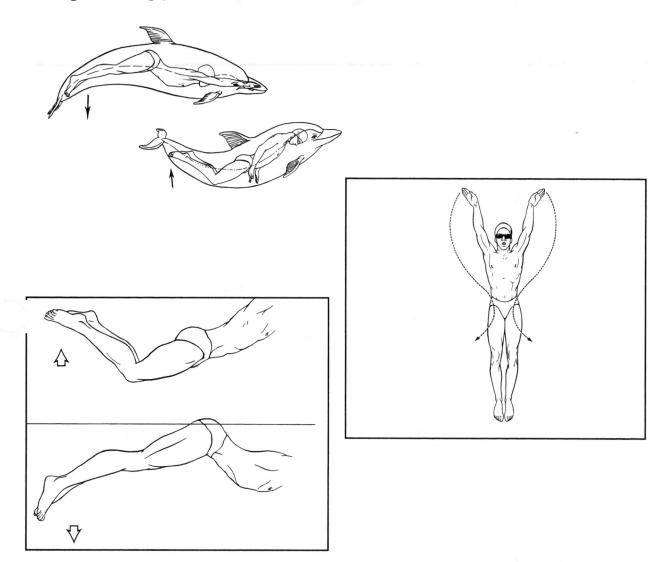

PROGRESSION DESCRIPTIONS

Progression descriptions are listed in the following sections for:
1. Wave motion
2. Dolphin kick
3. Arm action
4. Butterfly stroke
5. Mechanics
6. Arm—power

1. Wave Motion

USE TO PRACTICE BODY POSITION
WAVE MOTION:

- **Relax with a smooth, flowing motion.**
- **Roll forward through the water.**
- **Wave motion *starts at the head* and goes to the ends of the feet.**

CUES
Dolphin Kick:
Visual–Picture a wave rolling along the surface of the water.
Auditory–Think "head" and "hips" while moving the head to the surface followed by the hips.
Kinaesthetic–Feel your body moving from head to toes as your lower legs push down.

📖 *178*
📑 *255-259*

2. Dolphin Kick

USE TO PRACTICE COORDINATION

- **Kick starts at the hips.**
- **Both knees stay slightly bent through most of the *down* beat.**
- **Straighten both legs on the *up* beat.**
- **Heels just break the surface at the end of the recovery.**
- **Motion uses the whole body, not just the legs.**
- **Aim for a *continuous* kick.**

CORRECTIVE
Problem: RIGID DOLPHIN KICK, resulting in reduced propulsion.
Corrective Method:
Physical manipulation–Pull the students through the water while they move their whole body like a wave.
Overcorrection–Have students arch up and dive down in exaggerated dolphin dives.
Shaping–Have students focus on beginning their leg snap from the hips.

Problem: HIPS SINKING DURING BUTTERFLY, resulting in reduced effectiveness of the dolphin kick.
Corrective Method:
Physical manipulation–Hold an object above students as they swim, asking them to try to touch the object with their bum every time their arms enter the water.
Overcorrection–Have students push their bum right above the water each time they dive forward with their arms.
Shaping–Have students pretend the hips are being pulled up by a rope every time their arms enter the water.

📖 *178*
📑 *260, 261, 282*

3. Arm Action

USE TO PRACTICE COORDINATION

- **Reach in front of the head to start with a large scull in the water.**
- **Complete a large keyhole pattern in the water until the pull is past the hips.**
- **Elbows always stay higher than hands.**
- **In recovery, arms are almost straight, just above the surface, to the side of the body.**
- **Wrists stay relaxed.**

📖 *175-177*
📇 *281*

4. Butterfly stroke

USE TO PRACTICE COORDINATION

- **There are two kicks per pull.**
- **As the hands enter the water, perform first downkick.**
- **As arms exit, perform second downkick.**
- **Take a breath as arms finish pull.**
- **Tilt head and shoulders out of the water as the pull finishes.**

CUES

Skill: Butterfly breathing

Visual–Picture a table in front of you and put your chin on top of the table while breathing to the front.

Kinaesthetic–"Stretch" the chin and nose forward (not up).

CUES

Skill: Butterfly coordination

Visual–Picture the arms pulling during one kick and recovering during the other kick.

Auditory–"Kick in, kick out"...kick as the arms enter the water, and kick arms out of the water.

Kinaesthetic–Feel one kick propelling the arms forward and the second kick propelling the arms back and out.

📖 *179*
📇 *283, 284*

5. Mechanics

- **Legs are together, toes pointed.**
- **Dolphin kick is symmetric.**
- **Hands enter in front of the head and finish the pull at the thigh.**
- **Breathe to the side if necessary.**
- ***Optional* to use both arms simultaneously.**

CORRECTIVE
Problem: TOO MANY DOLPHIN KICKS PER PULL.
Corrective Method:
>*Physical manipulation*–Guide the students hands through the path of the pull, indicating when the kicks should occur.
>*Overcorrection*–Have students perform the stroke with only one kick occurring as the arms enter and stretch forward.
>*Shaping*–Have students perform the stroke in slow motion, concentrating on the proper timing of each kick.

📖 *179*

6. Arms—Power

- **Use bent-arm, keyhole pattern pull.**

📖 *175*
📖 *281*

 ENDURANCE

Research shows that a person in distress in the water uses up to 10 times the amount of energy he or she would normally use to swim to safety. Most drowning also occur within 50 metres of the shore, dock, boat, or other safe area. To survive in such a situation, endurance swimming is vital. Students should learn to swim at least 500 metres in any stroke that is comfortable and effective for them.

PROGRESSION DESCRIPTIONS

Progression descriptions are listed in the following section for:

1. Endurance

1. Endurance

ANY WAY YOU WANT

- *Any* way is OK.
- **Stroke performance criteria is *not* applied during the endurance swim.**
- **Emphasize using efficient strokes (e.g., front crawl) rather than inefficient methods (e.g., dog paddle).**

89, 90, 131, 157, 177, 205, 223, 239, 263, 295

SAFETY SCENES

General The purpose of Safety Scenes is to assess your students' ability to link knowledge and skills. When focusing on a specific skill, you instruct students how to do things right, which includes making wise choices in many cases (e.g., Stop! Look! Go Slow!). Outside of your lessons, you don't know for sure that your students will remember or choose to apply their knowledge and skills in a safe way. When you ask your students to perform a Safety Scene in a lesson, you are essentially asking them to demonstrate the integration of knowledge and skills that they have learned. This integration is essential in better preparing your students to *apply* what they learn in your lessons to potential real-life situations in, on, or around the water. This is why Safety Scenes are an important part of the Water Safety program.

Using Safety Scenes Safety Scenes must be used throughout each set of lessons and not just as something you do on the *last* day of classes. Safety Scenes can range in difficulty from a simple sequence of activities (e.g., slip-in, surface, spin around three times, return to edge, climb out) to an evolved scenario or story involving knowledge, skills, and judgment. Either way, be creative and use different Safety Scenes within one lesson set.

Appendix J contains examples of Safety Scenes for AquaTots, AquaQuest, and AquaAdults; they are ready for you to put onto strategy cards and use in the water. Adapt the scenes, especially entries, to make them appropriate to your site.

You are also encouraged to develop your own Safety Scenes and include them in your strategy cards. Build up a bank of Safety Scenes for each level! There are lots of good reasons to develop your own Safety Scenes. You can change the focus of Safety Scenes, depending on which season it is. For example, emphasize "stay warm" and ice safety in the winter, and use local names of water areas.

Steps to Follow When Developing Safety Scenes

1. *Choose the Skills: Review the content in the level that you are teaching and decide which knowledge and skills you want to link together in the Safety Scene.* To have an effective Safety Scene, you need to have only two or more items linked together. The items you choose depends on a number of factors such as the

time you have allotted or what knowledge and skills the students have learned at a particular point in the set of lessons. Your Safety Scene can focus on water safety, swimming, or wise choices or a combination of all three, depending on the level of difficulty your students can handle. In terms of strokes, level specific distance requirements can be shortened to better fit the Safety Scene.

2. *Set the Scene: Create a situation or scene in which students can apply their knowledge and skills together, in a relevant way.* As you'll see by the examples, Safety Scenes can be set in the "here and now" in your lesson, or they can be set around an activity or scenario in "real life." The scene itself can take place as a simple sequence of activities, a relay or circuit, or a survival scenario. Find out what aquatic activities (including emergency situations) the students have been involved in and think about instances in which people are drowning or injuring themselves.

3. *Identify Wise Choices: Make a list of wise choices that you and your students can incorporate into the Safety Scene. Your students will naturally demonstrate wise choices to some degree.* Wise choices can play a very simple role. For example, in the AquaQuest level 1 example, a wise choice is as simple as students waiting for your cue to enter the water. In level 10, wise choices take on a much greater role, in the sense that students should demonstrate how to prepare and stay safe while boating without being prompted. Also, when the boat capsizes, they have to make some quick choices about how to survive. You can highlight wise choices in your Safety Scene or simply review them. Either way, it is important for you and your students to identify and reflect on the wise choices that they made or could have made.

4. *Be Prepared and Stay Safe:* Prepare by determining the *equipment* needed to carry out the Safety Scene, and consult with fellow instructors to ensure that you have *space* to safely complete the scene. Stay Safe by noting and dealing with any *safety supervision* concerns (including effective *formations*) that may arise as the Safety Scene progresses.

You may want students to do a Safety Scene more than once. Repeating the Safety Scene will allow students the opportunity to reflect on their knowledge, skills, and attitude and to exercise their ability to keep making wise choices. *Remember, the idea is to link knowledge and skills together in an applicable, safe, and practical way.* So keep it simple, be creative, build in a progression of difficulty, and use Safety Scenes throughout your lessons. Have fun!

SAFETY SCENE FORM

Safety Scenes	Level:	AquaTots
		AquaQuest
		AquaAdults
Skills to be performed (WS and Sw)	Wise Choices (judgment)	
Safety Scene	Equipment/safety supervision	
	Other	

AquaAdults

Statistics show that the adult proportion of the Canadian population is growing rapidly. Drowning statistics indicate a great need for adult water safety education to promote water-safe behaviours and effective supervision of children. We also know that, although many have had limited exposure to the water, more and more adults are turning to aquatic activity for rejuvination, recreation, rehabilitation and relaxation. This is where you, the "Aquatic Link", come into the picture.

Get ready for some fun! Adolescents and adults may be bigger and have more experience than your AquaTot and AquaQuest students, but they are just as enjoyable. Instructing adults is always an exciting challenge and is a very rewarding experience. It's an amazing feeling to watch an adult who has been terrified of the water all of his or her life as he or she finally does his or her first front float without assistance. Equally gratifying is having adults thank you for providing them with information and skills that helped them to save a life. With AquaAdults, not only do you have an opportunity to share your knowledge, skills, and experience, but you can also learn a great deal from them.

Each person comes into your class with an incredible range of experiences, interests, needs, and abilities. Accommodating this diversity will not always be easy, but learning who your students are and what they want will help you apply an individualized approach to instructing. That is what the AquaAdults program is all about.

THE PROGRAM

AquaAdults was created to provide both adolescents and adults the opportunity to gain knowledge and skills in swimming and water safety in a safe and enjoyable environment. AquaAdults has four objectives:

- To develop swimming skills according to the student's interest and ability
- To provide water safety skills and knowledge according to the student's interests and ability
- To create a positive learning environment by helping students set and achieve personal goals
- To provide encouragement and flexible opportunities for students to continue their participation and enjoyment of aquatic activities

AquaAdults is a three-level program in which students register on the basis of their swimming ability. Basic water safety knowledge and skills are taught to any student who is new to the program, regardless of the level in which they register. Students can gain additional water safety knowledge and skills specific to four modules on the basis of their interests and information needs.

AquaAdults 1—
Basic Swimming Skills and Water Safety

Purpose: To develop or increase students' comfort in the water through basic flotation, movement and breathing skills, and to foster the basic knowledge, skills and attitudes necessary to prepare, stay safe and survive in and around the water.

Prerequisites: Completion of a fitness screening form, as required by the program site, and a keen interest in developing skills and knowledge that promote safe enjoyment of aquatic environments.

AquaAdults 2—
Swimming Strokes and Water Safety

Purpose: To develop one or more swimming strokes, working toward proficiency and increased endurance, and to introduce or enhance water safety knowledge and skills relevant to the student.

Prerequisites: Completion of a fitness screening form, as required by the program site; an ability to swim 15 metres continuously on the front and/or back; and a willingness to increase comfort in deep water.

AquaAdults 3—
Lifetime Swimming Fitness and Water Safety

Purpose: To maintain or increase your students' fitness through stroke improvement in a distance swimming setting; to introduce other forms of aquatic fitness activities, and to introduce or enhance water safety knowledge and skills relevant to the student.

Prerequisites: Completion of a fitness screening form, as required by the program site; an ability to swim 100 metres continuously in at least two of the following strokes: front crawl, back crawl, breaststroke or butterfly (with proper mechanics and effective propulsion at stroke standards at least of AquaQuest 9); and confidence in deep water.

AquaAdults Program Journal

When a person registers for the AquaAdults program (or on the first day of lessons), he or she will receive a program journal/booklet. Contained in this booklet is general information about the program, a learning inventory (questionnaire), swimming and water safety tips, and charts for setting goals, keeping track of their progress, and making notes of the feedback they receive from you.

> ### Working Together
> Try having your students fill out the learning inventory together on the first day of lessons. They will learn a little bit about each other, and you can take a look at the journal together.

The booklet is a learning tool for your student and you. Especially important for you will be the learning inventory. This is what every student will fill out and return to you, so that you learn about them, what their interests are, and what they expect from their lessons. Use the learning inventory as a starting point for helping your students set realistic goals and to make notes on your worksheets about each student's areas of interest and goals. A blank copy of this form can be found in Appendix O.

Worksheets

There are three instructor worksheets for the AquaAdults program. The first worksheet contains a check-off chart and performance guidelines for the basic swimming skills and water safety. The second worksheet focuses on swimming strokes and water safety, while the third is for lifetime swimming fitness and water safety. Each of these worksheets include performance guidelines and include room to make notes on each of your student's goals and progress. A reference worksheet in Chapter 5 contains the performance guidelines for each of the four water safety modules; Boating Safety, Ice Safety, Home Pool Safety, and Waterfront Safety.

The whole secret to the AquaAdults levels lies in setting attainable goals. In this sense, these levels are not "evaluative" but "participatory." As the lessons progress, you should be revisiting the goals set by your adult student and determine if these goals need to be modified or changed so success can be assured.

The worksheets are designed to: complement instead of repeat information that is found on AquaQuest worksheets; emphasize guidelines based on individual interests and abilities versus standard criteria; and provide you with space to make notes.

ADULT LEARNING CHARACTERISTICS

Adult learners are not the same as younger learners. They have certain characteristics that influence their learning experience, and certain general approaches work better when teaching adults. Remember that these characteristics vary greatly from individual to individual, so be flexible and consider them when planning your lessons.

The characteristics of adult learners can be grouped into five major categories:
- Motivation
- Previous experience
- Self-concept
- Physical state
- Learning limits

MOTIVATION

Understanding motivation means understanding *why* people do things. Fortunately, most of your adolescent or adult students take lessons because they really want to. As a result, they are generally highly motivated and determined to listen and learn!

Although motivation is usually high, you must remember that your students may have very different reasons for being in your class. Their learning inventory will give you a clear indication of their original motivation. Take time at the beginning of the lesson set to discuss everyone's expectations. As you get to know your students, you will gain a better understanding for their personal motivation, as well as what type of external motivation they respond to best.

When adults feel good about their successes, however small or large, personal commitment and active involvement increases. When they master a skill, they gain a sense of control; competence builds confidence. Your continual encouragement and reinforcement of their learning success provides incentive and helps maintain their high level of motivation.

PREVIOUS EXPERIENCE

Previous experience relates to the existing knowledge, skills, and attitudes of your students. Unlike younger learners, adults have acquired a great deal of general life experience. Once again, in terms of the water, previous experience can vary greatly among students.

Some of your students will have a wealth of experience when it comes to swimming and/or water safety. For example, a student may have taken a sailing course and knows a lot about safe boating; another student may be a fitness enthusiast who wants to learn deep water running. Beginners may have had no previous experience in or around the water and therefore share the same fears and anxieties as a young student learning to swim. Take time to carefully review the students' learning inventories for their previous experience. Informal discussions are also great for assessing and sharing previous experience. Remember that some students may have had a negative incident in or around the water, so be sensitive to their readiness to talk about the experience.

Once you know something about your students' backgrounds, you can use the more experienced people to enhance your instruction by drawing on their knowledge and real-life examples or experiences. This is ideal for Safety Scenes, especially if someone has actually been involved in a water-related emergency. You may also have them assist some of the less experienced people.

Previous experience also affects the way in which adults learn. In general adults have already developed their own strategies or approach to learning. Sometimes this means you have to change your method of teaching to use an individualized approach to instructing.

SELF-CONCEPT

Self-concept is the perception that people have of themselves. Adult learners are normally fairly confident in their abilities as a result of successful life experience. Adults are used to setting and achieving their own goals, which enhances their self-concept.

Some adults, although confident and self-assured out of the water, may be very insecure in the water. They can become very stressed and unsure of themselves when trying something new. It's important for these students to experience success in the water early in the experience.

You need to take them through progressions that encourage success at each step. This helps them build a positive self-concept in the water. For example, a beginner may feel "clumsy" or uncoordinated if he or she can do a front float but can't recover properly; to help the student avoid this feeling, teach him or her how to recover and stand up first. Ensure that each student is given adequate freedom and practice time, to help them feel successful. You need to build success into each lesson by helping students set and attain realistic goals.

Finally, your students will view you as the water "expert," so it's important for you to exhibit confidence during your lessons. You can do this by being prepared for your lessons and by communicating with them in a mature, respectful way. Work as a team with each of your students and build confidence together.

PHYSICAL STATE

Physical state refers to the physical characteristics of the students. Depending on the ages of your students and their activity level throughout adulthood, their physical state can vary dramatically. Around the age of 30, physical capacity begins to decline slowly. As described below, there are some predictable changes that occur as a result of the aging process, but you must remember four things:

1. Aging occurs at different rates for different people, so don't focus on age. A 50-year-old can be in much better physical condition than a 30-year-old.
2. A physical limitation can be the result of a disease (e.g., arthritis), disability, or injury as opposed to aging.
3. Be aware of and respect the physical limitations of your students, always focusing on what they CAN do, and adapting when needed.
4. If something feels uncomfortable or painful for a student, encourage him or her to *stop* the activity.

A gradual decline in flexibility is one of the common changes that can greatly affect physical ability. Using all of our joints in a variety of regular activities can help prevent this loss of flexibility. You know what they say: "Move it or lose it!" Your students may need time to loosen their joints and muscles, especially in colder water. Allow students the opportunity to stretch and warm up as often as needed.

Talk to your site supervisor about a fitness screening form. This type of form will provide you with important health-related information about your adult students.

As a person ages, body fat increases, and lean body mass decreases gradually until about age 70. As a result, buoyancy increases during this time and then decreases past 70 years of age, when people tend to become thinner.

Changes in muscle strength will depend on the person's activity level throughout life. Although strength declines gradually, muscles used on a regular basis will remain relatively strong, whereas less frequently used muscles will become less functional.

Nerve impulses decrease in speed as a person ages. This means that some older students may take longer to process information and learn new skills. It does *not* mean that older people are any less able to learn, only that it may take a little longer. Pace your lessons in a way that allows students to call on their past learning experiences, process information, and practice. For example, pause occasionally between instructions to give sufficient time for everyone to absorb information.

Vision, hearing, and the body's ability to regulate its temperature generally decline with age, each of which can affect learning. Pay particular attention to the way you communicate; coordinate body language with your verbal cues, try to decrease noise distractions at your site; have a special cue (e.g., thumbs up) for the class or a specific individual that indicates to you that they understood you. You may have to do your demonstrations closer, or you may need larger print on water safety handouts. Ensure that visual aids are easily visible to all students. In terms of body temperature, older adults may not be able to generate enough heat to stay warm, and they are at higher risk of heat illness (e.g., heat exhaustion).

One of the greatest benefits of the water is that it's a relatively "soft" environment that can allow for greater ease and freedom of movement, even for students with significant declines in physical capacity.

LEARNING LIMITS

Learning limits involve the amount of time and energy (both physical and psychological) that your adult students are willing or able to devote to the lessons or to a specific skill. Naturally, adults have some limits on their time and energy, which can vary from one lesson to the next. For example, one student may always have to leave your lesson early, whereas another takes an extended break half way through each lesson. Still some may need more mental time to prepare themselves for doing an activity, while others "jump right into it".

As an instructor, it's important for you to develop a sense of what learning limits a particular class or individual has and respect these limits. Sometimes you will find that your students want "to get on with it," whereas other times they need a break and will spend some time socializing. Keep the idea of learning limits in mind as you deliver your lessons. Within each lessson, focus on what each student wants to know and what your students are able to do, and be flexible. Your enthusiastic and caring attitude will encourage a learning atmosphere of trust and respect.

WATER SAFETY MODULES

As described earlier, AquaAdults aims to provide each student with basic water safety knowledge and skills, regardless of their swimming ability. In addition, the four water safety modules enable you to provide students with specific knowledge and skills relevant to them and their family or friends. Not all students will take the opportunity to learn more, but many will. The modules are Boating Safety, Ice Safety, Home Pool Safety, and Waterfront Safety. Each module is structured on how to Prepare! Stay Safe! and Survive! and includes Safety Scenes.

The water safety modules (see Chapter 5) are designed to be easily incorporated into your lessons, on the basis of your students' interests. Depending on what your students' indicate on their learning inventories, not everything can be taught or learned in one set of lessons. Consult with your students to determine priorities and goals.

There are many different ways to incorporate water safety modules into any of the AquaAdult levels. (Refer also to your strategy cards for more ideas.)

- You could devote 10 minutes during each lesson over a series of 10 lessons.
- Each lesson you could focus on a different module.
- With two groups, one could practice swimming skills together, while the other learns/practices water safety or a safety scene.
- You could team teach with other AquaAdult instructors by splitting the students into groups based on their interests and then having them move through the different water safety module stations.
- Guest speakers/instructors can be invited.
- You and your site supervisor could decide to run the module as a separate dryland and/or wet workshop (1 to 2 hours), if there is enough interest.

The possibilities are endless. Be creative, have a plan, be flexible, and have fun! Each of the modules, including basic water safety, follows a simple structure; How To Prepare, How To Stay Safe, How To Survive, and Safety Scenes. The statistical information from the drowning reports may spark discussion about personal experiences in and around the water to get you started. If available, include drowning statistics from your local Red Cross office.

Boating Safety Module

- For performance guidelines see the AquaAdult reference sheet in Chapter Five.
- More specific content information on this module is found in the "Boat Smart" theme in this manual (Chapter 4), and on your AquaQuest worksheets in Chapter Five.
- Also refer to the *Swimming and Water Safety* text, pages 31 to 41 and 67 to 77.

Ice Safety Module

- For performance guidelines see the AquaAdult reference sheet in Chapter Five.
- More specific content information on this module is found in the "Stay Warm" theme in this manual (Chapter 4), and on your AquaQuest worksheets in Chapter Five.
- Also refer to the *Swimming and Water Safety* text, pages 31 to 41 and 67 to 77.

Home Pool Safety Module

- For performance guidelines see the AquaAdult reference sheet in Chapter Five.
- More specific content information is outlined below.
- Also refer to the *Swimming and Water Safety* book, pages 33 to 43 and 52 to 53.

Most drownings in backyard or apartment pools involve children. In and around the home, children also drown in bathtubs, spas, and other water containers (including toilets). Easy access and a momentary lapse or lack of supervision are the main factors leading to the drownings. In addition, spinal cord injuries (some leading to drowning) are more likely in backyard or apartment pools. These incidents too are preventable, when one knows how to prepare and stay safe.

- How to Prepare
  - Personal
    - Be wise, supervise: Adult supervision is always a key to safety and a child's best life preserver.
    - Establish your own pool rules.
    - Being personally prepared means getting trained to be able to handle emergency situations (e.g., Take Red Cross First Aid/CPR course).
    - Learn how to swim.
  - Equipment
    - Good safety barriers make good pools; fences around the pool/hot tub should prevent direct access from the house, meet municipal height standards and have a self-closing gate with inside latch or lock.
    - Have the following safety equipment readily available; nonmetallic reaching pole, ringbuoy, reaching and throwing aids, first aid kit, buoy line separating shallow and deeper water.
    - Install a slide or diving board only if the depth is safe.
    - A portable telephone for use around the pool or bathtub is essential.
  - Environment
    - Most backyard/apartment pools are not deep enough for diving boards or slides; the upslope from deep to shallow water can be especially hazardous; clearly mark depths along the edge of the pool.
    - Keep the water clean with the right chemical balances.
    - Look for other water hazards around the home (or neighbourhood) and ensure safety barriers and/or supervision.
- How to stay safe
  - Personal
    - Be wise, supervise.
    - Ensure their fate, communicate; be a good role model and active supervisor, and ensure that family and friends know and follow the safety rules.
    - Teach family and friends Stop! Look! Go Slow! for safe entries—feet first, first time (or always).
    - Wise choices—stay sober; alcohol impairs mobility and judgment and is involved in over 50% of drownings and diving incidents. Offer fruit juices/water to family and friends.
    - Respect your own personal limits and encourage others to do the same.

- Equipment
  - Maintain equipment (e.g., gate, PFDs, slide) in safe working order and post the pool rules (including "No diving" markings/signs where needed).
  - Be alert that pool toys can attract small children to the water; they should never replace supervision or swimming ability.
  - Keep the telephone nearby.
  - Store pool chemicals under lock and key.
  - Only allow plastic (no glass) near pools, bathtub, spas.
- Environment
  - Know and communicate which water entries are safe for family and friends, based on the characteristics of the pool. No one should ever dive into an above-ground pool or the shallow end of any pool. Keep area around the pool uncluttered.
  - Be sun safe—remember the sunscreen, hat.
  - Limit your time in a spa or hot tub (15 minutes), and keep children under age 5 out.

- How to survive: Refer to the AquaQuest performance criteria for the survival skills. Emphasize that students must respect their personal limitations and obtain further training to reduce risk in survival situations.
- Safety Scenes: Refer to Appendix O and AquaAdult strategy cards.

Waterfront Safety Module

- For performance guidelines see the AquaAdult reference sheet in Chapter Five.
- More specific content information is outlined below.
- Also refer to the *Swimming and Water Safety* book, pages 33 to 41 and 55 to 65.

Most recreational swimming drownings occur in rivers and lakes, including drownings that occur when children or adults unexpectedly fall into the water. Over 60% of toddlers who drown are only playing or walking near the water, and 90% of toddlers who drown are not being supervised by an adult. In addition, injuries as a result of diving are more likely in open-water areas because of poor water clarity and other water conditions.

- How to Prepare
  - Personal
    - Be wise, supervise: Adult supervision is always a key to safety, and a child's best life preserver.
    - Establish some rules while in or around the water, at the beach.

- Being personally prepared means getting trained to be able to handle emergency situations (e.g., Red Cross First Aid/CPR course).
- Learn how to swim.
- Equipment
  - Safety equipment may include PFDs, throwing or reaching aids, whistle, first aid kit, sunscreen.
- Environment
  - Be aware of the general hazards of waterfront areas: underwater obstacles, bad weather, cold water, waves, ocean currents (e.g., drift, undertow, rip), river currents, hydraulics, tides, aquatic life (e.g., weeds, jellyfish sting), drop-offs, dams.
  - Check the weather.
- How to Stay Safe
  - Personal
    - Be wise, supervise; in and around waterfronts always stay in direct contact with children and use the buddy system.
    - Ensure their fate, communicate; be a good role model and ensure that family and friends know the hazards and follow safety rules.
    - Teach family and friends Stop! Look! Go Slow! for safe entries—feet first, first time (or always).
    - Wise choices—stay sober; alcohol impairs mobility and judgment and is involved in over 50% of drownings and diving incidents.
    - Respect personal limits.
  - Equipment
    - Wear a PFD (depending on activity).
    - Ensure that throwing and reaching aids are easily accessible; take them into the water when supervising children.
    - Ensure that buoyant water toys and PFDs are in good condition (they must not replace supervision).
    - Have clothing and towels for getting warm.
  - Environment
    - Recognize safe and unsafe conditions.
    - Choose safe entries into the water by checking the environment every time.
    - Keep a close eye on the weather; listen to weather reports.
    - Swim or play in lifeguard supervised areas, whenever possible; stay in designated swimming area.
    - Be sun safe; use sunscreen, cover up, drink plenty of fluids.

- How to Survive: Refer to the AquaQuest performance criteria for the survival skills. Emphasize that students must respect their personal limitations and obtain further training to reduce their risks in survival situations.
- Safety Scenes: Refer to Appendix O and AquaAdult strategy cards.

How-To's

Here are several key points to assist you when instructing AquaAdults:
- AquaAdults 1
    1. Give assistance to students whenever necessary, encouraging them to work towards total independence.
    2. Ensure that skills are initiated by the student (e.g., going into the deep water).
    3. Develop basic swimming skills using progressions in AquaQuest Levels 1 to 4.
    4. Incorporate water safety, based on your students' interests and abilities.
- AquaAdults 2
    1. If necessary, assist your students in choosing stroke(s) that are geared toward their goals and ability.
    2. Assist your student in setting attainable goals (e.g., to swim 50 metres per stroke) and improving his or her technique at a personal rate.
    3. Use the progressions in AquaQuest 12 to develop your student's stroke(s), working toward the Level 12 performance criteria.
    4. Use stroke drills found in your strategy cards.
    5. Incorporate water safety, based on your students' interests and abilities.
- AquaAdults 3
    1. Encourage your students to know and work at their own fitness levels, gradually increasing fitness and improving stroke proficiency.
    2. To enhance the fitness component, tap into the experience and knowledge of your students and fellow instructors who may have coaching or a fitness training background.
    3. As with all levels, if something doesn't feel comfortable, or if your student feels pain, *stop* the activity.
    4. Incorporate water safety, based on students' interests and abilities.

- General
  1. Take time with each student to determine his or her individual goals for the set of lessons. Some students may wish to simply practice a stroke; others may wish to work toward completing specific performance guidelines; still others may wish to supplement their current knowledge of water safety. Use the AquaAdults Journal, the Learning Inventory, and your Instructor Worksheets to assist in this task.
  2. Develop a long-term plan and individual lesson plans based on each student's interests and goals. This may seem complicated, but REMEMBER: adults like to practice on their own; they can help each other in partners or groups; they have already developed individual strategies for learning new things; and they are highly motivated and determined to learn!
  3. Provide feedback on an ongoing basis, encouraging students to provide each other with feedback.
  4. Reference the *Swimming and Water Safety* book, Drowning Reports, and the "Swimming Skills" video as much as possible, and encourage your students to obtain these and other educational materials from their local Red Cross office.
  5. Incorporate fun, fitness and social interaction into your lessons.
  6. Remember, the uniqueness of the program is that it allows you to tailor the program to meet the varied needs and interests of each student, without having to evaluate specific criteria!

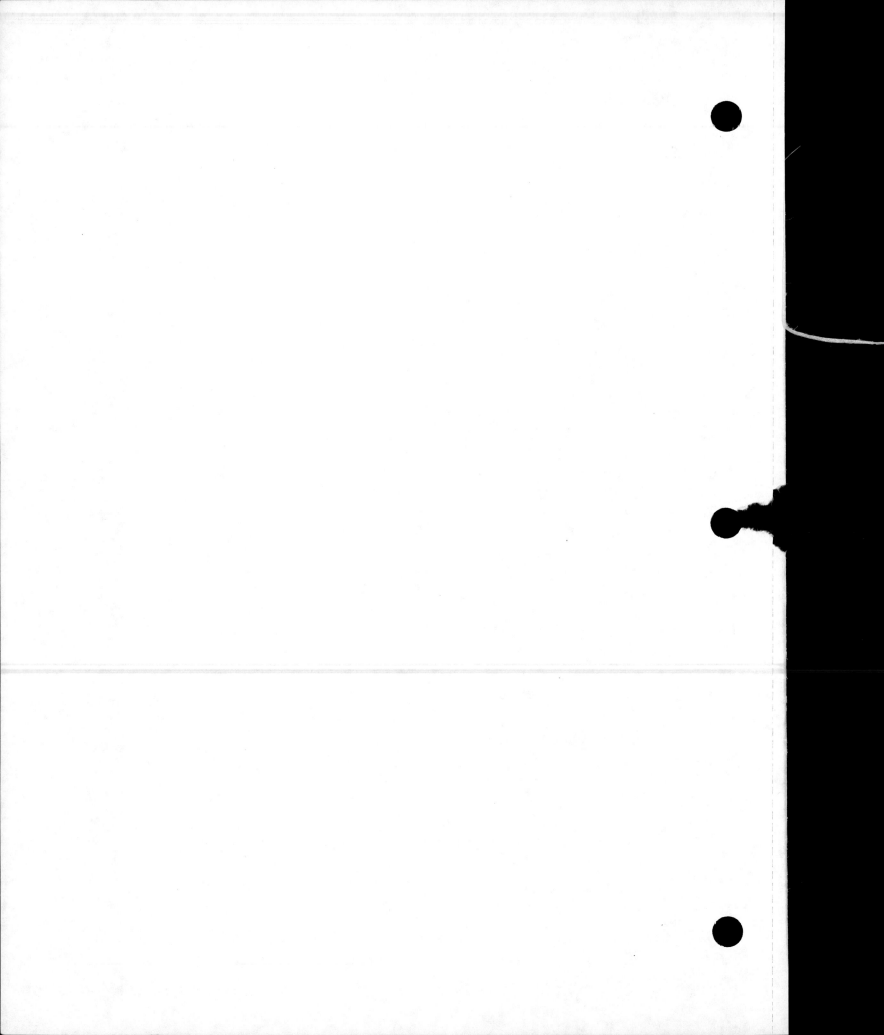

Instructor:

Day/Time:

Session:

Location:

Name and Attendance

Introduction to Discovering Water and Movement

Program Summary

• Water Safety

PREPARE!
Stop! Look! Listen! Show you know...

STAY SAFE!
Stop! Look! Go Slow! Shallow water entries and exits (parent/caregiver and child)
PFD and Me: Review features of an approved PFD

SURVIVE!
Show how to stay warm
When and how to get help

• Swimming

PREPARE!
Getting wet
Supports
Buoyancy and movement
Exhaling
Front position
Back positon
Basic kick and arm action
Submersion (optional)

SAFETY SCENES

Submersion Notes

■ While submersion is part of the total swimming experience, parents and caregivers should be given the option of NOT submerging a child if they are not comfortable or not ready for this skill. You must help the parent/caregiver decide if they are "relaxed and ready" for this skill.

Body Positions and Support

Basic Parent Position
Basic Front Layout Position/Side by Side Position
Back Cradle Position/Back Layout Position
Submersion Positions

Some Development Notes...

■ Infants should be able to hold their head up independently, usually between 4 and 6 months before entering AquaTots 1
■ Very responsive to sounds, rhythms and music
■ Initial attempts to stand and walk occur at approximately 11 months of age
■ Will play alone or with a familiar adult

Did You...

■ Make sure the site is safe and that you are prepared?
■ Plan your lesson, choosing your THEME and using both WATER SAFETY and SWIMMING items?
■ Review the parent/caregiver supports and holds that apply to your activities?
■ Gather all your equipment and place it in a safe, easily accessible spot?

Observation Information

The skill items in this level are designed as an instructional guide for you and an observational guide for parents/caregivers. Encourage parents/caregivers to observe and applaud their child's progress and experiences. Using the AquaTots memos, record the highlights of each lesson. It could be the first smile of the lesson set or it could be the first independent kick. Each action should be seen as a step towards positive water orientation, and not as a specific goal. The measure of your success as an instructor is providing activities and information that increase awareness of water risks for young children, that develop water safe attitudes, and that promote individual development.

**Canadian
Red Cross**

© Canadian Red Cross 1995

Recommended Class Size: **10-12**   Recommended age: **4 months to 16 months**   Total Enrolled: ☐

Observation Guidelines

🦉 = **Wise Choices Focus**

In every lesson, I...

- Incorporate Prepare! Stay Safe! Survive!
- Try to keep the class in the water 95% of the time
- Provide positive, constructive feedback to the parent/caregiver and the child
- Use both Water Safety and Swimming items
- Encourage parent/caregivers to use a consistent cue when initiating activities
- Include at least 3 songs/active learning games
- Reinforce the need for constant adult supervision
- Adapt teaching strategies to meet individual needs

Please refer to Red Cross Water Safety Instructor Manual; Swimming and Water Safety book; National Drowning Reports.

WATER SAFETY

PREPARE!
STOP! LOOK! LISTEN! *Show you know...*
- Parent/caregiver and child participate in a facility orientation where rules, hazards, first aid station and special features of the facility are discussed
- Each lesson the parent/caregiver and child wait for instructor permission to enter water
- 🦉 Parent/caregiver can explain the importance of adult supervision when in, on or around the water

STAY SAFE!
STOP! LOOK! GO SLOW! *Shallow water entries and exits (caregiver and child)*
- Parent/caregiver checks depth, hazards, and the location of other people before entering the water
- Performs shallow-water entries and exits appropriate to site, e.g. wading in, using ramp, steps, ladder or slipping in from seated position at water level
- Parent/caregiver enters the water first and maintains contact with the child at all times

PFD AND ME
Review features of an approved PFD/Lifejacket
- Parent/caregiver knows the features of an approved PFD/Lifejacket and the differences among adult, child and infant PFDs/Lifejackets
- Parent/caregiver puts an appropriate PFD/Lifejacket on the child

- Parent/caregiver puts on an appropriate PFD/Lifejacket
- Parent/caregiver helps child move and float while wearing the PFD/Lifejacket

SURVIVE!
SHOW HOW TO STAY WARM
- Out of the water the parent/caregiver shows how to stay warm — uses towels to dry and keep the child warm

WHEN AND HOW TO GET HELP
- Parent/caregiver knows when to get help
- Parent/caregiver knows how to contact EMS in an emergency and what information is needed
- Parent/caregiver is given a demonstration of how to identify an airway obstruction and a conscious airway obstruction technique. Parent/caregiver receives information where to learn this technique.

SWIMMING

PREPARE!
GETTING WET
- With help, child experiences water on the face, head, and body

SUPPORTS
- Parent/caregiver can demonstrate appropriate supports for the child in the water, including basic parent and child position, side by side position, back float positions, submersion positions, entry and exit positions

BUOYANCY AND MOVEMENT
- Parent/caregiver and child explore buoyancy and movement in the water by rocking side to side, turning, floating, towing, using toys and buoyant aids.

EXHALING THROUGH MOUTH
- Parent/caregiver demonstrates blowing bubbles through mouth at water level to child; child may mimic this action

FRONT POSITION (ASSISTED)
- Child is supported by parent/caregiver on front and allowed to move arms and legs freely
- Child is towed by parent/caregiver

BACK POSITION (ASSISTED)
- Child is supported by parent/caregiver on back and allowed to move arms and legs freely
- Child is towed by parent/caregiver

BASIC KICK AND ARM ACTION (ASSISTED)
- Parent/caregiver moves arms in a propulsive action
- Parent/caregiver moves legs in a propulsive action
- With parent/caregiver support, child is encouraged to move arms and legs independently

SUBMERSION
***Note:** This is an optional, voluntary activity and should occur only if and when the parent/caregiver and child are interested, relaxed and ready.*
- Parent/caregiver gently submerges child - parent/caregiver should submerge with the child and use the face to face basic front layout position; eye contact must be maintained; movement is smooth, flowing
- Submersion and assisted underwater movement toward parent/caregiver
- Submersion and unsupported underwater movement from instructor to parent/caregiver

SAFETY SCENES
Safety Scenes are a sequence of activities in, on or around the water the parent/caregiver with child demonstrates to show you they have the knowledge, skills and judgement to be water safe and make wise choices for the child and themself. Safety Scenes may include: entries, rescue skills, use of safety equipment, swimming and/or water safety skills.

Instructor Worksheet

AquaTots 2

**Canadian
Red Cross**

Instructor:

Day/Time:

Session:

Location:

Name and Attendance

*Introduction to Safe Movement
Experiences with and in Water*

Program Summary

• **Water Safety**

PREPARE!
Stop! Look! Listen! Show you know...

STAY SAFE!
Stop! Look! Go Slow! Shallow water entries
and exits
PFD and Me: Put on, move, and float...

SURVIVE!
Show how to stay warm
When and how to get help
Uses buoyant object for support

• **Swimming**

PREPARE!
Getting wet
Supports
Buoyancy and movement
Exhaling
Front float
Back float
Front and back glide
Rollover floats
Basic kick on front/back
Basic arm action on front/back

SURVIVE!
Front swim

SAFETY SCENES
Note: Independent submersions ONLY are
encouraged at this level.

BODY POSITIONS AND SUPPORTS
Basic Parent Position
Basic Front Layout/Side by Side Position
Back Layout Position
Back and Head Support Position

SOME DEVELOPMENT NOTES...
■ Can use a few clear words and listens closely
  to songs, rhymes
■ Recognizes and shows familiar items; under-
  stands simple commands
■ Can stand and walk alone
■ Will play alone or with a familiar adult

DID YOU...
■ Make sure the site is safe and that you are
  prepared?
■ Plan your lesson, choosing your THEME and
  using both WATER SAFETY and SWIMMING
  items?
■ Review the parent/caregiver supports and
  holds that apply to your activities?
■ Gather all your equipment and place it in a
  safe, easily accessible spot?

OBSERVATION INFORMATION
The skill items in this level are designed as an
instructional guide for you and an observational
guide for parents/caregivers. Encourage par-
ents/caregivers to observe and applaud their
child's progress and experiences. Using the
AquaTots memos, record the highlights of each
lesson. It could be the first smile of the lesson
set or it could be the first independent kick.
Each action should be seen as a step towards
positive water orientation, and not as a specific
goal. The measure of your success as an
instructor is providing activities and information
that increase awareness of water risks for young
children, that develop water safe attitudes, and
that promote individual development.

© Canadian Red Cross 1995

Recommended Class Size: **10-12**   Recommended age: 16 months to 24 months   Total Enrolled: ☐

<owl icon> = **Wise Choices Focus**

In every lesson, I...

- Incorporate Prepare! Stay Safe! Survive!
- Try to keep the class in the water 95% of the time
- Provide positive, constructive feedback to the parent/caregiver and the child
- Use both Water Safety and Swimming items
- Encourage parent/caregivers to use a consistent cue when initiating activities
- Include at least 3 songs/active learning games
- Reinforce the need for constant adult supervision
- Adapt teaching strategies to meet individual needs

Please refer to: Red Cross Water Safety Instructor Manual; Swimming and Water Safety book; National Drowning Reports.

WATER SAFETY

PREPARE!

STOP! LOOK! LISTEN! Show you know...
- Parent/caregiver and child participate in a facility orientation where rules, hazards, first aid station and special features of the facility are discussed
- Each lesson the parent/caregiver and child wait for instructor permission to enter the water
- Parent/caregiver can explain the importance of adult supervision when in, on and around the water
- Parent/caregiver can identify site specific buoyant/non-buoyant objects that can be used for rescues

STAY SAFE!

STOP! LOOK! GO SLOW! Shallow water entries and exits (assisted)
- Both parent/caregiver and child demonstrate Stop! Look! Go Slow! while performing shallow water entries and exits
- STOP — makes sure parent/caregiver is in water
- LOOK — checks that water is clear of hazards
- GO SLOW — enters when parent/caregiver or instructor says it's safe; entry is feet first on a consistent signal

PFD AND ME

Put on, move, and float ...(assisted)
- Parent/caregiver and child put on and properly fasten a PFD/Lifejacket
- Parent/caregiver and child demonstrates safe entries and exits from the water

- Parent/caregiver and child explores buoyancy and movement in any comfortable position while wearing a PFD/Lifejacket
- Parent/caregiver and child move in different directions while floating in a PFD/Lifejacket

SURVIVE!

SHOW HOW TO STAY WARM
- Out of the water, child and parent/caregiver show how to stay warm — uses towels, curls up close to others

WHEN AND HOW TO GET HELP
- Parent/caregiver describes two situations where people might need help; describes how to contact EMS and what information is needed.
- Parent/caregiver is given a demonstration of how to identify an airway obstruction, and a conscious airway obstruction technique. Parent/caregiver receives information where to learn this technique

USES BUOYANT OBJECT FOR SUPPORT (ASSISTED)
- Child supports personal buoyancy by holding on to a stable buoyant object (not a PFD/Lifejacket) with parent/caregiver assistance

SWIMMING

PREPARE!

GETTING WET
- With help child experiences water on face, head, and body
- Child initiates getting water on face, head, and body

SUPPORTS
- Parent/caregiver can demonstrate appropriate supports for the child in the water including basic parent and child position, side by side position, back float positions, entry and exit positions

BUOYANCY AND MOVEMENT
- Parent/caregiver and child explore buoyancy and movement in the water by rocking, turning, floating, walking, running, skipping, jumping, towing, using supplementary floation aids (kickboard, swim bar, etc.)
- Child makes the water move up, down, forward, backwards using his or her body

- Child uses equipment to move the water and explore buoyancy

EXHALING THROUGH MOUTH
- Child blows bubbles through mouth at and below the water surface in any body position

FRONT FLOAT (ASSISTED)
- Child performs front float and recovers to a stable position
- Performs front float and blows bubbles

BACK FLOAT (ASSISTED)
- Child performs back float and recovers to a stable position

FRONT AND BACK GLIDE (ASSISTED)
- Child performs front and back glide - thrust and movement provided by parent/caregiver

ROLLOVER FLOATS (ASSISTED)
- Child floats on front (back), then rolls over to back (front); parent/caregiver directs movement throughout

BASIC KICK ON FRONT/BACK (ASSISTED)
- Child performs basic kick on front and back assisted by parent/caregiver
- Child uses a buoyant aid to kick on front and back assisted by parent/caregiver

BASIC ARM ACTION ON FRONT/BACK (ASSISTED)
- Child performs basic propulsive arm movements on front/back; assisted by parent/caregiver

SURVIVE!

Front Swim (assisted)
- Child uses any arm or leg movements (or combination)
- Body approaches horizontal

SAFETY SCENES

Safety Scenes are a sequence of activities in, on or around the water the parent/caregiver with child demonstrates to show you they have the knowledge, skills and judgement to be water safe and make wise choices for the child and themself. Safety Scenes may include: entries, rescue skills, use of safety equipment, swimming and/or water safety skills.

Instructor Worksheet

AquaTots **3**

Instructor:

Day/Time:

Session:

Location:

Name and Attendance

Introduction to Moving, Floating and Swimming Independently

Program Summary

• Water Safety

PREPARE!
Stop! Look! Listen! Show you know...
When it is safe to swim or go near water...
Identify Buoyant Objects

STAY SAFE!
Stop! Look! Go Slow! Shallow water entries and exits
PFD and ME: When to wear, activities
Weight transfer

SURVIVE!
Show how to stay warm
When and how to get help
Surface support

• Swimming

PREPARE!
Getting wet
Supports
Buoyancy and movement
Rhythmic breathing
Front float
Back float
Front and back glides
Rollover glide
Basic kick on front and back
Front/back glides with basic flutterkick

SURVIVE!
Change direction
Front swim

SAFETY SCENES
Note: Independent submersions ONLY are encouraged at this level.

BODY POSITIONS AND SUPPORTS
Basic Parent Position
Basic Front Layout/Side by Side Position
Back Layout Position
Back and Head Support Position

SOME DEVELOPMENT NOTES...
■ Likes to listen to stories and talks more, asks why?
■ Likes to independently explore and experience everything
■ Will play beside other children
■ Pushes and pulls objects; improved mobility

DID YOU...
■ Make sure the site is safe and that you are prepared?
■ Plan your lesson, choosing your THEME and using both WATER SAFETY and SWIMMING items?
■ Review the parent/caregiver supports and holds that apply to your activities?
■ Gather all your equipment and place it in a safe, easily accessible spot?

OBSERVATION INFORMATION
The skill items in this level are designed as an instructional guide for you and an observational guide for parents/caregivers. Encourage parents/caregivers to observe and applaud their child's progress and experiences. Using the AquaTots memos, record the highlights of each lesson. It could be the first smile of the lesson set or it could be the first independent kick. Each action should be seen as a step towards positive water orientation, and not as a specific goal. The measure of your success as an instructor is providing activities and information that increase awareness of water risks for young children, that develop water safe attitudes, and that promote individual development.

＋ Canadian
Red Cross

Total Enrolled:

Recommended age: 24 months and up

Recommended Class Size: 10-12

Observation Guidelines

= Wise Choices Focus

FRONT FLOAT (ASSISTED)
- Child assumes natural floating position on front with face in the water and recovers to a stable position
- Explores other floating positions on front and recovers to original position

BACK FLOAT (ASSISTED)
- Child assumes natural floating position on back and recovers to a stable position
- Explores other floating positions on back and recovers to original position

FRONT AND BACK GLIDES (ASSISTED)
- Child performs front and back glides; arms are fully extended in front of head (front) or resting along side the body (back); initial thrust and movement is provided by parent/caregiver
- Glides in a relaxed manner
- Parent/caregiver encourages a streamlined body position

ROLLOVER GLIDES (ASSISTED)
- Child glides on front (back), then rolls over to back (front) and glides; parent/caregiver directs. Parent/caregiver encourages a streamlined body position

BASIC KICK ON FRONT/BACK (ASSISTED)
- Performs basic (age appropriate) flutterkick motions on front. Parent/caregiver encourages face in the water
- Performs basic (age appropriate) flutterkick motions on back
- Parent/caregiver encourages a streamlined body position
- May use buoyant aid or be assisted by parent/caregiver

FRONT/BACK GLIDES WITH BASIC FLUTTERKICK (ASSISTED)
- Performs front and back glides with basic flutterkicking, alternating up and down leg motions
- Body approaches horizontal
- Arms are fully extended (on front) and down the sides (on back)
- Initial thrust provided by parent/caregiver

SURVIVE!

CHANGE DIRECTION (ASSISTED)
- Child experiments with reversing direction, moving side to side, and moving in circles
- Child changes direction while on front and back to return to safety; parent/caregiver guides movement
- Child is encouraged to hold on to side

FRONT SWIM (ASSISTED)
- Child uses any arm or leg movement; parent/caregiver encourages alternating arm action and horizontal body position
- Face is in the water

SAFETY SCENES
Safety Scenes are a sequence of activities in, on or around the water the parent/caregiver and child demonstrates to show you they have the knowledge, skills and judgement to be water safe and make wise choices for the child and themself. Safety Scenes may include: entries, rescue skills, use of safety equipment, swimming and/or water safety skills.

In every lesson, I...

- Incorporate Prepare! Stay Safe! Survive!
- Try to keep the class in the water 95% of the time
- Provide positive, constructive feedback to the parent/caregiver and the child
- Use both Water Safety and Swimming items
- Encourage parent/caregivers to use a consistent cue when initiating activities
- Include at least 3 songs/active learning games
- Reinforce the need for constant adult supervision
- Adapt teaching strategies to meet individual needs

Please refer to:Red Cross Water Safety Instructor Manual; Swimming and Water Safety book; National Drowning Reports.

WATER SAFETY

PREPARE!
STOP! LOOK! LISTEN! Show you know...
- Parent/caregiver and child participate in a facility orientation where rules, hazards, first aid station and special features of the facility are discussed
- Each lesson the parent/caregiver and child wait for instructor permission to enter the water
- Parent/caregiver and child can explain the importance of adult supervision in, on and around the water
- Parent/caregiver can identify site specific buoyant/non-buoyant objects that can be used for rescues

DESCRIBE WHEN IT IS SAFE TO SWIM OR GO NEAR WATER — AND WHEN IT ISN'T
- Safe: with adult permission and supervision, with a buddy, in a supervised area, in daylight, good weather
- Not safe: without adult permission and supervision, alone, outside supervised areas, bad weather

IDENTIFY BUOYANT OBJECTS
- Child identifies some site specific objects that float and some that sink

STAY SAFE!
STOP! LOOK! GO SLOW! Shallow water entries and exits (assisted)
- Both parent/caregiver and child demonstrate:Stop! Look! Go Slow! while performing shallow water entries and exits
  - STOP — makes sure parent/caregiver is in water
  - LOOK — checks that water is clear of hazards
  - GO SLOW — enters when parent/caregiver or instructor says it's safe; entry is feet first on a consistent signal

PFD AND ME
When to wear, activities (assisted)
- Parent/caregiver and child identify at least two situations where PFDs/Lifejackets must be worn (boating, playing near water)

- Child demonstrates Stop! Look! Go Slow! while doing entries with a PFD/Lifejacket.
- Child explores floatation and movement (kicking, propulsion with arms on front/back)
- Child moves in different directions while floating in a PFD/Lifejacket (reverses direction, moves side to side, moves in circles)
- Child enters water, rolls over onto back and swims wearing PFD/Lifejacket (assisted)
- Child demonstrates safe exits (assisted)

WEIGHT TRANSFER
- Child is able to transfer weight in one way, e.g. retrieve objects

SURVIVE!

SHOW HOW TO STAY WARM
- Out of the water, child and parent/caregiver show how to stay warm — uses towels, curls up close to others

WHEN AND HOW TO GET HELP
- Parent/caregiver and child describe 2 situations where people might need help; describe how to contact EMS and what information is needed
- Parent/caregiver is given a demonstration of how to identify an airway obstruction and a conscious airway obstruction technique. Parent/caregiver receives information where to learn this technique

SWIMMING

PREPARE!

GETTING WET
- Child initiates getting water on face, head and body
- Child initiates putting entire face in the water in a relaxed manner including chin, mouth, nose, eyes and forehead

SUPPORTS
- Parent/caregiver can demonstrate appropriate supports for the child in the water including basic parent and child position, side by side position, back float positions, entry and exit positions

SURFACE SUPPORT (ASSISTED)
- Child floats, swims in place, treads water or combination — head stays above surface with parent/caregiver assistance

BUOYANCY AND MOVEMENT
- Parent/caregiver and child explores buoyancy and movement in the water by rocking, turning, floating, walking, running, skipping, jumping, rolling, towing, using supplementary aids (kickboard, swim bar,etc.)
- Child makes the water move up, down, forwards, backwards using his or her body
- Child uses equipment to move water, and explore buoyancy

INTRODUCTION TO RHYTHMIC BREATHING
- Child blows bubbles through mouth or nose at and below the water surface in any body position
- Child exhales through mouth or nose under water; inhales through mouth just above surface in any body position
- Performance is relaxed

Instructor Worksheet

AquaQuest 1

Canadian Red Cross
Water Safety Program

Instructor:

Day/Time:

Session:

Location:

Water Safety						**Swimming**									**Next Level**				
Prepare	Stay Safe	Survive	Prepare																COMPLETE (C) • INCOMPLETE (I)
Stop! Look! Listen! Show you know	Stop! Look! Go Slow! Shallow water entries/exits (assisted)	PFD & Me (assisted)	Show how to stay warm	Move water 4 ways	Move through water 2 ways	Submerge face	Exhale through mouth or nose	Front floats (assisted)	Back floats (assisted)	Front/Back Glides (assisted)	Basic kick on front/back (assisted)	SAFETY SCENES							

Name and Attendance

Recommended Class Size: 1:4 (P) • 1:4-6 (S)

Total Enrolled: ☐

Total Completed: ☐

Performance Criteria

✦ = **Note to Instructor**   ✓ = **Performance Criteria (Student)**   🦉 = **Wise Choices Focus**

In every lesson, I...
- Incorporate Prepare!...Stay Safe!...Survive!
- Try to keep the class in the water 95% of the time
- Use a least 5 stroke drills/activities
- Provide constructive feedback to each student
- Adapt teaching strategies to meet individual needs
- Use both Water Safety and Swimming items

WATER SAFETY

STOP! LOOK! LISTEN!
Show you know...
✓ Participates in basic orientation to site and site safety rules.
✓ Waits for specific permission to enter water, every time.
✓ Listens to you throughout each lesson.

STOP! LOOK! GO SLOW!
Shallow water entries/exits (assisted)
✦ You/caregiver may assist.
✦ Introduce participant to Stop! Look! Go Slow!
✓ Demonstrates STOP! — makes sure you (an adult) are already in the water, and ready.
✓ Performs shallow water entries and exits, appropriate to the site. eg. wading in, using ramp, steps or ladder, jumping in, slipping in from seated position at water level.
✓ Demonstrates safe exits.

PFD & ME (ASSISTED)
✦ You/caregiver may assist.
✦ Shallow water: water that is no more than shoulder height, relative to each student.
✓ Puts on Personal Flotation Device (PFD); all zippers, ties and buckles properly fastened.
✓ Wearing PFD, moves (walks, runs, hops, kicks, etc.) through shallow water
✓ Wearing PFD, floats in any position in shallow water, in a relaxed manner.

SHOW HOW TO STAY WARM
✓ Out of water, shows how to stay warm — uses towel, curls up, huddles with others, gets dry.

SWIMMING

MOVE WATER FOUR WAYS
✓ In stationary position, makes water move in four of following ways: up, down, forward, backward, in circles.
✓ Uses arms, legs, hands, feet and hips to move water.

MOVE THROUGH WATER TWO WAYS
✦ You/caregiver may assist.
✓ Moves through shallow water in at least two of following ways: walking, running, pedalling, hopping, skiing, jumping, gliding, etc.

SUBMERGE FACE
✦ Initiated by participant.
✓ Puts entire face in the water, in a relaxed manner, at least 3 seconds, including; chin, mouth, nose, eyes and forehead.

EXHALE THROUGH MOUTH OR NOSE
✓ Exhales/blows bubbles, through mouth, just below the surface, and;
✓ Exhales through mouth and/or nose with entire face in the water.

FRONT FLOATS (ASSISTED)
✦ May use a buoyant aid (NOT a PFD) or be assisted by you/caregiver.
✓ Performs front floats in shallow water.
✓ Floats in a relaxed manner with face in.
✓ Recovers to a stable position.

BACK FLOATS (ASSISTED)
✦ May use a buoyant aid (NOT a PFD) or be assisted by you/caregiver.
✓ Performs back floats in shallow water.
✓ Floats in a relaxed manner, with head back.
✓ Recovers to a stable position.

FRONT/BACK GLIDES (ASSISTED)
✦ You/caregiver may provide initial thrust and support.
✓ Performs front glides, face in the water, with arms extended in front of head, for at least three seconds.
✓ Performs back glides with arms along sides, for at least three seconds.
✓ Glides in a relaxed manner.
✓ Performs recoveries to a stable position.

BASIC KICK ON FRONT/BACK (ASSISTED)
✦ May use buoyant aid (NOT a PFD) or be assisted by you/caregiver.
✓ Performs basic (age appropriate) flutter kick motions for at least five seconds on front, face in the water.
✓ Performs basic (age appropriate) flutter kick motions on back, for at least five seconds.

SAFETY SCENES

✦ Develop Safety Scenes based on the guidelines and examples in the Instructor Manual, ensuring effective safety supervision.
✦ Safety Scenes are scenarios that link knowledge and skills from the water safety and swimming learned in this level.
✓ Performs Safety Scenes, demonstrating knowledge and skills learned.

Instructor Worksheet

AquaQuest 2

Canadian Red Cross

© Canadian Red Cross 1995

Instructor:

Day/Time:

Session:

Location:

			Next Level
			COMPLETE (C) • INCOMPLETE (I)

Swimming

Survive
- SAFETY SCENES

Prepare
- Endurance swim, 2 metres (unassisted)
- Front/back glides with basic flutter kick (unassisted)
- Roll-over glides (assisted)
- Roll-over floats (assisted)
- Back glide (unassisted)
- Front glide (unassisted)
- Back float/recovery (unassisted)
- Front float/recovery (unassisted)
- Rhythmic breathing, 5 times
- Chest-deep water activities (unassisted)
- Submerge head, exhale

Water Safety

Stay Safe
- PFD & Me Introduction to deep water (assisted)

Prepare
- Stop! Look! Go! Slow! Shallow water entries/exits (unassisted)
- Identify buoyant objects
- Stop! Look! Listen! Show you know

Name and Attendance

Recommended Class Size: 1:4 (P) • 1:4-6 (S)

Total Enrolled: ☐   Total Completed: ☐

Performance Criteria

✓ = Performance Criteria (Student)   = Wise Choices Focus

◆ = Note to Instructor   ✓ = Performance Criteria

In every lesson, I...
- Incorporate Prepare!...Stay Safe!...Survive!
- Try to keep the class in the water 95% of the time
- Use a least 5 stroke drills/activities
- Provide constructive feedback to each student
- Adapt teaching strategies to meet individual needs
- Use both Water Safety and Swimming items

WATER SAFETY

STOP! LOOK! LISTEN!
Show you know...
✓ Describes and follows at least two site-specific safety rules (e.g. always walks on deck).
✓ Where applicable, shows where deep water (water over shoulders) is.
✓ Waits for specific permission to enter water, *every* time.
✓ Listens to you throughout each lesson.
✓ Swims with buddy (ie. stays with the class).

IDENTIFY BUOYANT OBJECTS
✓ Identifies some site-specific objects that float and some that sink.

STOP! LOOK! GO SLOW!
Shallow water entries/exits (unassisted)
✓ Performs various shallow water entries appropriate to site: e.g. front standing jump, wading in, using ramp, steps or ladder, slipping in from seated position at water level.
✓ Demonstrates STOP! — makes sure you and a buddy are already in water, and ready, and;
✓ Demonstrates LOOK! — checks that water is clear enough; also checks below and ahead for hazards or other people that might be in the way, and;
✓ Demonstrates GO SLOW! — enters when you say it's safe; enters feet first, first time, to check how deep the water is. ALWAYS enters shallow water feet first.
✓ Demonstrates safe exits.

PFD & ME
Introduction to deep water (assisted)
◆ You/caregiver may assist.
◆ Deep water: water that is higher than shoulder height, relative to each student.
✓ Identifies at least two situations in which PFD's must be worn: e.g. when playing in or around the water, when in a boat.
✓ Where site permits, puts on appropriate PFD and demonstrates Stop! Look! Go Slow! during deep water entries (ladder, front standing jump).
✓ Explores flotation and movement (eg. kicking, pedalling, propulsion with arms, on back, on front, etc.).
✓ Moves in different directions while floating in PFD: reverses direction, moves side to side, moves in circles, etc.
✓ Demonstrates safe exits from deep water area

SWIMMING

SUBMERGE HEAD, EXHALE
✓ Initiated by participant, in a relaxed manner.
✓ Submerges entire head under water in any comfortable way, including: face, ears and back of head.
✓ Exhales slowly through mouth and/or nose.
✓ Opens eyes underwater.

CHEST-DEEP WATER ACTIVITIES (UNASSISTED)
✓ Explores flotation and movement (e.g. sitting on bottom, balancing on one leg, touching toes, kicking, pedalling, propulsion with arms, on back, on front, on side, etc.) in chest-deep water.

RHYTHMIC BREATHING, FIVE TIMES
◆ Encourage student to turn head to side, during inhalation.
✓ Exhales through mouth and/or nose under water, inhales through mouth just above surface.
✓ Performance is rhythmic and relaxed, with noticeable and effective exhalation and inhalation, on EACH repetition.
✓ Performs at least five repetitions in any body position.

FRONT FLOAT/RECOVERY (UNASSISTED)
✓ Assumes stable floating position on front, with face in water.
✓ Floats for at least three seconds, in a relaxed manner.
✓ Comfortably recovers to original position.

BACK FLOAT/RECOVERY (UNASSISTED)
✓ Assumes stable floating position on back, with head back.
✓ Floats for at least three seconds, in a relaxed manner.
✓ Comfortably recovers to original position.

FRONT GLIDE (UNASSISTED)
◆ Minimal assistance may be provided to initiate glide.
✓ Glides on front for at least three seconds, with face in water, in a relaxed manner.
✓ Body is streamlined, with arms fully extended in front of head.
✓ Comfortably recovers to original position.

BACK GLIDE (UNASSISTED)
◆ Minimal assistance may be provided to initiate glide.
✓ Glides on back for at least 3 seconds, in a relaxed manner.
✓ Body is streamlined, with arms and hands rested along side of body.
✓ Comfortably recovers to original position.

ROLL-OVER FLOATS (ASSISTED)
◆ May use buoyant aid or be assisted by you/caregiver.
✓ Assumes floating position on front (with face in), then rolls onto back.
✓ Holds each position for at least three seconds, in a relaxed manner.
✓ Exhales through mouth or nose when face is in water, and inhales through mouth when face is out.
✓ Repeats roll-over from back to front.

ROLL-OVER GLIDES (ASSISTED)
◆ May use buoyant aid or be assisted by you/caregiver.
✓ Glides on front for at least three seconds with face n, then rolls over to back and glides (or floats) for at least three more seconds.
✓ Exhales through mouth or nose when face is in water, and inhales through mouth when face is out.
✓ Repeats; back to front glide.
✓ Glides in streamlined and relaxed manner.
✓ Initiates roll with shoulders and head.

FRONT/BACK GLIDES, WITH BASIC FLUTTER KICK (UNASSISTED)
◆ Minimal assistance may be provided to initiate glide.
✓ Performs front and back glides with basic flutter kick: alternating up and down leg motions.
✓ Performs kick for at least three seconds, with body approaching horizontal.
✓ Arms are fully extended (on front) and along the sides (on back).

ENDURANCE SWIM, TWO METRES (UNASSISTED)
◆ Proper front crawl technique is taught and encouraged, but is NOT evaluated.
✓ Body approaches horizontal on front or back.
✓ Moves at least two metres using any arm or leg movements (or a combination).

SAFETY SCENES
◆ Develop Safety Scenes based on the guidelines and examples in the Instructor Manual, ensuring effective safety supervision.
◆ Safety Scenes are scenarios that link knowledge and skills from the water safety and swimming learned in this level.
✓ Performs Safety Scenes, demonstrating knowledge and skills learned.

Instructor Worksheet

AquaQuest 3

Instructor:

Day/Time:

Session:

Location:

				Next Level					
				COMPLETE (c) • INCOMPLETE (I)					

Swimming

Survive
- Endurance swim, 5 metres (unassisted)

Prepare
- Roll-over glides with flutter kick (unassisted)
- Back glide with flutter kick (unassisted)
- Front glide with flutter kick (unassisted)
- Side glide with flutter kick (assisted)
- Front/Back floats, relaxed 5 seconds (unassisted)
- Rhythmic breathing, 10 times, 2 ways

Water Safety

Survive
- Deep water activities (assisted)
- Change direction shallow water (unassisted)

Stay Safe
- Use buoyant object for support
- Jump entry, deep water (assisted)

Prepare
- Stop! Look! Go Slow! When it's safe to go near water and when it isn't
- Stop! Look! Listen! Show you know

SAFETY SCENES

Name and Attendance

Canadian
Red Cross

© Canadian Red Cross 1995

Total Enrolled: ☐   Total Completed: ☐

Recommended Class Size: 1:4 (P) • 1:4-6 (S)

◆ = Note to Instructor   ✓ = Performance Criteria (Student)   🦉 = Wise Choices Focus

In every lesson, I...

■ Incorporate Prepare!...Stay Safe!...Survive!
■ Try to keep the class in the water 95% of the time.
■ Use a least 5 stroke drills/activities
■ Provide constructive feedback to each student
■ Adapt teaching strategies to meet individual needs
■ Use both Water Safety and Swimming items

WATER SAFETY

STOP! LOOK! LISTEN!
Show you know...
✓ Describes and follows at least 4 site-specific safety rules.
✓ Waits for specific permission to enter water, every time.
✓ Describes why it is important to always swim with a buddy under adult supervision.

WHEN IT'S SAFE TO SWIM OR GO NEAR WATER —
AND WHEN IT ISN'T
✓ Safe: with adult permission and supervision, with a buddy, in lifeguard supervised areas, in daylight, good weather.
✓ Not safe: without adult permission and supervision, alone, bad weather, too much sun, too cold, outside swimming area, too far from safety.

STOP! LOOK! GO SLOW!
Jump entry, deep water (assisted)
◆ You/caregiver may assist.
✓ Demonstrates Stop! Look! Go Slow! while entering the deep water with a feet first jump.

USE BUOYANT OBJECT FOR SUPPORT
◆ In shallow or deep water, NOT using a PFD, as PFD's should be worn vs. held onto.
✓ Supports personal buoyancy for 30 seconds, by holding onto a stable buoyant object, without touching the bottom.
✓ Knows that some inflatable buoyant objects can be dangerous because they can deflate.

CHANGE DIRECTION, SHALLOW WATER (UNASSISTED)
✓ Pushes away from point of safety (e.g. edge of

pool/you), in a front or back glide position, changes direction (re-orients), and returns to the point of safety.
✓ Exits water safely.

SWIMMING

DEEP WATER ACTIVITIES (ASSISTED)
◆ You/caregiver may assist, without a PFD.
✓ Where site permits, demonstrates Stop! Look! Go Slow! during deep-water entries (ladder, slip in, front standing jump).
✓ Explores flotation and movement in deep water, in a near-horizontal position (kicking, propulsion with arms, on back, front).
✓ Demonstrates safe exit.

RHYTHMIC BREATHING, 10 TIMES, TWO WAYS
✓ Exhales through mouth and/or nose under water, inhales through mouth just above surface.
✓ Performance is rhythmic and relaxed, with noticeable and effective exhalation and inhalation, on EACH repetition.
✓ Performs 10 repetitions to the side, at least two different ways: e.g. standing with face in the water, changing from one side to the other, while kicking with a board.

FRONT/BACK FLOATS, RELAXED, FIVE SECONDS
(UNASSISTED)
✓ Floats in a relaxed manner for at least five seconds, in shallow water, on front and back.
✓ Holds stable position with minimal or no leg movement.
✓ Comfortably recovers to original position.

SIDE GLIDES WITH FLUTTER KICK (ASSISTED)
◆ May be assisted by you/caregiver, or a buoyant aid.
✓ Glides on each side with one arm extended above the head, and the other beside the body, with no movements of the hands.
✓ Performs flutter kick on each side for at least three seconds.
✓ Head is turned to side, with ear resting in water, near shoulder.

FRONT GLIDE WITH FLUTTER KICK (UNASSISTED)
✓ Performs front glide with flutter kick: alternating up and down motion with both legs, at or just below the surface, toes pointed.
✓ Flutter kick is continuous and lasts at least five seconds.

BACK GLIDE WITH FLUTTER KICK (UNASSISTED)
✓ Performs back glide with flutter kick: alternating up and down motion with both legs, at or just below the surface, toes pointed.
✓ Flutter kick is continuous and lasts at least five seconds.

ROLL-OVER GLIDES WITH FLUTTER KICK (UNASSISTED)
✓ Performs front glide with flutter kick, for at least three seconds.
✓ Rolls over to back and continues kicking for at least three seconds.
✓ Repeat; back to front glides with flutter kick.
✓ Initiates roll with shoulders and head.

ENDURANCE SWIM, FIVE METRES (UNASSISTED)
◆ Proper front crawl technique is taught and encouraged, including breathing to the side, but is NOT evaluated.
✓ Body approaches horizontal, on front.
✓ Exhales under the water with face in.
✓ Moves at least five metres using any arm or leg movements (or a combination).

SAFETY SCENES

◆ Develop Safety Scenes based on the guidelines and examples in the Instructor Manual, ensuring effective safety supervision.
◆ Safety Scenes are scenarios that link knowledge and skills from the water safety and swimming learned in this level.
✓ Performs Safety Scenes, demonstrating knowledge and skills learned.

Instructor Worksheet

Canadian Red Cross
Water Safety Program

AquaQuest 4

Canadian Red Cross

© Canadian Red Cross 1995

Instructor:

Day/Time:

Session:

Location:

			COMPLETE (c) • INCOMPLETE (I)
		Next Level	
Swimming	*Survive*		SAFETY SCENES
	Stay Safe		Endurance swim, 15 metres
	Prepare		Front crawl, 3 X 5 metres (one lesson)
			Back glide and kick, 3 X 10 metres (one lesson)
			Introduction to sculling, shallow water
			Side glides with flutter kick (unassisted)
			Weight transfer, shallow water
Water Safety	*Survive*		Rhythmic breathing, 15 times, 2 ways
			Surface support, 20 seconds, deep water
			Show how to contact EMS
	Prepare		Change direction, deep water (unassisted)
			Safe boating equipment
			PFD & Me: Know your PFD
			Check the weather
			Stop! Look! Listen! Show you know

Name and Attendance

Total Enrolled: ☐

Total Completed: ☐

Recommended Class Size: **1:6-8**

✦ = Note to Instructor

✔ = Performance Criteria (Student)

🦉 = Wise Choices Focus

In every lesson, I...

- ■ Incorporate Prepare!...Stay Safe!...Survive!
- ■ Try to keep the class in the water 95% of the time
- ■ Use a least 5 stroke drills/activities
- ■ Provide constructive feedback to each student
- ■ Adapt teaching strategies to meet individual needs
- ■ Use both Water Safety and Swimming items

WATER SAFETY

STOP! LOOK! LISTEN!

Show you know...
- 🦉 MAKING WISE CHOICES: Explains why it is important to: 1) swim with a buddy with adult supervision, 2) wait for and listen to you (caregiver /lifeguard), 3) respect other students and swimmers.
- ✔ Performs site check and identifies site-specific danger areas: deep water, drop-offs, ladders, slippery decks, diving areas, sauna, whirlpool, currents, waves, cloudy water, boating area, etc.)

CHECK THE WEATHER
- ✔ Describes why it is important to always check the weather before being in or around the water outside.
- ✔ Knows at least two places to get information on weather: parents, radio and television forecasts, newspapers, Marine Weather Services.

PFD & ME: KNOW YOUR PFD
- ✔ Describes four characteristics of a good PFD: 1) Department of Transport (DOT) approved, 2) right size with bright colors, 3) whistle attached, 4) working ties, buckles, zippers, straps and no rips or tears.
- ✔ Identifies 3 ways to take care of PFD's: 1) rinse off salt or chlorine water, 2) hang up to dry, 3) keep out of the sun.

SAFE BOATING EQUIPMENT
- ✦ Small craft = 5.5 metres (or less) in length (e.g. canoe, rowboat, kayak).
- ✔ Identifies the minimum safety equipment that is required BY LAW on a small craft: 1) 1 PFD per person (DOT approved), 2) 2 paddles or oars (and rowlocks), 3) bailer or manual pump, 4) soundsignalling device, and 5) fire extinguisher if inboard motor or cooking appliance is on small craft.
- ✔ Describes importance of each item.

CHANGE DIRECTION, DEEP WATER (UNASSISTED)
- ✔ Performs front jump entry into deep water, and surfaces in a vertical position.
- ✔ After surfacing, turns in one direction and then in the opposite direction (complete rotations).
- ✔ Orients self toward original point of entry, and swims back to the point of safety in any manner.
- ✔ Explains why this skill is important to know.

SHOW HOW TO CONTACT EMS
- ✔ Describes at least two ways to get help: call adult or lifeguard, go to lifeguard/first aid station, contacts EMS (Emergency Medical System @ 911 or community alternative).
- ✔ Knows what EMS means and simulates a telephone conversation with 911 (you!): listens carefully, answers questions slowly, hangs up last.
- ✔ Describes at least two situations in which people might need help around the water.

SURFACE SUPPORT, 20 SECONDS, DEEP WATER
- ✔ Performs relaxed float on front for five seconds, rolls to back float for five seconds, and then continues to float, swim in place, or tread water (or combination) for at least 10 more seconds, in a relaxed manner.

SWIMMING

RHYTHMIC BREATHING, 15 TIMES, TWO WAYS
- ✔ Exhales through mouth and/or nose under water, inhales through mouth just above surface.
- ✔ Performance is rhythmic and relaxed, with noticeable and effective exhalation and inhalation, on EACH repetition.
- ✔ Performs 15 repetitions to the side, at least two different ways: e.g. standing with face in water, while kicking at the edge, while kicking with a board, while performing front crawl arm movements.

WEIGHT TRANSFER, SHALLOW WATER
- ✔ Transfers weight at least two ways, experimenting with buoyancy and centre of gravity: eg. retrieves objects from bottom, touches different body parts on bottom, does handstand, somersaults, log rolls.

SIDE GLIDES WITH FLUTTER KICK (UNASSISTED)
- ✔ Glides on each side with one arm extended above the head, and the other beside the body, with no movements of the hands.

- ✔ Performs flutter kick on each side for at least five seconds.
- ✔ Head is turned to side, with ear resting in water, near shoulder.

INTRODUCTION TO SCULLING, SHALLOW WATER
- ✔ Explores how to feel, manipulate and move the water, by sculling with lower arms and hands.
- ✔ Puts lower arms/hands under water, with fingers together, palms facing down.
- ✔ Orient palms (fingers) in various directions (palms up, down, one up and one down).
- ✔ Lower arms/hands swing out and in with even pressure.
- ✔ Body can be in different positions (standing, floating, sitting/leaning on buoyant aid).
- · Movement over a distance is not required.

BACK GLIDE AND KICK, 3 X 10 METRES (ONE LESSON)
- ✔ Maintains body in stretched-out position.
- ✔ Flutter kicks in continuous manner, with toes pointed.
- ✔ Breathes in a relaxed manner.

FRONT CRAWL, 3 X 5 METRES (ONE LESSON)
- ✦ Focus is on arm recovery/maintaining body position; breathing is not required.
- ✔ Maintains near horizontal body position, face in the water, keeping head straight.
- ✔ Flutter kick is at or near surface, with toes pointed.
- ✔ Recovers arms above water in a controlled, alternating manner.
- ✔ Breathes to the side, if needed, exhaling under water.

ENDURANCE SWIM, 15 METRES
- ✦ Proper techniques are encouraged and practiced, but NOT evaluated.
- ✔ Swims 15 metres continuously, on front and/or back using any form of propulsion (arms/legs or combination).

SAFETY SCENES
- ✦ Develop Safety Scenes based on the guidelines and examples in the Instructor Manual, ensuring effective safety supervision.
- ✦ Safety Scenes are scenarios that link knowledge and skills from the water safety and swimming learned in this level.
- ✔ Performs Safety Scenes, demonstrating knowledge and skills learned.

Canadian
Red Cross

Instructor Worksheet

AquaQuest 5

Instructor:

Day/Time:

Session:

Location:

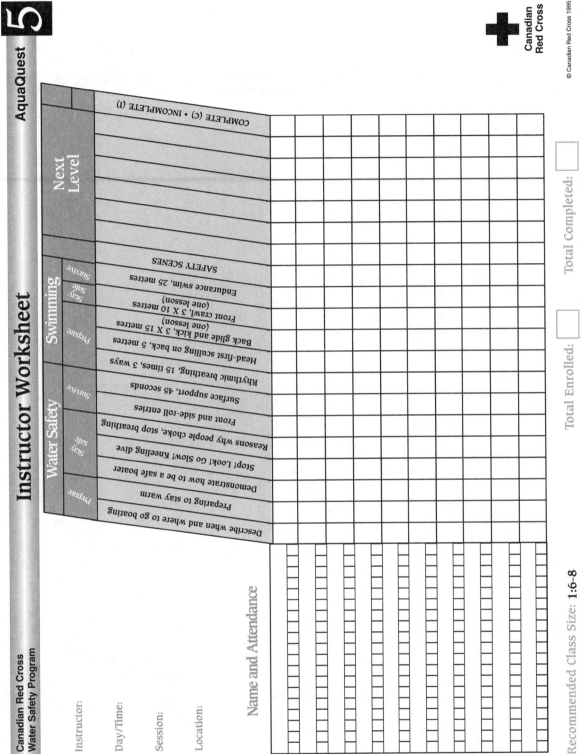

				COMPLETE (c) • INCOMPLETE (i)									

Next Level

Water Safety / **Swimming**

Prepare		Stay safe		Survive	Prepare	Stay Safe	Survive			
Describe when and where to go boating	Preparing to stay warm	Demonstrate how to be a safe boater	Stop! Look! Go Slow! Kneeling dive	Reasons why people choke, stop breathing	Front and side-roll entries	Surface support, 45 seconds	Rhythmic breathing, 15 times, 3 ways	Head-first sculling on back, 5 metres	Back glide and kick, 3 X 15 metres (one lesson)	Front crawl, 3 X 10 metres (one lesson)	Endurance swim, 25 metres	SAFETY SCENES

Name and Attendance

Total Enrolled: ☐

Total Completed: ☐

Recommended Class Size: **1:6-8**

Performance Criteria

✦ = Note to Instructor

✔ = Performance Criteria (Student)

🦉 = Wise Choices Focus

In every lesson, I...

■ Incorporate Prepare!...Stay Safe!...Survive!
■ Try to keep the class in the water 95% of the time
■ Use a least 5 stroke drills/activities
■ Provide constructive feedback to each student
■ Adapt teaching strategies to meet individual needs
■ Use both Water Safety and Swimming items

WATER SAFETY

DESCRIBE WHEN AND WHERE TO GO BOATING

✔ Identifies when it is safe: with adult permission and supervision, with minimum required safety equipment, with buddy, in a safe craft, with a float plan, good weather, daylight, etc.
✔ Identifies where it is safe: close to shore (except for boats with a motor), not in swimming area, away from larger boats, away from strong currents and tides, etc.

PREPARING TO STAY WARM

✔ Shows the major heat-loss areas (head, neck, sides of chest and groin) and how to keep them warm by curling up or huddling.
✔ Describes at least two ways to stay warm while boating: e.g. wear a PFD, be a safe and dry boater.
✔ Describes at least two ways to stay warm during activities on the ice: wear a hat, wear warm layers of clothes, know the weather.

DEMONSTRATE HOW TO BE A SAFE BOATER

🦉 MAKING WISE CHOICES: Shows how to prepare before getting into the boat.
🦉 Selects and puts on an appropriate PFD, and knows why a whistle should be attached.
🦉 Gathers all required safety equipment to take in boat (as per Level 4).
✔ Knows to never overload a boat and enters stabilized craft slowly (one at a time), staying low and balanced, with each hand on a stable position.
✔ Demonstrates staying safe: kneels or sits low and centred, doesn't stand up, makes no sudden movements, avoids leaning over edge, and doesn't show off.
✔ Exits stabilized craft slowly (one at a time), staying low and balanced, with each hand on a stable position.

STOP! LOOK! GO SLOW!

Kneeling dive
✦ Ensure safe depth and width of site (refer to Instructor Manual).
🦉 MAKING WISE CHOICES: States 3 wise choices related to diving: 1) always entering the water FEET FIRST, FIRST TIME, 2) obeying all posted signs about diving, 3) performing Stop! Look! Go Slow! when entering the water at any site.
🦉 Identifies injuries/consequences associated with unsafe diving (eg. spinal injury).
🦉 Demonstrates Stop! Look! Go Slow! and describes why site area is (or is not) safe for diving.
✔ Where site permits, performs front kneeling dive into water.
✔ Extends hands and arms above head, and enters with arms first, then head, then body, then feet.
✔ Keeps hands/arms above head throughout dive path, to protect head.

REASONS WHY PEOPLE CHOKE, STOP BREATHING

✔ Identifies three items that can cause people to choke: e.g. gum, food, tongue, toys.
✔ States why it's important not to eat or chew gum while playing in/around the water.
✔ Identifies three reasons why people might stop breathing: e.g. choking, drowning, overexposure to heat or cold, seizure.

FRONT & SIDE-ROLL ENTRIES

✦ Performs front and side-roll entries, reorients self in the water, and returns to point of safety.
✔ Tucks chin and protects head by holding firmly with both hands, elbows squeezed together below chin.
✔ Forward roll: rolls forward with back of head and shoulders contacting water first. Side roll: rolls forward and to side, with one shoulder contacting water first.

SURFACE SUPPORT, 45 SECONDS

✔ Treads water using large leg and arm movements, or swims in place, in a relaxed manner.
✔ Keeps head above water.

SWIMMING

RHYTHMIC BREATHING, 15 TIMES, THREE WAYS

✔ Exhales through mouth and/or nose under water, inhales through mouth just above surface.
✔ Performance is rhythmic and relaxed, with noticeable and effective exhalation and inhalation, on EACH repetition.

✔ Performs 15 repetitions, at least 3 different ways: deepwater bobs, one-arm front crawl, switching sides, front crawl, side glides with kick, etc.

HEAD-FIRST SCULLING ON BACK, FIVE METRES

✦ Minimal flutter kick or buoyant aid may be used to support flotation.
✔ Body is extended with ears in water, and legs together.
✔ Wrists are hyperextended with palms toward feet and fingers to ceiling.
✔ Upturned fingers remain closed and just below surface.
✔ Lower arms swing out and in with even pressure, while upper arms are relatively still and slightly away from body.
✔ Hand action is by hips and underwater, while body moves head-first in smooth manner.

BACK GLIDE AND KICK, 3 x 15 METRES (ONE LESSON)

✔ *Maintains near horizontal body position with neck in line with spine.*
✔ *Kicks from hips, knees below surface.*
✔ *Rolls body from side to side leading with shoulders and keeping head stationary.*
✔ Flutter kicks in a continuous manner, with toes pointed.
✔ Breathes in a relaxed manner.

FRONT CRAWL, 3 x 10 METRES (ONE LESSON)

✔ *Exhales under water, breathes to side as needed (may pause in side-glide position for up to two seconds).*
✔ Maintains horizontal body position, keeping head straight.
✔ Recovers arms above water in a controlled, alternating manner.
✔ Flutter kicks from hips, toes pointed.

ENDURANCE SWIM, 25 METRES

✦ Proper techniques are encouraged and practiced but not evaluated.
✔ Swims 25 metres continuously, using any stroke or combination of strokes, including legs or arms only.

SAFETY SCENES

✦ Develop Safety Scenes based on the guidelines and examples in the Instructor Manual, ensuring effective safety supervision.
✦ Safety Scenes are scenarios that link knowledge and skills from the water safety and swimming learned in this level.
✔ Performs Safety Scenes, demonstrating knowledge and skills learned.

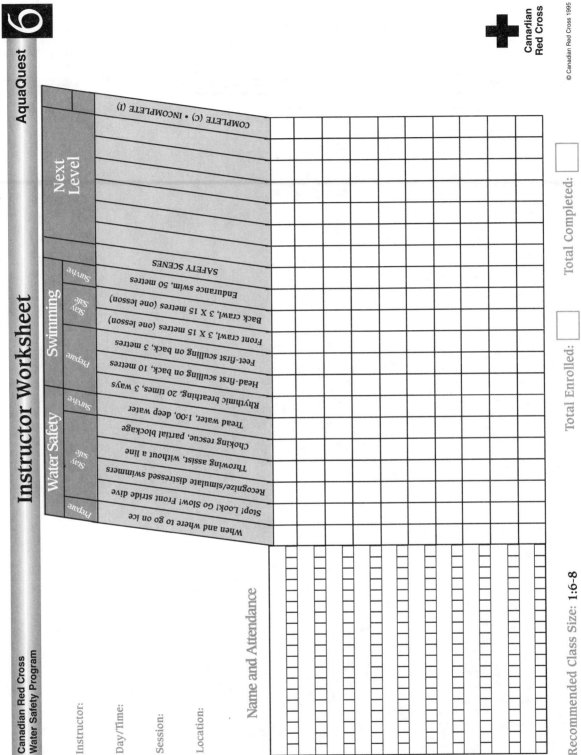

Canadian Red Cross
Water Safety Program

Instructor Worksheet

AquaQuest 6

Canadian
Red Cross

© Canadian Red Cross 1995

Instructor:

Day/Time:

Session:

Location:

Name and Attendance

Recommended Class Size: **1:6-8**

COMPLETE (C) • INCOMPLETE (I)

Next Level

Swimming

Survive — SAFETY SCENES

Survive — Endurance swim, 50 metres

Stay Safe — Back crawl, 3 X 15 metres (one lesson)

Stay Safe — Front crawl, 3 X 15 metres (one lesson)

Prepare — Feet-first sculling on back, 3 metres

Prepare — Head-first sculling on back, 10 metres

Prepare — Rhythmic breathing, 20 times, 3 ways

Water Safety

Survive — Tread water, 1:00, deep water

Stay Safe — Choking rescue, partial blockage

Stay Safe — Throwing assist, without a line

Recognize/simulate distressed swimmers

Prepare — Stop! Look! Go Slow! Front stride dive

Prepare — When and where to go on ice

Total Enrolled: ☐

Total Completed: ☐

Performance Criteria

✦ = Note to Instructor

✔ = Performance Criteria (Student)

= Wise Choices Focus

- Incorporate Prepare!...Stay Safe!...Survive!
- Try to keep the class in the water 95% of the time
- Use a least 5 stroke drills/activities
- Provide constructive feedback to each student
- Adapt teaching strategies to meet individual needs
- Use both Water Safety and Swimming items

WATER SAFETY

WHEN & WHERE TO GO ON ICE
✔ States that ice should always be checked by trained adult and that posted signs should be obeyed.
✔ Explains why adult supervision and a buddy are always necessary on the ice.
✔ Describes safe uniform ice thicknesses for various activities (ice safety zones): 1) 15cm for walking/skating in small groups, 2) 20cm for larger groups (skating parties), 3) 25cm for snowmobiles.
✔ Identifies three items for safety on the ice: e.g. warm clothes, whistle, rope.

STOP! LOOK! GO SLOW!
Front stride dive
✦ Ensure safe depth and width of site (refer to Instructor Manual).
✔ Demonstrates Stop! Look! Go Slow! and describes why site area is (or is not) safe for diving.
✔ Where site permits, performs front dive from stride position, into the water.
✔ Enters water with extended hands/arms above head, followed by head, shoulders, trunk, legs and feet.
✔ Keeps hands/arms extended above head throughout dive path, to protect head.

RECOGNIZE/SIMULATE DISTRESSED SWIMMERS
✔ Demonstrates ability to recognize and simulate 4 different types of distressed swimmers: weak or tired, non-swimmer, injured and unconscious.

THROWING ASSIST, WITHOUT A LINE
✦ Practices throwing to target first.
✔ Identifies characteristics of a good throwing assist: buoyant, accessible, easy to throw, not easily blown away, easy to hold onto.
✔ Gives/finds three examples of a good throwing assist: eg. ring-buoy (with our without a line), PFD.
✔ Consistently throws an assist, without a line, to a distressed conscious person (simulated), at least two metres away.

✔ 1) Calls for help and communicates clearly to the distressed swimmer, maintaining eye contact, 2) places feet shoulder width apart, with one foot in front of the other, 3) faces person, throws assist and follows through by pointing to target, 4) tells person to grab assist and move toward safety.
✔ Assist must land within one arm's length in front of the person (or repeats 2-4).
Explains reasons for not going into the water during a rescue and avoiding direct contact, and identifies need for further training.

CHOKING RESCUE, PARTIAL BLOCKAGE
✔ Shows universal sign for choking: clasping both hands near throat.
✔ Determines whether blockage is partial or complete, by asking if person can cough or speak.
✔ Encourages person to stay calm, sit down and continue coughing.
✔ Describes why it is important to stay with the person and call for help.

TREAD WATER, 1:00, DEEP WATER
✔ Treads water (1:00): vertical body position, head stays above water, uses any large, slow movements of the arms and legs, and stays in one place.
✔ Attempts to maximize efficiency by minimizing movement.

SWIMMING

RHYTHMIC BREATHING, 20 TIMES, THREE WAYS
✔ Exhales through mouth and/or nose under water, inhales through mouth just above surface.
✔ Performance is rhythmic and relaxed, with noticeable and effective inhalation and exhalation, on EACH repetition.
✔ Performs 20 repetitions, at least 3 different ways: e.g. deepwater bobs, one-arm front crawl (both sides), front crawl, side glides with kick, etc.

HEAD-FIRST SCULLING ON BACK, 10 METRES
✔ Body is extended at surface, ears in the water, with legs together.
✔ Wrists are hyperextended with palms toward feet/fingers to ceiling.
✔ Upturned fingers remain closed and just below surface.
✔ Lower arms swing out and in with even pressure while upper arms are relatively still and slightly away from body. Hand action is by hips and underwater, while body moves head first in smooth manner.

FEET-FIRST SCULLING ON BACK, THREE METRES
✦ Minimal flutter kick or buoyant aid may be used to support

flotation of legs.
✔ Body is extended on back, ears in the water, with legs together.
✔ Wrists bend downward (palms toward head/fingers toward bottom).
✔ Downturned fingers remain closed and just below surface.
✔ Lower arms swing out and in with even pressure while upper arms are relatively still and slightly away from body.
✔ Hand action is by hips and underwater, while body moves feet-first in smooth manner.

FRONT CRAWL, 3 x 15 METRES (ONE LESSON)
✔ Extends hand entry forward of head.
✔ Extends pull past hips.
✔ Exhales under water, breathes to side as needed *(no pause)*.
✔ Co-ordinates relaxed breathing with alternating relaxed arm recovery above water.
✔ Maintains horizontal body position, keeping head straight.
✔ Flutter kicks from hips, toes pointed.

BACK CRAWL, 3 x 15 METRES (ONE LESSON)
✔ Recovers arms above water, *in opposition to one another*.
✔ Arms may pause for up to two seconds *(one arm above head, one beside body)*.
✔ Maintains near horizontal body position with neck in line with spine.
✔ Rolls body from side to side leading with shoulders and keeping head stationary.
✔ Flutter kicks in continuous manner, with toes pointed.
✔ Kicks from hips, knees below surface.
✔ Breathes in a relaxed manner.

ENDURANCE SWIM, 50 METRES
✦ Proper techniques are encouraged and practiced but not evaluated.
✔ Swims 50 metres continuously, using any stroke or combination of strokes, including legs or arms only.

SAFETY SCENES

✦ Develop Safety Scenes based on the guidelines and examples in the Instructor Manual, ensuring effective safety supervision.
✦ Safety Scenes are scenarios that link knowledge and skills from the water safety and swimming learned in this level.
✔ Performs Safety Scenes, demonstrating knowledge and skills learned.

Canadian Red Cross
Water Safety Program

Instructor Worksheet

Instructor:

Day/Time:

Session:

Location:

Name and Attendance

	Next Level	COMPLETE (C) • INCOMPLETE (I)

Swimming

Survive		SAFETY SCENES
		Endurance swim, 75 metres
Stay Safe		Whip kick on front, 3 X 10 metres (one lesson)
		Whip kick on back, 3 X 10 metres (one lesson)
		Back crawl, 3 X 25 metres (one lesson)
Prepare		Front crawl, 3 X 25 metres (one lesson)
		Front scull, 5 metres
Survive		Feet-first sculling on back, 5 metres

Water Safety

Survive		Tread water, 1:30, deep water
Stay Safe		Checking airway, unconscious breathing person
		Stop! Look! Go Slow! Stride entry
Prepare		Preparing for safe boating
		Dangers of open water
		Exposure to cold

Total Enrolled:

Total Completed:

Recommended Class Size: 1:8-10

Performance Criteria

✔ = **Performance Criteria (Student)**

🦉 = **Wise Choices Focus**

♦ = **Note to Instructor**

In every lesson, I...

- Incorporate Prepare!...Stay Safe!...Survive!
- Try to keep the class in the water 95% of the time
- Use a least 5 stroke drills/activities
- Provide constructive feedback to each student
- Adapt teaching strategies to meet individual needs
- Use both Water Safety and Swimming items

WATER SAFETY

EXPOSURE TO COLD

✔ States major heat loss areas.
✔ States basic definition of hypothermia: a life-threatening condition in which the body's warming mechanism cannot maintain normal body temperature (37 degrees celcius) and the body cools.
✔ Identifies four signs and symptoms of hypothermia: which range from vigorous shivering to no shivering, bluish lips and reddish skin, sluggish speech, abnormal behaviour, poor co-ordination, stiff muscles, slow breathing, unconsciousness.
✔ Describes two water situations where hypothermia may occur (e.g. fall through ice, boat capsize).

DANGERS OF OPEN WATER

✔ Describes three potential dangers of open water: e.g. cold water, currents, waves, undertows, varying depths, sudden drop offs, weeds, exposure to sun or cold.
✔ Describes two ways to prepare and stay safe in and around the open water: e.g. Stop! Look! Listen! (including adult supervision and buddy), wear a PFD, Stop! Look! Go Slow!

PREPARING FOR SAFE BOATING

✔ Personal — 1) Makes a Float Plan including: who is travelling, point of destination, when they are going, stops along the way, expected arrival time, type and description of boat, equipment on-board, 2) Identifies a responsible person to give it to.
✔ Equipment — 1) Identifies minimum equipment required by law (level 4), 2) Identifies 3 additional safety items, 3) Identifies appropriate clothing.
✔ Environment — 1) States importance of checking weather and being familiar with the area of the trip.

STOP! LOOK! GO SLOW!
Stride entry
✔ Demonstrates Stop! Look! Go Slow!
✔ Enters water with legs in stride or whip kick position.
✔ Leans forward slightly during entry to increase surface resis-

tance and presses down with outstretched arms.
✔ Head stays above water at all times.

CHECKING AIRWAY, UNCONSCIOUS BREATHING PERSON
🦉 MAKING WISE CHOICES: Identifies why it's important to stay safe by always checking for dangers before proceeding.
✔ Demonstrates opening and maintaining airway: 1) checks for unresponsiveness (tap and shout), 2) if person is unresponsive, shouts for help and calls EMS, 3) rolls person onto back (if necessary) and opens airway (head tilt/chin lift), 4) checks for breathing (look, listen, feel — 5 seconds), 5) maintains open airway.

SWIMMING

TREAD WATER, 1:30, DEEP WATER
✔ Treads water (1:30).
✔ Maximizes efficiency by minimizing movement.
✔ States why it is important to keep head above water in a survival/cold water situation.

FEET-FIRST SCULLING ON BACK, FIVE METRES
♦ Minimal flutter may be needed to support flotation of legs.
✔ Body is extended and near horizontal, with legs together.
✔ Wrists bend downward (palms toward head/fingers toward bottom).
✔ Downturned fingers remain closed and just below surface.
✔ Lower arms swing out and in with even pressure while upper arms are relatively still and slightly away from body.
✔ Hand action is by hips and underwater, and body moves feet-first in smooth manner.

FRONT SCULL, FIVE METRES
♦ Focus is on performing sculling motion of breaststroke pull.
✔ Performs sculling motion with lower arms/hands, causing forward movement.
✔ Leans forward in water with arms extended in front, just wider than shoulder width.
✔ Bends elbows and forcefully sculls hands and lower arms down and in underneath the chin, then gently swings them out and back up to the surface.
✔ Elbows are bent out to the side and remain slightly forward of the shoulders at all times.

FRONT CRAWL, 3 x 25 METRES (ONE LESSON)
✔ Rolls body on long axis, no hip sway.
✔ Extends hand entry forward of head and in line with shoulders.
✔ Maintains horizontal body position, keeping head straight.
✔ Flutter kicks from hips, toes pointed.
✔ Extends pull past hips.
✔ Exhales under water, breathes to side as needed (no pause).

✔ Co-ordinates relaxed breathing with alternating relaxed arm recovery above water.

BACK CRAWL, 3 x 25 METRES (ONE LESSON)
✔ Recovers arms in a straight and relaxed manner, no pause.
✔ Maintains near horizontal body position with neck n line with spine.
✔ Rolls body from side to side leading with shoulders and keeping head stationary.
✔ Flutter kicks in continuous manner, with toes pointed.
✔ Kicks from hips, knees below surface.
✔ Recovers arms above water in opposition.
✔ Breathes in a relaxed manner.
✔ Co-ordinates body roll with arm recovery.

WHIP KICK ON BACK, 3 x 10 METRES (ONE LESSON)
✔ Body is in horizontal back glide position.
✔ Keeps back, hips and thighs nearly straight, just below surface.
✔ Recovers legs symmetrically by bending and separating knees slightly wider than hips.
✔ Pulls heels beneath and just wider than knees.
✔ Flexes ankles and rotates feet outward (dorsiflexed)
✔ Whips feet and lower leg back (power phase) to glide position with toes pointed (plantar-flexed).
✔ Glides until forward momentum slows.

WHIP KICK ON FRONT, 3 x 10 METRES (ONE LESSON)
♦ May use buoyant aid to support arms.
✔ Body is in horizontal glide position, face in or out.
✔ Recovers legs symmetrically by bending hips and knees.
✔ Pulls heels toward the buttocks, while separating knees just wider than hips; ankles slightly outside knees.
✔ Flexes ankles and rotates feet outward (dorsiflexed)
✔ Whips feet and lower leg back (power phase) to glide position with toes pointed (plantar-flexed).
✔ Glides until forward momentum slows.

ENDURANCE SWIM, 75 METRES
♦ Proper techniques are encouraged and practiced but not evaluated.
✔ Swims 75 metres continuously, using any stroke or combination of strokes, including legs or arms only.

SAFETY SCENES

♦ Develop Safety Scenes based on the guidelines and examples in the Instructor Manual, ensuring effective safety supervision.
✔ Safety Scenes are scenarios that link knowledge and skills from the water safety and swimming learned in this level.
✔ Performs Safety Scenes, demonstrating knowledge and skills learned.

Instructor:

Day/Time:

Session:

Location:

Water Safety

Prepare
- Causes of boating incidents

Stay Safe
- Stop! Look! Go Slow! Front dive
- Throwing assist, with a line
- Rescue breathing, adult, with pulse

Survive
- Cold water, H.E.L.P.
- Tread water, 2:00, deep water

Swimming

Stay Safe
- Front crawl, 50 metres
- Back crawl, 50 metres
- Elementary backstroke, 3 X 15 metres (one lesson)
- Breaststroke, 3 X 15 metres (one lesson)

Survive
- Endurance swim, 150 metres
- SAFETY SCENES

Next Level

COMPLETE (C) • INCOMPLETE (I)

Name and Attendance

✦ = Note to Instructor

✓ = Performance Criteria (Student)

🦉 = Wise Choices Focus

In every lesson, I...

- Incorporate Prepare!...Stay Safe!...Survive!
- Try to keep the class in the water 95% of the time
- Use a least 5 stroke drills/activities
- Provide constructive feedback to each student
- Adapt teaching strategies to meet individual needs
- Use both Water Safety and Swimming items

WATER SAFETY

CAUSES OF BOATING INCIDENTS

🦉 MAKING WISE CHOICES: Identifies three unwise choices that cause boating related drownings and injuries: e.g. mixing alcohol and boating, not wearing a PFD in the boat, and standing up in the boat.

✓ Describes the effects of alcohol on physical ability and judgement, and knows that it is illegal to drink and boat.

STOP! LOOK! GO SLOW!

Front dive

✦ Ensure safe depth and width of site (refer to Instructor Manual).

✓ Demonstrates Stop! Look! Go Slow! and describes why site area is (or is not) safe for diving.

✓ Where site permits, performs front dive, launching from both legs, and diving just below the surface (ie. shallow dive), in a streamlined manner.

✓ Demonstrates complete control of dive path, keeping arms/hands extended in front of head.

THROWING ASSIST, WITH A LINE

✓ Consistently throws an assist, with a line, to a distressed conscious swimmer (simulated) at least three metres away: 1) Calls for help and communicates clearly to the distressed swimmer while maintaining eye contact, 2) places feet shoulder width apart, with the line secured under the front foot, 3) faces person, throws assist and follows through by pointing to person, 4) gets into stable position (lying down) before person grabs onto the assist 5) smoothly pulls person to a secure point of safety.

✓ Assist must land within one arm's length just behind or to the side of the person.

✓ Explains reasons for not going into the water during a rescue and avoiding direct contact, and identifies need for further training.

RESCUE BREATHING, ADULT, WITH PULSE

✦ Use dolls or simulate with partners, without mouth-to-mouth contact.

✓ Demonstrates rescue breathing sequence for an adult: 1)

ensures no further danger, 2) checks for unresponsiveness (tap and shout), 3) if unresponsive, shouts for help and tells bystander to call EMS, 4) rolls person onto back (if necessary) and opens airway (head tilt/chin lift), 5) checks for breathing (look, listen, feel - 5 seconds), 6) if not breathing, simulates two full breaths (tight seal, nose pinched), 7) checks for pulse, 5-10 seconds (pulse is present), 8) continues rescue breathing, one full breath every 5 seconds (12 breaths/minute).

✓ States when to stop rescue breathing: when EMS arrives or person starts breathing.

COLD WATER, H.E.L.P.

✓ Explains what "Heat Escape Lessening Postures" or Positions do.

✓ States what exposure to cold water can do and why it is essential keep the head and neck above the water, and get the body out as soon as possible.

✓ Shows an individual H.E.L.P. (1:00): Wearing PFD, holds knees close to chest, arms held tight to body, head out of water. (May need to scull to maintain balance.)

✓ Shows a group H.E.L.P.- Huddle (1:00): Wearing PFD, huddles with other participants with chests close, arms around each other, legs squeezed together, with the smallest person in the middle of huddle.

✓ Explains why PFD's must be worn to be able to effectively maintain a heat escape lessening position in the water.

✓ Identifies situations when HELP (including the Huddle) may be needed.

TREAD WATER, 2:00, DEEP WATER

✓ Treads water (2:00)

✓ Maximizes efficiency by minimizing movement.

SWIMMING

FRONT CRAWL, 50 METRES

✓ Maintains horizontal body position, keeping head straight.

✓ Rolls body on long axis, no hip sway.

✓ Flutter kicks from hips, toes pointed.

✓ Extends hand entry forward of head and in line with the shoulders.

✓ Extends pull past hips.

✓ Exhales under water, breathes to side as needed (no pause).

✓ Co-ordinates relaxed breathing with alternating relaxed arm recovery above water.

BACK CRAWL, 50 METRES

✓ Enters hands and catches the water at 11:00 and 1:00 positions.

✓ Maintains near horizontal body position with neck in line with spine.

✓ Rolls body from side to side leading with shoulders and keeping head stationary.

✓ Flutter kicks in continuous manner, with toes pointed.

✓ Kicks from hips, knees below surface.

✓ Recovers arms above water in opposition.

✓ Recovers arms in a straight and relaxed manner, no pause.

✓ Breathes in a relaxed manner.

✓ Co-ordinates body roll with arm recovery.

ELEMENTARY BACKSTROKE, 3 x 15 METRES (ONE LESSON)

✓ Body is in horizontal back glide position, face above surface at all times.

✓ Keeps the back, hips, thighs nearly straight just below surface.

✓ Recovers legs symmetrically by bending and separating knees slightly wider than the hips.

✓ Pulls heels beneath and slightly wider than the knees.

✓ Flexes ankles and rotates feet outward.

✓ Whips feet and lower leg back (power phase) to glide position with toes pointed.

✓ Slides palms slowly up the sides of the body, extends arms slowly out to side and presses hands toward feet, as legs kick.

✓ Co-ordinates symmetric arm pull with kick, inhaling during recovery and exhaling during power phase.

✓ Glides until forward momentum slows.

BREASTSTROKE, 3 x 15 METRES (ONE LESSON)

✓ Body/head remains at or near surface.

✓ Recovers legs symmetrically by bending hips and knee.

✓ Pulls heels toward the buttocks while separating knees just wider than hips; ankles slightly outside knees.

✓ Flexes ankles and rotates feet outward.

✓ Whips feet and lower leg back (power phase) to glide position with toes pointed.

✓ Presses extended arms/palms apart slightly wider than shoulders.

✓ Bends elbows and sweeps the forearms and hands downward and towards chest.

✓ Hands sweep together under the chin, keeping the elbows forward of shoulders.

✓ Arms recover forward to full extension.

✓ Co-ordinates symmetric arm pull and whip kick, inhaling during pull, exhaling during kick (ie. pull and breathe, kick and glide).

✓ Glides until forward momentum slows.

ENDURANCE, 150 METRES

✦ Proper techniques are encouraged and practiced but not evaluated.

✓ Swims 150 metres continuously, using any stroke or combination of strokes, including legs or arms only.

SAFETY SCENES

✦ Develop Safety Scenes based on the guidelines and examples in the Instructor Manual, ensuring effective safety supervision.

✦ Safety Scenes are scenarios that link knowledge and skills from the water safety and swimming learned in this level.

✓ Performs Safety Scenes, demonstrating knowledge and skills learned.

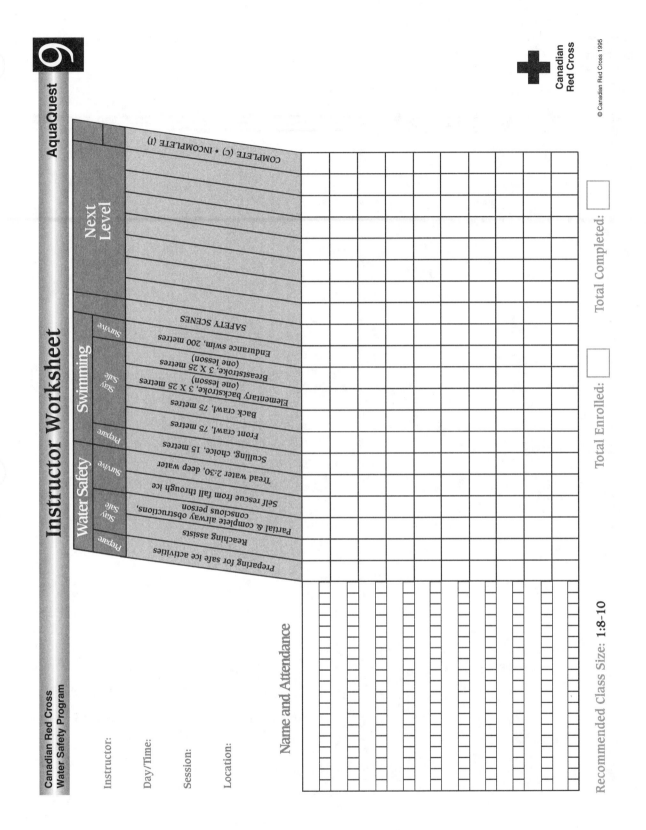

Canadian Red Cross
Water Safety Program

Instructor Worksheet

AquaQuest

9

Instructor:

Day/Time:

Session:

Location:

Name and Attendance

Recommended Class Size: **1:8–10**

Total Enrolled:

Total Completed:

COMPLETE (c) • INCOMPLETE (I)

Next Level

Swimming

Survive	SAFETY SCENES
	Endurance swim, 200 metres
Stay Safe	Breaststroke, 3 X 25 metres (one lesson)
	Elementary backstroke, 3 X 25 metres (one lesson)
	Back crawl, 75 metres
Prepare	Front crawl, 75 metres
	Sculling, choice, 15 metres

Water Safety

Survive	Tread water 2:30, deep water
	Self rescue from fall through ice
Stay Safe	Partial & complete airway obstructions, conscious person
	Reaching assists
Prepare	Preparing for safe ice activities

Canadian Red Cross

© Canadian Red Cross 1995

✦ = Note to Instructor

✔ = Performance Criteria (Student)

🐟 = Wise Choices Focus

In every lesson, I...

■ Incorporate Prepare!...Stay Safe!...Survive!
■ Try to keep the class in the water 95% of the time
■ Use a least 5 stroke drills/activities
■ Provide constructive feedback to each student
■ Adapt teaching strategies to meet individual needs
■ Use both Water Safety and Swimming items

WATER SAFETY

PREPARING FOR SAFE ICE ACTIVITIES

🐟 MAKING WISE CHOICES: Describes how to make wise choices in terms of personal, equipment and environment factors.
✔ Personal — Identifies the need for a buddy and adult supervision.
✔ Equipment — Identifies three safety items to have on or around the ice: eg. warm clothing, reaching/throwing assists, PFD, whistle, etc.
✔ Environment — 1) Reviews and states the ice safety zones (Level 6), 2) Identifies at least one place in the community where it would not be safe to go on the ice: e.g. open water, snow-covered ice, secluded or unsupervised area.

REACHING ASSISTS

✔ Identifies characteristics of good reaching assists: buoyant, accessible, light, easy to hold onto.
✔ Gives/finds four examples of good reaching assists: flutterboard, paddle, ring-buoy, innertube, etc.
✔ Demonstrates safe reaching assists to various types of distressed swimmers: 1) gets into stable position (lying down on angle), 2) communicates clearly and continually, maintaining eye contact, 3) pulls person to point of safety, keeping the assist between themselves and the person at all times.
✔ Explains reasons for not going into the water during a rescue and avoiding direct contact, and identifies need for further training.

PARTIAL & COMPLETE AIRWAY OBSTRUCTIONS, CONSCIOUS PERSON

✔ Determines whether blockage is partial or complete, by asking if person can cough or speak. If partial blockage, performs rescue as per Level 6.
✔ If complete blockage, call for help and: 1) stand behind person and wrap arms around waist, 2) make fist with one hand and place thumb side of fist on middle of abdomen, slightly above navel and below tip of breast-bone, 3) grasp fist with other hand and give quick, inward and upward

thrusts into the abdomen, to dislodge object.
✔ Continue until airway is cleared.

SELF RESCUE FROM FALL THROUGH ICE

✔ Simulates a self rescue by staying calm, and shouting for help or blowing whistle.
✔ Breaks weak ice in front and kicks feet, in order to assume a front float position.
✔ Grabs as far up on the ice as possible and continues to kick.
✔ Pulls self onto ice while kicking.
✔ Stays low and flat on ice, rolls to safety, seeks help, shelter and warmth.

TREAD WATER, 2:30, DEEP WATER

✔ Treads water (2:30)
✔ Maximizes efficiency by minimizing movement.

SWIMMING

SCULLING, CHOICE, 15M

✔ Performs choice of continuous sculling over a combined distance of 15 metres.

FRONT CRAWL, 75 METRES

✔ Executes bent-arm pull, in "s" pattern.
✔ Maintains horizontal body position, keeping head straight.
✔ Rolls body on long axis, no hip sway.
✔ Flutter kicks from hips, toes pointed.
✔ Extends hand entry forward of head and in line with shoulders.
✔ Extends pull past hips.
✔ Exhales under water, breathes to side as needed (no pause).
✔ Co-ordinates relaxed breathing with alternating relaxed arm recovery above water.

BACK CRAWL, 75 METRES

✔ Extends pull past the hips.
✔ Maintains near horizontal body position with neck in line with spine.
✔ Rolls body from side to side leading with shoulders and keeping head stationary.
✔ Flutter kicks in continuous manner, with toes pointed.
✔ Kicks from hips, knees below surface.
✔ Recovers arms above water in opposition.
✔ Enters arms in a straight and relaxed manner, no pause.
✔ Breathes in a relaxed manner.
✔ Co-ordinates body roll with arm recovery.

ELEMENTARY BACKSTROKE, 3 X 25 METRES (ONE LESSON)

✔ Arms and legs accelerate through power phase.

✔ Body is in horizontal back glide position, face above surface at all times.
✔ Keeps the back, hips, thighs nearly straight just below surface.
✔ Recovers legs symmetrically by bending and separating knees slightly wider than the hips.
✔ Pulls heels beneath and slightly wider than the knees.
✔ Flexes ankles and rotates feet outward.
✔ Whips feet and lower leg back to glide position with toes pointed (power phase).
✔ Slides palms slowly up the sides of the body, extends arms slowly out to side and presses hands toward feet, as legs kick.
✔ Co-ordinates symmetric arm pull with kick, inhaling during recovery and exhaling during power phase.
✔ Glides until forward momentum slows.

BREASTSTROKE, 3 X 25 METRES (ONE LESSON)

✔ Legs accelerate through power phase.
✔ Body/head remains at or near surface.
✔ Recovers legs symmetrically by bending hips and knees.
✔ Pulls heels toward the buttocks while separating knees just wider than hips, ankles slightly outside knees.
✔ Flexes ankles and rotates feet outward.
✔ Whips feet and lower leg back (power phase) to glide position with toes pointed.
✔ Presses extended arms/palms apart slightly wider than shoulders.
✔ Bends elbows and sweeps the forearms and hands downward and towards chest.
✔ Hands sweep together under the chin, keeping the elbows forward of shoulders.
✔ Arms recover forward to full extension.
✔ Co-ordinates symmetric arm pull and whip kick, inhaling during pull, exhaling during kick (i.e. pull and breathe, kick and glide).
✔ Glides until forward momentum slows.

ENDURANCE, 200 METRES

✦ Proper techniques are encouraged and practiced but not evaluated.
✔ Swims 200 metres continuously, using any stroke or combination of strokes, including legs or arms only.

SAFETY SCENES

✦ Develop Safety Scenes based on the guidelines and examples in the Instructor Manual, ensuring effective safety supervision.
✦ Safety Scenes are scenarios that link knowledge and skills from the water safety and swimming learned in this level.
✔ Performs Safety Scenes, demonstrating knowledge and skills learned.

Choke

Instructor Worksheet

AquaQuest

Canadian Red Cross
Water Safety Program

Instructor:

Day/Time:

Session:

Location:

		Water Safety				Swimming				Next Level	
		Prepare	Stay Safe	Survive		Stay Safe		Survive			COMPLETE (c) • INCOMPLETE (i)
Name and Attendance		Exposure to heat	Feet-first surface dive	Rescue breathing, child	Controlled capsize, survival skills	Tread water, 3:00, deep water	Front crawl, 100 metres	Back crawl, 100 metres	Elementary backstroke, 50 metres	Breaststroke 50 metres	Sidestroke, 3 X 15 metres (one lesson)	Dolphin kick, 3 X 10 metres (one lesson)	Endurance swim, 300 metres	SAFETY SCENES						

Total Enrolled: [ ]   Total Completed: [ ]

Recommended Class Size: **1:8–10**

♦ = Note to Instructor   ✓ = Performance Criteria (Student)   🐚 = Wise Choices Focus

In every lesson, I...

■ Incorporate Prepare!...Stay Safe!...Survive!
■ Try to keep the class in the water 95% of the time
■ Use a least 5 stroke drills/activities
■ Provide constructive feedback to each student
■ Adapt teaching strategies to meet individual needs
■ Use both Water Safety and Swimming items

WATER SAFETY

EXPOSURE TO HEAT

✓ Identifies potential dangers or consequences of exposure to heat/sun, including: heat exhaustion, heat stroke, sunburn, skin cancer.

✓ Identifies ways to reduce risks associated with exposure to heat: only go in whirlpool or sauna for very short duration (with adult supervision), drink plenty of cold water, wear protective hat/clothing, apply/re-apply waterproof sunscreen (SPF 15 or higher).

FEET-FIRST SURFACE DIVE

✓ Presses down with arms and performs any powerful kick (scissor, whip, eggbeater) to provide upward body lift, then uses upward arm press to assist vertical descent, keeping legs together.

✓ Where site permits, descends two metres.

RESCUE BREATHING, CHILD

✓ Performs rescue breathing as for adult, demonstrating modifications for a child.

✓ Opens airway gently, breathes at a rate of one every three seconds or 20/minute, and expels less air.

CONTROLLED CAPSIZE, SURVIVAL SKILLS

🐚✓ MAKING WISE CHOICES: Demonstrates the wisest choices to reduce exposure to cold and increase chances of survival.

🐚✓ Wise choices: 1) stays calm and reorients self, 2) stays with the craft, and straddles body onto overturned hull, if possible, OR 3) stays with the craft and minimizes movement and protects heat loss areas by performing a H.E.L.P. (individual or group huddle) with head above the water.

✓ Calls for help, and blows the whistle attached to the PFD.

TREAD WATER, 3:00, DEEP WATER

✓ Treads water (3:00)

✓ Maximizes efficiency by minimizing movement.

SWIMMING

FRONT CRAWL, 100 METRES

✓ Maintains horizontal body position, keeping head straight.
✓ Rolls body on long axis, with no hip sway.
✓ Flutter kicks from the hips, toes pointed.
✓ Extends hand entry forward of head and in line with the shoulders.
✓ Executes bent-arm pull, in "s" pattern.
✓ Extends pull past hips.
✓ Exhales under water, breathes to side as needed (no pause).
✓ Co-ordinates relaxed breathing with alternating relaxed arm recovery above water.

BACK CRAWL, 100 METRES

✓ Maintains near horizontal body position with neck in line with spine.
✓ Rolls body from side to side leading with shoulders and keeping head stationary.
✓ Flutter kicks in a continuous manner, with toes pointed.
✓ Kicks from hips, knees below surface.
✓ Recovers arms above water in opposition.
✓ Recovers arms in a straight and relaxed manner, with no pause.
✓ Enters hands and catches the water at 11:00 and 1:00 positions.
✓ Extends pull past the hips.
✓ Breathes in a relaxed manner.
✓ Co-ordinates body roll with arm recovery.

ELEMENTARY BACKSTROKE, 50 METRES

✓ Body is in horizontal back glide position, face above surface at all times.
✓ Keeps the back, hips, thighs nearly straight just below surface.
✓ Recovers legs symmetrically by bending and separating knees slightly wider than the hips.
✓ Pulls heels beneath and slightly wider than the knees.
✓ Flexes ankles and rotates feet outward.
✓ Whips feet and lower leg back (power phase) to glide position with toes pointed.
✓ Legs accelerate through power phase.
✓ Slides palms slowly up the sides of the body, extends arms slowly out to side and presses hands toward feet, as legs kick.
✓ Arms accelerate through power phase.
✓ Co-ordinates symmetric arm pull with kick, inhaling during recovery and exhaling during power phase.
✓ Glides until forward momentum slows.

BREASTSTROKE, 50 METRES

✓ Arms accelerate through power phase.
✓ Body/head remains at or near surface.
✓ Recovers legs symmetrically by bending hips and knees.

✓ Pulls heels toward the buttocks while separating knees just wider than hips; ankles slightly outside knees.
✓ Flexes ankles and rotates feet outward.
✓ Whips feet out and lower leg back (power phase) to glide position with toes pointed.
✓ Legs accelerate through power phase.
✓ Presses extended arms/palms apart slightly wider than shoulders.
✓ Bends elbows and sweeps the forearms and hands downward and towards chest.
✓ Hands sweep together under the chin, keeping the elbows forward of shoulders.
✓ Arms recover forward to full extension.
✓ Co-ordinates symmetric arm pull and whip kick, inhaling during pull, exhaling during kick (ie. pull and breathe, kick and glide).
✓ Glides until forward momentum slows.

SIDESTROKE, 3 x 15 METRES (ONE LESSON)

✓ Body and head are aligned in horizontal sideglide position.
✓ Recovers legs slowly by bending at hips and knees.
✓ Extends one leg forward/one back, then scissors them together (power phase).
✓ Pulls leading arm (above head), to meet trailing arm at chin.
✓ Extends into side-glide position, with trailing arm pushing toward feet (power phase).
✓ Recovers trailing arm and legs together, while leading arm pulls.
✓ Inhales during recovery and exhales during power phase.

DOLPHIN KICK, 3 x 10 METRES (ONE LESSON)

✓ Body moves in a continuous wave-like motion on the front, with hips remaining near the surface.
✓ Legs kick together (symmetric), originating from the hips.
✓ Knees lead the legs during downbeat of the kick (power phase), with toes pointed.
✓ Arms are extended above the head or along the sides.

ENDURANCE, 300 METRES

♦ Proper techniques are encouraged and practiced but not evaluated.
✓ Swims 300 metres continuously, using any stroke or combination of strokes, including legs or arms only.

SAFETY SCENES

♦ Develop Safety Scenes based on the guidelines and examples in the Instructor Manual, ensuring effective safety supervision.
♦ Safety Scenes are scenarios that link knowledge and skills from the water safety and swimming learned in this level.
✓ Performs Safety Scenes, demonstrating knowledge and skills learned.

Instructor:

Day/Time:

Session:

Location:

		COMPLETE (c) • INCOMPLETE (1)
Next Level		
Swimming	*Survive*	SAFETY SCENES
	Stay Safe	Endurance swim, 400 metres
		Butterfly, 3 X 10 metres (one lesson)
		Sidestroke, 50 metres
		Breaststroke, 50 metres
		Elementary backstroke 50 metres
		Back crawl, 100 metres
		Front crawl, 100 metres
Water Safety	*Survive*	Tread water, 4:00, deep water
	Stay Safe	Rescue breathing with complications
		Stop! Look! Go Slow! Front dives
		Head-first surface dive
	Prepare	Safe snowmobiling
		Causes of ice incidents

Name and Attendance

Total Enrolled: ☐   Total Completed: ☐

Recommended Class Size: 1:8-10

◆ = Note to Instructor

✔ = Performance Criteria (Student)   **= Wise Choices Focus**

In every lesson, I...

■ Incorporate Prepare!...Stay Safe!...Survive!
■ Try to keep the class in the water 95% of the time
■ Use a least 5 stroke drills/activities
■ Provide constructive feedback to each student
■ Adapt teaching strategies to meet individual needs
■ Use both Water Safety and Swimming items

WATER SAFETY

CAUSES OF ICE INCIDENTS

✔ MAKING WISE CHOICES: Identifies 3 unwise choices that cause drowning or injuries around the ice: eg. not having buddy and supervision, not checking for safe ice thickness, drinking alcohol.

SAFE SNOWMOBILING

✔ Identifies 4 ways to prevent snowmobiling incidents: e.g. stay on land or ensure ice is thick enough (25cm), don't drink alcohol and drive, stay off ice at night, wear flotation device, carry safety equipment.

HEAD-FIRST SURFACE DIVE

✔ Pikes at waist or tucks into vertical descent, keeping body streamlined, with legs together.
✔ Where site permits, descends 2 metres.

STOP! LOOK! GO SLOW!

Front dives
◆ Ensure safe depth and width of site (refer to Instructor Manual).
✔ MAKING WISE CHOICES: Demonstrates Stop! Look! Go Slow! and describes why site area is (or is not) safe for diving.
✔ Where site permits, performs a shallow dive staying just under the surface.
✔ Where site permits, performs a deep dive at a 45 degree angle to the surface.
✔ Enters the water in a streamlined manner, keeping arms/hands extended in front of head.

RESCUE BREATHING WITH COMPLICATIONS

✔ Simulates rescue breathing for child and adult.
✔ Recognizes two types of complications (distended stomach and vomiting), and shows how to respond: 1) Distended stomach — recognizes distention and decreases amount of air expelled during breaths, 2) Vomiting — protects head, rolls person on back, opens airway, and continues rescue breathing.

TREAD WATER, 4:00, DEEP WATER

✔ Treads water (4:00).
✔ Maximizes efficiency by minimizing movement.

SWIMMING

FRONT CRAWL, 100 METRES

✔ *Accelerates hands through the pull.*
✔ Maintains horizontal body position, keeping head straight.
✔ Rolls body on long axis, with no hip sway.
✔ Flutter kicks from the hips, toes pointed.
✔ Enters hand entry forward of head and in line with the shoulders.
✔ Executes bent-arm pull, in "s" pattern.
✔ Extends pull past hips.
✔ Exhales under water, breathes to side as needed (no pause).
✔ Co-ordinates relaxed breathing with alternating relaxed arm recovery above water.

BACK CRAWL, 100 METRES

✔ *Uses bent-arm pull in an "s"/question mark pattern, keeping elbows high.*
✔ Maintains near horizontal body position with neck in line with spine.
✔ Rolls body from side to side leading with shoulders and keeping head stationary.
✔ Flutter kicks in a continuous manner, with toes pointed.
✔ Kicks from hips, knees below surface.
✔ Recovers arms above water in opposition.
✔ Enters arms in a straight and relaxed manner, with no pause.
✔ Enters hands, catching the water at 11:00 and 1:00 positions.
✔ Extends pull past the hips.
✔ Breathes in a relaxed manner.
✔ Co-ordinates body roll with arm recovery.

ELEMENTARY BACKSTROKE, 50 METRES

✔ Body is in horizontal back glide position, face above surface at all times.
✔ Keeps the back, hips, thighs nearly straight just below surface.
✔ Recovers legs symmetrically by bending and separating knees slightly wider than the hips.
✔ Pulls heels beneath and slightly wider than the knees.
✔ Flexes ankles and rotates feet outward.
✔ Whips feet and lower leg back (power phase) to glide position with toes pointed.
✔ Legs accelerate through power phase.
✔ Slides palms slowly up the sides of the body, extends arms slowly out to side and presses hands toward feet, as legs kick.
✔ Arms accelerate through power phase.
✔ Co-ordinates symmetric arm pull with kick, inhaling during recovery and exhaling during power phase.
✔ Glides until forward momentum slows.

BREASTSTROKE, 50 METRES

✔ Body/head remains at or near surface.
✔ Recovers legs symmetrically by bending hips and knees.
✔ Pulls heels toward the buttocks while separating knees just wider than hips; ankles slightly ouside knees.
✔ Flexes ankles and rotates feet outward.
✔ Whips feet and lower leg back (power phase) to glide position with toes pointed.
✔ Legs accelerate through power phase.
✔ Presses extended arms/palms apart slightly wider than shoulders.
✔ Bends elbows and sweeps the forearms and hands downward and

towards chest.
✔ Hands sweep together under the chin, keeping the elbows forward of shoulders.
✔ Arms accelerate through power phase.
✔ Arms recover forward to full extension.
✔ Co-ordinates symmetric arm pull and whip kick, inhaling during pull, exhaling during kick (i.e. pull and breathe, kick and glide).
✔ Glides until forward momentum slows.

SIDESTROKE, 50 METRES

✔ *Accelerates kick and trailing arm through power phase.*
✔ *Glides until forward momentum slows.*
✔ Body and head are aligned in horizontal sideglide position.
✔ Recovers legs slowly by bending at hips and knees.
✔ Extends one leg forward/one back, then scissors them together (power phase).
✔ Pulls leading arm (above head) while recovering trailing arm to the chin.
✔ Extends into side-glide, with trailing arm pushing toward feet (power phase).
✔ Recovers trailing arm and legs together, while leading arm pulls.
✔ Inhales during recovery and exhales during power phase.

BUTTERFLY, 3 x 10 METRES (ONE LESSON)

◆ Evaluation is based ONLY on a willingness to attempt/practice the full stroke, as follows:
✔ Moves in a continuous motion, hips remaining near the surface.
✔ Legs kick together, from the hips.
✔ Knees lead legs during downbeat of the kick (power phase) with toes pointed.
✔ Relaxes arms during recovery, extending arms/hands in front of head as they enter.
✔ Pulls in a key-hole pattern, accelerating through the power phase, and pulling past hips.
✔ Co-ordinates two dolphin kicks with one symmetric arm stroke.
✔ Performs first downkick as arms enter water and second downkick as hands exit water.
✔ Breathes in any comfortable pattern, as the arms finish the pull, tilting the head up with the chin out.

ENDURANCE, 400 METRES

◆ Proper techniques are encouraged and practiced but not evaluated.
✔ Swims 400 metres continuously, using any stroke or combination of strokes, including legs or arms only.

SAFETY SCENES

◆ Develop Safety Scenes based on the guidelines and examples in the Instructor Manual, ensuring effective safety supervision.
✔ Safety Scenes are scenarios that link knowledge and skills from the water safety and swimming learned in this level.
✔ Performs Safety Scenes, demonstrating knowledge and skills learned.

Instructor Worksheet

AquaQuest **12**

Canadian
Red Cross

© Canadian Red Cross 1995

Instructor:

Day/Time:

Session:

Location:

					Water Safety						Swimming							Next Level				
	Prepare		Stay Safe		Survive		Prepare		Stay Safe					Survive									

Name and Attendance

COMPLETE (c) • INCOMPLETE (i)

Statistically speaking: preventing drownings...
Next steps: get trained
Surface dives with underwater swim 2 metres
Throwing/reaching assists
Ice rescue from safe zones
Tread water, 5:00, deep water
Sculling, choice, 20 metres
Front crawl, 100 metres
Back crawl, 100 metres
Elementary backstroke, 75 metres
Breaststroke, 75 metres
Sidestroke, 50 metres
Butterfly, 20 metres
Endurance, 500 metres
SAFETY SCENES

Total Enrolled: ☐   Total Completed: ☐

Recommended Class Size: 1:8–10

✦ = Note to Instructor   ✔ = Performance Criteria (Student)   = Wise Choices Focus

In every lesson, I...

- Incorporate Prepare!....Stay Safe!....Survive!
- Try to keep the class in the water 95% of the time
- Use a least 5 stroke drills/activities
- Provide constructive feedback to each student
- Adapt teaching strategies to meet individual needs
- Use both Water Safety and Swimming items

WATER SAFETY

STATISTICALLY SPEAKING:
Preventing drownings...
✦ Refer to current Canadian Red Cross drowning research and reports.
✔ Identifies at least three main causes for drownings and water-related injuries, stating who is at most risk for these incidents.
✔ Identifies a water-related situation they see themselves in, and communicates their understanding of how to apply PREPARE! STAY SAFE! SURVIVE! to that situation.

NEXT STEPS:
Get trained
✔ Identifies ways to get trained, stay involved and have fun in various aquatic activities: e.g. water polo, synchronized swimming, speed swimming, scuba, canoeing, sailing, Red Cross Water Safety Leadership courses or First Aid courses, Lifeguarding courses, Boating courses.

SURFACE DIVES WITH UNDERWATER SWIM, TWO METRES
✔ Swims two metres under water, following both head-first and feet-first surface dives.

THROWING/REACHING ASSISTS
✔ Demonstrates wise choices to stay safe while performing at least two safe and effective reaching and/or throwing assists.
✦ Explains reasons for not going into the water during a rescue and avoiding direct contact, and identifies need for further training.

ICE RESCUE FROM SAFE ZONE
✔ Identifies need to quickly assess situation, call for help, and tell someone to contact EMS.
✔ Identifies why it's ALWAYS safest to perform the rescue from shore/land.
✔ Identifies four items that would be effective throwing or reaching assists: e.g. ladder, hockey stick, rope, PFD, pole, strong branch.
✔ Demonstrates how to guide/talk a person through a self-rescue (as per Level 9).
✔ Identifies need to get the person warm and dry and to contact EMS in case of hypothermia.
✦ Explains reasons for not going into the water during a rescue and avoiding direct contact, and identifies need for further training.
✦ Describes how someone could perform a throwing or reaching assist, if needed, from a secure "safe zone" on the ice: i.e. crawling slowly while ensuring the ice ahead is stable, staying as far away from the breakthrough as possible, throwing or reaching the assist while lying down, pulling person onto safe ice and rolling back to land.

TREAD WATER, 5:00, DEEP WATER
✔ Treads water (5:00).
✔ Maximizes efficiency by minimizing movement.

SWIMMING

SCULLING, CHOICE, 20 METRES
✔ Performs choice of continous sculling over a combined distance of 20 metres.

FRONT CRAWL, 100 METRES
✔ *Keeps elbows high during recovery and pull.*
✔ Maintains horizontal body position, keeping head straight.
✔ Flutter kicks from the hips, toes pointed.
✔ Executes bent-arm pull, in "s" pattern.
✔ Accelerates hands through the pull.
✔ Extends pull past hips.
✔ Exhales under water, breathes to side as needed (no pause).
✔ Co-ordinates relaxed breathing with alternating relaxed arm recovery above water.

BACK CRAWL, 100 METRES
✔ *Accelerates arms/hands through the pull.*
✔ Maintains near horizontal body position with neck in line with spine.
✔ Rolls body from side to side leading with shoulders and keeping head stationary.
✔ Flutter kicks in a continuous manner, with toes pointed.
✔ Kicks from hips, knees below surface.
✔ Recovers arms above water in opposition.
✔ Recovers arms in a straight and relaxed manner, with no pause.
✔ Enters hands, catching the water at 11:00 and 1:00 positions.
✔ Uses bent-arm pull in an "s"/question mark pattern, keeping elbows high.
✔ Extends pull past the hips.
✔ Breathes in a relaxed manner.
✔ Co-ordinates body roll with arm recovery.

ELEMENTARY BACKSTROKE, 75 METRES
✔ Body is in horizontal back glide position, face above surface at all times.
✔ Keeps the back, hips, thighs nearly straight just below surface.
✔ Recovers legs symmetrically by bending and separating knees slightly wider than the hips.
✔ Pulls heels beneath and slightly wider than the knees.
✔ Flexes ankles and rotates feet outward.
✔ Whips feet and lower leg back (power phase) to glide position with toes pointed.
✔ Legs accelerate through power phase.
✔ Slides palms slowly up the sides of the body, extends arms slowly out to side and presses hands toward feet, as legs kick.
✔ Arms accelerate through power phase.
✔ Co-ordinates symmetric arm pull with kick, inhaling during recovery and exhaling during power phase.
✔ Glides until forward momentum slows.

BREASTSTROKE, 75 METRES
✔ Body/head remains at or near surface.
✔ Recovers legs symmetrically by bending hips and knees.
✔ Pulls heels toward the buttocks while separating knees just wider than hips; ankles slightly outside knees.

✔ Flexes ankles and rotates feet outward.
✔ Whips feet and lower leg back (power phase) to glide position with toes pointed.
✔ Legs accelerate through power phase.
✔ Presses extended arms/palms slightly wider than shoulders.
✔ Bends elbows and sweeps the forearms and hands downward and towards chest.
✔ Hands sweep together under the chin, keeping the elbows forward of shoulders.
✔ Arms accelerate through power phase.
✔ Arms recover forward to full extension.
✔ Co-ordinates symmetric arm pull and whip kick, inhaling during pull, exhaling during kick (i.e. pull and breathe, kick and glide).
✔ Glides until forward momentum slows.

SIDESTROKE, 50 METRES
✔ Body and head are aligned in horizontal sideglide position.
✔ Recovers legs slowly by bending at hips and knees.
✔ Extends one leg forward/one back, then scissors them together (power phase).
✔ Accelerates kick through power phase.
✔ Pulls leading arm (above head) while recovering trailing arm to the chin.
✔ Extends into side-glide, with trailing arm pushing toward feet (power phase).
✔ Accelerates trailing arm power phase.
✔ Recovers trailing arm and legs together, while leading arm pulls.
✔ Glides until forward momentum slows.
✔ Inhales during recovery and exhales during power phase.

BUTTERFLY, 20 METRES
✦ Evaluation is based ONLY on a willingness to attempt/practice the full stroke, as follows:
✔ Moves in a continuous motion, with hips remaining near the surface.
✔ Legs kick together, from the hips.
✔ Knees lead legs during downbeat of the kick (power phase), with toes pointed.
✔ Relaxes arms during recovery, extending arms/hands in front of head as they enter.
✔ Pulls in a key-hole pattern, accelerating through the power phase, and pulling past hips.
✔ Co-ordinates two dolphin kicks with one symmetric arm stroke.
✔ Performs first downkick as arms enter water and second downkick as hands exit water.
✔ Breathes in any comfortable pattern, as the arms finish the pull, tilting the head up with the chin out.

ENDURANCE, 500 METRES
✦ Proper techniques are encouraged and practiced but not evaluated.
✔ Swims 500 metres continuously, using any stroke or combination of strokes, including legs or arms only.

SAFETY SCENES
✦ Develop Safety Scenes based on the guidelines and examples in the Instructor Manual, ensuring effective safety supervision.
✦ Safety Scenes are scenarios that link knowledge and skills from the water safety and swimming learned in this level.
✔ Performs Safety Scenes, demonstrating knowledge and skills learned.

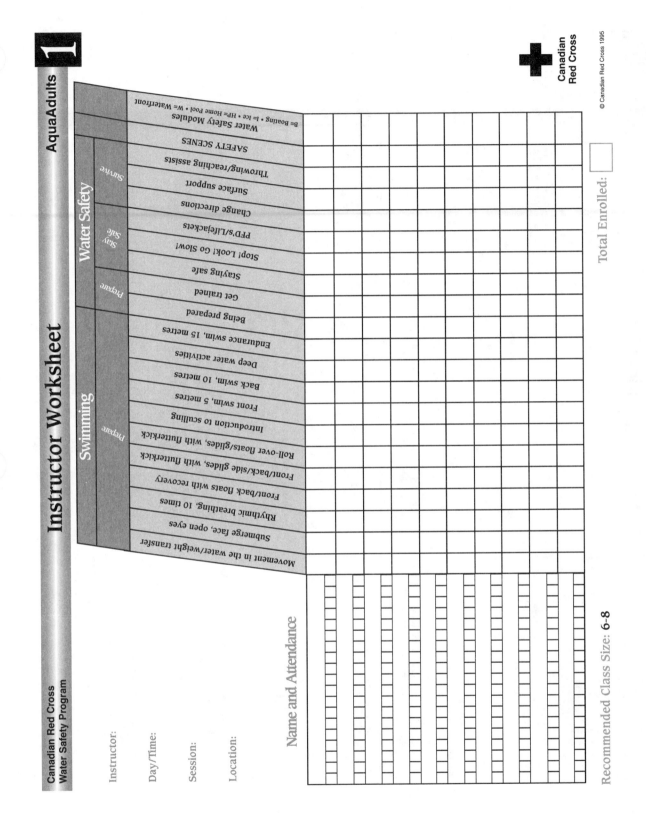

Canadian Red Cross
Water Safety Program

Instructor Worksheet

AquaAdults 1

Instructor:

Day/Time:

Session:

Location:

Name and Attendance

Recommended Class Size: 6-8

Water Safety

Survive
- SAFETY SCENES
- Throwing/reaching assists
- Surface support
- Change directions

Stay Safe
- PFD's/Lifejackets
- Stop! Look! Go Slow!
- Staying safe

Prepare
- Get trained
- Being prepared

Water Safety Modules
B= Boating • I= Ice • HP= Home Pool • W= Waterfront

Swimming

Prepare
- Endurance swim, 15 metres
- Deep water activities
- Back swim, 10 metres
- Front swim, 5 metres
- Introduction to sculling
- Roll-over floats/glides, with flutterkick
- Front/back/side glides, with flutterkick
- Front/back floats with recovery
- Rhythmic breathing, 10 times
- Submerge face, open eyes
- Movement in the water/weight transfer

Total Enrolled:

Canadian Red Cross

Notes to Instructor...

- Provide assistance to the student whenever necessary encouraging them to work towards total independance.
- Ensure that skills are initiated by the student; for example, going into the deep water.
- Incorporate water safety, based on students' interests.
- Refer to Swimming and Water Safety book.

SWIMMING

- Develop the basic swimming skills as per the progressions in AquaQuest Levels 1-4.

Prepare!

✔ Movement in the water ✔ Submerge face, open eyes ✔ Rhythmic breathing, 10 times ✔ Weight transfer ✔ Front floats with recovery, 5 seconds ✔ Back floats with recovery, 5 seconds ✔ Back glides with flutterkick ✔ Front glides with flutterkick ✔ Back glides with flutterkick ✔ Side glides with flutterkick ✔ Roll-over floats ✔ Roll-over glides with flutterkick ✔ Introduction to sculling ✔ Front swim, 5 metres (any method) ✔ Back swim, 10 metres (any method) ✔ Deep water activities ✔ Endurance Swim, 15 metres (any method)

WATER SAFETY

Statistically Speaking...

1) Did they know...
- Canadian Red Cross conducts research and produces drowning reports on an annual basis, which are available from their local Red Cross office.

2) What the research tells us...
- Drownings are among the leading causes of injury death among Canadians. ■ There are approximately 600 unintentional water-related fatalities in Canada each year. ■ Males account for more than 80% of all drownings; the greatest numbers of drowning victims were among males ages 15-44 years of age. ■ Most recreational swimming drownings occur in rivers and lakes.

In every lesson, I...
- Incorporate Prepare!...Stay Safe!...Survive!
- Adapt teaching strategies to meet individual needs
- Use a least 5 stroke drills/activities
- Provide at least 3 in-water demonstrations
- Provide constructive feedback to each student
- Use both Water Safety and Swimming items

🦉 = **Wise Choices Focus**

3) What they can do about it...
- PREPARE! STAY SAFE! SURVIVE!

How to Prepare...

Being prepared... ✔ 🦉 Identifies three key ways to ensure that they are personally prepared (with family/friends) for activities in and around the water: e.g. ensure adult supervision/buddy system; have/bring safety equipment, be familiar with the site; check the weather; recognize personal limitations.

Get trained... ✔ Describes three ways to get trained, to be better prepared in and around the water: e.g. explore other AquaAdults water safety modules, take a First Aid (CPR) course, take a boating course.

How to Stay Safe...

Staying safe... ✔ Identifies three key ways to stay safe while in and around the water: e.g. maintain supervision, stay sober, use appropriate equipment (wear a PFD); respect the aquatic environment and your personal limitations.

Stop! Look! Go Slow!... ✔ 🦉 Explains the importance of, and demonstrates STOP! LOOK! GO SLOW! while performing safe entries into various depths of water, based on personal readiness and interest: e.g. using ladder, jumping feet first, stride entry, diving (where site permits).

PFD's/Lifejackets... ✔ Identifies the characteristics of and differences between PFD's and Lifejackets, including how to take care of them. ✔ Wears a PFD in shallow and/or deep water, and explores movement and flotation. ✔ Performs H.E.L.P. and Huddle and explains the importance of the skill.

How to Survive...

Change directions... ✔ Demonstrates ability to push away from a point of safety, turn circles in each direction, reorient and return to point of safety.

Surface support... ✔ Progresses from floats and swimming in place to treading water. ✔ Keeps head above water (maintaining vision and decreasing heat loss from the head). ✔ Works toward a minimum of 30 seconds.

Throwing/reaching assists... ✔ Recognizes/simulates distressed swimmers: tired or weak, non-swimmer, injured, unconscious. ✔ Describes and identifies good throwing or reaching aids. ✔ 🦉 Demonstrates safe and effective throwing and reaching assists. ✔ Explains reasons for not going into the water during a rescue and avoiding direct contact, and identifies need for further training.

SAFETY SCENES

- ◆ Develop Safety Scenes based on the guidelines and examples in the Instructor Manual, ensuring effective safety supervision.
- ◆ Safety Scenes are scenarios that link knowledge and skills from the water safety and swimming learned in this level.
- ✔ Performs Safety Scenes, demonstrating knowledge and skills learned.

Canadian Red Cross
Water Safety Program

Instructor Worksheet

AquaAdults 2

Instructor:

Day/Time:

Session:

Location:

Name:

- ☐ Front crawl
- ☐ Back crawl
- ☐ El. Backstroke
- ☐ Breaststroke
- ☐ Sidestroke
- ☐ Butterfly

- ☐ Basic
- ☐ Boating
- ☐ Ice
- ☐ Home Pool
- ☐ Waterfront

Name:

- ☐ Front crawl
- ☐ Back crawl
- ☐ El. Backstroke
- ☐ Breaststroke
- ☐ Sidestroke
- ☐ Butterfly

- ☐ Basic
- ☐ Boating
- ☐ Ice
- ☐ Home Pool
- ☐ Waterfront

Name:

- ☐ Front crawl
- ☐ Back crawl
- ☐ El. Backstroke
- ☐ Breaststroke
- ☐ Sidestroke
- ☐ Butterfly

- ☐ Basic
- ☐ Boating
- ☐ Ice
- ☐ Home Pool
- ☐ Waterfront

Name:

- ☐ Front crawl
- ☐ Back crawl
- ☐ El. Backstroke
- ☐ Breaststroke
- ☐ Sidestroke
- ☐ Butterfly

- ☐ Basic
- ☐ Boating
- ☐ Ice
- ☐ Home Pool
- ☐ Waterfront

Name:

- ☐ Front crawl
- ☐ Back crawl
- ☐ El. Backstroke
- ☐ Breaststroke
- ☐ Sidestroke
- ☐ Butterfly

- ☐ Basic
- ☐ Boating
- ☐ Ice
- ☐ Home Pool
- ☐ Waterfront

Name:

- ☐ Front crawl
- ☐ Back crawl
- ☐ El. Backstroke
- ☐ Breaststroke
- ☐ Sidestroke
- ☐ Butterfly

- ☐ Basic
- ☐ Boating
- ☐ Ice
- ☐ Home Pool
- ☐ Waterfront

Name:

- ☐ Front crawl
- ☐ Back crawl
- ☐ El. Backstroke
- ☐ Breaststroke
- ☐ Sidestroke
- ☐ Butterfly

- ☐ Basic
- ☐ Boating
- ☐ Ice
- ☐ Home Pool
- ☐ Waterfront

Name:

- ☐ Front crawl
- ☐ Back crawl
- ☐ El. Backstroke
- ☐ Breaststroke
- ☐ Sidestroke
- ☐ Butterfly

- ☐ Basic
- ☐ Boating
- ☐ Ice
- ☐ Home Pool
- ☐ Waterfront

Name:

- ☐ Front crawl
- ☐ Back crawl
- ☐ El. Backstroke
- ☐ Breaststroke
- ☐ Sidestroke
- ☐ Butterfly

- ☐ Basic
- ☐ Boating
- ☐ Ice
- ☐ Home Pool
- ☐ Waterfront

Name:

- ☐ Front crawl
- ☐ Back crawl
- ☐ El. Backstroke
- ☐ Breaststroke
- ☐ Sidestroke
- ☐ Butterfly

- ☐ Basic
- ☐ Boating
- ☐ Ice
- ☐ Home Pool
- ☐ Waterfront

Canadian Red Cross

Total Enrolled:

Recommended Class Size: 6-10

Performance Guidelines

🐢 = **Wise Choices Focus**

Notes to Instructor...

■ Student chooses stroke(s) in consultation with you based on their learning inventory.
■ Help the student set attainable goals (eg. to swim 50 metres per stroke), improving stroke technique at a personal rate.
■ Develop strokes as per the AquaQuest 12 progressions, working toward the Level 12 proficiency checklists seen below, and utilizing stroke drills found in Levels 4-12 strategy cards.
■ Incorporate water safety, based on students' interests.
■ Refer to Swimming and Water Safety book.

SWIMMING

Stay Safe!

FRONT CRAWL
✔ Maintains horizontal body position, keeping head straight ✔ Rolls body on long axis, with no hip sway ✔ Flutter kicks from the hips, toes pointed ✔ Recovers arms in a relaxed manner, elbows high ✔ Extends hand entry forward of head and in line with the shoulders ✔ Executes bent-arm pull, in "s" pattern, keeping elbows high ✔ Accelerates hands through the pull ✔ Extends pull past hips ✔ Exhales under water, breathes to side as needed (no pause) ✔ Co-ordinates relaxed breathing with alternating relaxed arm recovery above water

BACK CRAWL
✔ Maintains near horizontal body position with neck in line with spine ✔ Rolls body from side to side leading with shoulders and keeping head stationary ✔ Flutter kicks in a continuous manner, with toes pointed ✔ Kicks from hips, knees below surface ✔ Recovers arms above water in opposition ✔ Recovers arms in a straight and relaxed manner, with no pause ✔ Enters hands, catching the water at 11:00 and 1:00 positions ✔ Uses bent-arm pull in an "s"/question mark pattern, keeping elbows high ✔ Accelerates arms/hands through the pull ✔ Extends pull past the hips ✔ Breathes in a relaxed manner ✔ Co-ordinates body roll with arm recovery

ELEMENTARY BACKSTROKE
✔ Body is in horizontal back glide position, face above surface at all times ✔ Keeps the back, hips and thighs near/ straight and just below the surface ✔ Recovers legs symmetrically by bending and separating knees slightly wider than the hips ✔ Pulls heels beneath and slightly wider than the knees, ankles slightly outside knees ✔ Flexes ankles and rotates feet outward ✔ Whips feet and lower leg back (power phase) to glide position with toes pointed ✔ Legs accelerate through power phase ✔ Slide: palms slowly up the sides of the body and extends arms slowly out to side ✔ Presses hands toward feet as legs kick ✔ Arms accelerate through power phase ✔ Co-ordinates symmetric arm pull with kick, inhaling during recovery and exhaling during power phase ✔ Glides until forward momentum slows

BREASTSTROKE
✔ Body/head remains at or near surface ✔ Recovers legs symmet-

rically by bending hips and knees ✔ Pulls heels toward the buttocks while separating knees just wider than hips ✔ Flexes ankles and rotates feet outward ✔ Whips feet and lower leg back (power phase) to glide position with toes pointed ✔ Legs accelerate through power phase ✔ Presses extended arms/palms apart slightly wider than shoulders ✔ Bends elbows and sweeps the forearms and hands downward and towards chest ✔ Hands sweep together under the chin, keeping the elbows forward of shoulders ✔ Arms accelerate through power phase ✔ Arms recover forward to full extension ✔ Co-ordinates symmetric arm pull and whip kick, inhaling during pull, exhaling during kick (pull and breathe, kick and glide) ✔ Glides until forward momentum slows

SIDESTROKE
✔ Body and head are aligned in horizontal side-glide position ✔ Recovers legs slowly by bending at hips and knees ✔ Extends one leg forward/one back, then scissors them together (power phase) ✔ Accelerates kick through power phase ✔ Pulls leading arm (above head) while recovering trailing arm to the chin ✔ Extends into side-glide, with trailing arm pushing toward feet (power phase) ✔ Accelerates trailing arm power phase ✔ Recovers trailing arm and legs together, while leading arm pulls ✔ Glides until forward momentum slows ✔ Inhales during recovery and exhales during power phase

BUTTERFLY
✔ Moves in a continuous motion, with hips remaining near the surface ✔ Legs kick together, from the hips ✔ Knees lead legs during downbeat of the kick (power phase), with toes pointed ✔ Relaxes arms during recovery, extending arms/hands in front of head as they enter ✔ Pulls in a key-hole pattern, accelerating through the power phase, and pulling past hips ✔ Co-ordinates two dolphin kicks with one symmetric arm stroke ✔ Performs first downkick as arms enter water and second downkick as hands exit water ✔ Breathes in any comfortable pattern, as the arms finish the pull, tilting the head up with the chin out

ENDURANCE
✔ Works toward a personal distance goal, in a stroke or strokes chosen, aiming for a minimum of 100 metres

WATER SAFETY

How to Prepare...

Being prepared... 🐢 Identifies three key ways to ensure that they are personally prepared (with family/friends) for activities in and around the water: e.g. ensure adult supervision/buddy system; have/bring safety equipment, be familiar with the site; check the weather; recognize personal limitations.

Get trained... 🐢 Describes three ways to get trained: e.g. explore other AquaAdults water safety modules, take a First Aid (CPR) course, take a boating course.

In every lesson, I...

■ Incorporate Prepare!...Stay Safe!...Survive!
■ Adapt teaching strategies to meet individual needs
■ Use a least 5 stroke drills/activities
■ Provide at least 3 in-water demonstrations
■ Provide constructive feedback to each student
■ Use both Water Safety and Swimming items

How to Stay Safe...

Staying safe... 🐢 Identifies three key ways to stay safe while in and around the water: e.g. maintain supervision, stay safer, use appropriate equipment (i.e. wear a PFD); respect the aquatic environment and your personal limitations.

Stop! Look! Go Slow!... ✔ Explains the importance of, and demonstrates STOP! LOOK! GO SLOW! while performing safe entries into various depths of water, based on personal readiness and interest: e.g. using ladder, jumping feet first, stride entry, diving (where site permits).

PFD's/Lifejackets... ✔ Identifies the characteristics of and differences between PFD's and Lifejackets, including how to take care of them. ✔ Wears a PFD in shallow and/or deep water, and explores movement and flotation. ✔ Performs H.E.L.P. and Huddle and explains the importance of the skill.

How to Survive...

Change directions... ✔ Demonstrates ability to push away from a point of safety, turn circles in each direction, reorient and return to point of safety.

Surface support... ✔ Progresses from floats and swimming in place to treading water. ✔ Keeps head above water (maintaining vision and decreasing heat loss from the head). ✔ Works toward a minimum of 30 seconds.

Throwing/reaching assists... ✔ Recognizes/simulates distressed swimmers: tired or weak, nonswimmer, injured, unconscious. ✔ Describes and identifies good throwing or reaching aids. ✔ Demonstrates safe and effective throwing and reaching assists. ✔ Explains reasons for not going into the water during a rescue and avoiding direct contact, and identifies need for further training.

SAFETY SCENES

◆ Develop Safety Scenes based on the guidelines and examples in the Instructor Manual, ensuring effective safety supervision.
◆ Safety Scenes are scenarios that link knowledge and skills from the water safety and swimming learned in this level.
✔ Performs Safety Scenes, demonstrating knowledge and skills learned.

Instructor Worksheet

AquaAdults **3**

Instructor: **Day/Time:** **Session:** **Location:**

Name:

- ☐ Front crawl
- ☐ Back crawl
- ☐ El. Backstroke
- ☐ Breaststroke
- ☐ Sidestroke
- ☐ Butterfly

- ☐ Basic
- ☐ Boating
- ☐ Ice
- ☐ Home Pool
- ☐ Waterfront

Name:

- ☐ Front crawl
- ☐ Back crawl
- ☐ El. Backstroke
- ☐ Breaststroke
- ☐ Sidestroke
- ☐ Butterfly

- ☐ Basic
- ☐ Boating
- ☐ Ice
- ☐ Home Pool
- ☐ Waterfront

Name:

- ☐ Front crawl
- ☐ Back crawl
- ☐ El. Backstroke
- ☐ Breaststroke
- ☐ Sidestroke
- ☐ Butterfly

- ☐ Basic
- ☐ Boating
- ☐ Ice
- ☐ Home Pool
- ☐ Waterfront

Name:

- ☐ Front crawl
- ☐ Back crawl
- ☐ El. Backstroke
- ☐ Breaststroke
- ☐ Sidestroke
- ☐ Butterfly

- ☐ Basic
- ☐ Boating
- ☐ Ice
- ☐ Home Pool
- ☐ Waterfront

Name:

- ☐ Front crawl
- ☐ Back crawl
- ☐ El. Backstroke
- ☐ Breaststroke
- ☐ Sidestroke
- ☐ Butterfly

- ☐ Basic
- ☐ Boating
- ☐ Ice
- ☐ Home Pool
- ☐ Waterfront

Name:

- ☐ Front crawl
- ☐ Back crawl
- ☐ El. Backstroke
- ☐ Breaststroke
- ☐ Sidestroke
- ☐ Butterfly

- ☐ Basic
- ☐ Boating
- ☐ Ice
- ☐ Home Pool
- ☐ Waterfront

Name:

- ☐ Front crawl
- ☐ Back crawl
- ☐ El. Backstroke
- ☐ Breaststroke
- ☐ Sidestroke
- ☐ Butterfly

- ☐ Basic
- ☐ Boating
- ☐ Ice
- ☐ Home Pool
- ☐ Waterfront

Name:

- ☐ Front crawl
- ☐ Back crawl
- ☐ El. Backstroke
- ☐ Breaststroke
- ☐ Sidestroke
- ☐ Butterfly

- ☐ Basic
- ☐ Boating
- ☐ Ice
- ☐ Home Pool
- ☐ Waterfront

Name:

- ☐ Front crawl
- ☐ Back crawl
- ☐ El. Backstroke
- ☐ Breaststroke
- ☐ Sidestroke
- ☐ Butterfly

- ☐ Basic
- ☐ Boating
- ☐ Ice
- ☐ Home Pool
- ☐ Waterfront

Name:

- ☐ Front crawl
- ☐ Back crawl
- ☐ El. Backstroke
- ☐ Breaststroke
- ☐ Sidestroke
- ☐ Butterfly

- ☐ Basic
- ☐ Boating
- ☐ Ice
- ☐ Home Pool
- ☐ Waterfront

Recommended Class Size: 6-10

Total Enrolled: ☐

+ Canadian Red Cross

SWIMMING

Notes to Instructor...

- Encourage each student to know and work at his or her own fitness level, gradually increasing fitness and improving stroke proficiency.
- If something doesn't feel good to a student, stop it.
- Incorporate water safety, based on students interest.
- Refer to Swimming and Water Safety book.

WARM-UP/COOL-DOWN

✔ Demonstrates the importance of beginning and completing each swimming session with a warm-up and cool-down, consisting of low intensity activity and/or stretching, for 5-10 minutes, depending on the length and intensity of the exercise session.

✔ Participates in warm-up: preparing the body for action by warming up and loosening the major joints and muscles and by raising the heart rate gradually.

✔ Participates in cool-down: gradually decreasing the heart rate and allowing the body to recover from fatigue.

F.I.T. PRINCIPLE

✔ Lists the three factors of the F.I.T. principle:
  1) F = frequency of exercise
  2) I = intensity of exercise
  3) T = time or duration of exercise.

✔ Knows that attaining and maintaining a certain level of fitness, in any exercise program, depends on a balance of these factors.

✔ Knows that fitness level may vary from one specific activity to another.

TARGET HEART RATE

- **Refer to Target Heart Rate Range chart.**

✔ Explains what target heart rate range (THRR) is: the ideal heart rate range to maintain during exercise, for greatest cardiovascular benefit, based on age and current physical fitness level.

✔ Identifies personal THRR, recognizing that it may vary as per the directions of a medical doctor.

✔ Explains the importance of taking heart rate to monitor exertion level and improvements in fitness level. Also recognizes that listening to how your body "feels" is also very important.

✔ Demonstrates ability to monitor heart rate during exercise sessions, using the index and middle fingers to count the radial or carotid pulse. (10 second count multiplied by 6, or 15 second count multiplied by 4.)

SWIMMING SKILLS AND DRILLS

- **Suggested stroke drills appear on strategy card. (AquaQuest Levels 4-12).**

✔ Works with instructor to identify areas of improvement, and sets goals based on personal ability and interest.

In every lesson, I...

- Incorporate Prepare!...Stay Safe!...Survive!
- Adapt teaching strategies to meet individual needs
- Use a least 5 stroke drills/activities
- Provide at least 3 in-water demonstrations
- Provide constructive feedback to each student
- Use both Water Safety and Swimming items

🦉 = Wise Choices Focus

✔ Swims various distances and performs drills and skills, aimed at improving any or all of the following: body position/motion, kicking, arm stroke, breathing/timing, endurance, speed.

✔ Utilizes various types of training equipment, based on interest and physical ability: e.g. kick boards, flippers, pool "noodles".

FIT & FUN

- **Activities are determined by participants and instructor, based on interest, abilities and site-specific availability of activities.**

✔ Participates in additional aquatic activities for fun and fitness! (e.g. deep-water running, water polo, synchronized swimming, aquafit, swima-thon, parent/child relay night, etc.)

WATER SAFETY

How to Prepare...

Being prepared... ✔ Identifies three key ways to ensure that they are personally prepared (with family/friends) for activities in and around the water: e.g. ensure adult supervision/buddy system; have/bring safety equipment, be familiar with the site; check the weather; recognize personal limitations.

Get trained... ✔ Describes three ways to get trained, to be better prepared in and around the water: e.g. explore other AquaAdults water safety modules, take a First Aid (CPR) course, take a boating course.

How to Stay Safe...

Staying safe... ✔🦉 Identifies three key ways to stay safe while in and around the water: e.g. maintain supervision, stay sober, use appropriate equipment (wear a PFD); respect the aquatic environment and your personal limitations.

Stop! Look! Go Slow!... ✔🦉 Explains the importance of, and demonstrates STOP! LOOK! GO SLOW! while performing safe entries into various depths of water, based on personal readiness and interest: e.g. using ladder, jumping feet first, stride entry, diving (where site permits).

PFD's/Lifejackets... ✔ Identifies the characteristics of and differences between PFD's and Lifejackets, including how to take care of them. ✔ Wears a PFD in shallow and/or deep water, and explores movement and flotation. ✔ Performs H.E.L.P. and Huddle and explains the importance of the skill.

How to Survive...

Change directions... ✔ Demonstrates ability to push away from a point of safety, turn circles in each direction, reorient and return to point of safety.

Surface support... ✔ Progresses from floats and swimming in place to treading water. ✔ Keeps head above water (maintaining vision and decreasing heat loss from the head). ✔ Works toward a minimum of 30 seconds.

Throwing/reaching assists... ✔ Recognizes/simulates distressed swimmers: tired or weak, non-swimmer, injured, unconscious. ✔ Describes and identifies good throwing or reaching aids. ✔ Demonstrates safe and effective throwing and reaching assists. ✔ Explains reasons for not going into the water during a rescue and avoiding direct contact, and identifies need for further training.

SAFETY SCENES

- Develop Safety Scenes based on the guidelines and examples in the Instructor Manual, ensuring effective safety supervision.
- Safety Scenes are scenarios that link knowledge and skills from the water safety and swimming learned in this level.

✔ Performs Safety Scenes, demonstrating knowledge and skills learned.

TARGET HEART RATE CHART
(refer to Swimming & Water Safety book)

AGE	Minimum Working Heart Rate (60%)	Maximum Working Heart Rate (85%)
20-29	124	179
30-39	119	161
40-49	114	152
50-59	108	143
60-69	103	134
70 +	98	125

• Pulse counts are based on 60 seconds

Water Safety Modules

Boating Safety

Refer to "Boat Smart" theme in the Instructor Manual.
Refer to Swimming and Water Safety book

STATISTICALLY SPEAKING:
Here's what the research tells us...
- About 40% of all drownings occur during boating activities.
- Over 90% of boating victims were not properly wearing a PFD.
- Over 1/3 of boating drownings involve alcohol consumption.
- About 2/3 of all recreational boating drownings occured in small open outboard motor boats 5.5 metres or less in length, and in canoes.

HOW TO PREPARE:
✓ Identifies primary causes of boating incidents
✓ Describes what and why a float plan is important
✓ Identifies safety equipment required by law
✓ Describes when and where to go boating
✓ Recognizes need for further training to deal with emergency situations (e.g. CPR, first aid, water rescue)

HOW TO STAY SAFE:
✓ Describes effective supervision of children
✓ Identifies importance of wearing an appropriate PFD
✓ Describes/demonstrates how to enter/exit boat safely
✓ Describes/demonstrates safe behaviour in the boat
✓ Identifies the dangers and law regarding alcohol and boating

HOW TO SURVIVE:
✓ Demonstrates Heat Escape Lessening Positions with a PFD
✓ Demonstrates survival skills in a controlled capsize
✓ Performs rescue for partial and complete airway obstructions (conscious person)
✓ Performs rescue breathing for adult, child and infant (pulse present)

SAFETY SCENES:
✓ Performs boating related Safety Scenes, demonstrating water safety/swimming knowledge and skills learned.

Ice Safety

Refer to "Stay Warm" theme in the Instructor Manual.
Refer to Swimming and Water Safety book

STATISTICALLY SPEAKING:
Here's what the research tells us...
- Drownings during snowmobiling are almost seven times more common among males than females.
- Blood alcohol levels are above the legal limit in 1/3 of snowmobile drowning victims aged 15 and over.
- Findings suggest that flotation coats or suits will provide more adequate protection than standard PFD's, under conditions of extreme cold.
- For adults, falls into water during ice fishing is among the common recreational activities associated with drowning.

HOW TO PREPARE:
✓ Identifies primary causes of ice-related incidents.
✓ Identifies safety equipment for activities on the ice.
✓ Identifies the dangers of exposure to cold and how to stay warm.
✓ Describes when and where to go on ice: ice safety zones.
✓ Recognizes need for further training to deal with emergency situations (e.g. CPR, first aid, water rescue)

HOW TO STAY SAFE:
✓ Describes effective supervision of children.
✓ Identifies ways to ensure safety while snowmobiling.
✓ Identifies the dangers of mixing alcohol with ice activities.
✓ Recognizes signs/symptoms of hypothermia.
✓ Explains importance of continually checking the quality/strength of the ice.

HOW TO SURVIVE:
✓ Demonstrates a self rescue from fall through ice.
✓ Demonstrates a rescue (talking/throwing/reaching) from a safe zone.
✓ Performs rescue for partial and complete airway obstructions (conscious person)
✓ Performs rescue breathing for adult, child and infant (pulse present)

SAFETY SCENES:
✓ Performs ice related Safety Scenes, demonstrating water safety/swimming knowledge and skills learned.

Home Pool Safety

Refer to AquaAdults section of Instructor Manual.
Refer to Swimming and Water Safety book

STATISTICALLY SPEAKING:
Here's what the research tells us...
- Most drownings in home pools involve children. On these occasions children either gained easy access to the pool area, or were left unsupervised.
- One of every three diving incidents happens in home pools. The majority of spinal injuries occure while diving into water less than 5 feet deep.
- The 1-4 age group is at high risk of many types of unintentional injuries, especially in and around the home.
- Drowning hazards in and around the home account for approximately 50% of all toddler drownings.

HOW TO PREPARE:
✓ Identifies primary causes of injury/drownings in and around the home
✓ Explains role as an active supervisor and role model
✓ Identifies the dangers of home pools (including bath tubs, hot tubs, etc.)
✓ Describes ways to prepare for safety in and around the pool (water).
✓ Recognizes need for further training to deal with emergency situations (e.g. CPR, first aid, water rescue)

HOW TO STAY SAFE:
✓ Identifies ways to communicate safety messages
✓ Identifies possible consequences of mixing water and alcohol
✓ Describes effective supervision of children
✓ Describes/demonstrates how to enter water safely

HOW TO SURVIVE:
✓ Performs self rescue skills (e.g. tread water, change direction)
✓ Demonstrates safe and effective rescues (talking /throwing/reaching)
✓ Performs rescue for partial and complete airway obstructions (conscious person)
✓ Performs rescue breathing for adult, child and infant (pulse present)

SAFETY SCENES:
✓ Performs home pool related Safety Scenes, demonstrating water safety/swimming knowledge and skills learned.

Waterfront Safety

Refer to AquaAdults section of Instructor Manual.
Refer to Swimming and Water Safety book

STATISTICALLY SPEAKING:
Here's what the research tells us...
- Most recreational swimming drownings occur in rivers and lakes.
- Drowning due to falls into large bodies of water involve both children and adults.
- Over 60% of toddlers who drown are thought to be only playing or walking near the water.
- Over 90% of toddlers who drown are not being supervised by an adult.

HOW TO PREPARE:
✓ Identifies primary causes of injury/drownings at waterfront areas
✓ Identifies general hazards of waterfront areas
✓ Describes ways to prepare for safety in and around waterfront areas
✓ Recognizes need for further training to deal with emergency situations (e.g. CPR, first aid, water rescue)

HOW TO STAY SAFE:
✓ Describes ways to stay safe during waterfront activities
✓ Identifies possible consequences of mixing water and alcohol
✓ Describes effective supervision of children
✓ Describes/demonstrates how to enter water safely

HOW TO SURVIVE:
✓ Performs self rescue skills (e.g. tread water, change direction)
✓ Demonstrates safe and effective rescues (talking/throwing/reaching)
✓ Performs rescue for partial and complete airway obstructions (conscious person)
✓ Performs rescue breathing for adult, child and infant (pulse present)

SAFETY SCENES:
✓ Performs waterfront related Safety Scenes, demonstrating water safety/swimming knowledge and skills learned.

Canadian Red Cross
© Canadian Red Cross 1995

Appendix A:
Guiding Principles for Healthy Child Development

Background

In 1995, Parks and Recreation Ontario developed a tool to measure how well recreation programs are designed, implemented, and led to ensure that children will develop in a healthy way while in these settings. It is critical that you understand and incorporate the following concepts into your student's lessons. Healthy child development today means a brighter tomorrow. You can have a positive or a negative impact on the children you work with. One careless put-down or a moment of sincere understanding can make a difference and last a lifetime. The following Guiding Principles were adopted for use by the Parks and Recreation Ontario organization.

Guiding Principles for Healthy Child Development

It is through the use of the following guiding principles that environments, programs, and systems are created to help children along the path of healthy development.

A. Environments for children must be:
- Secure, safe, and stable
- Caring
- Stimulating
- Accessible
- Considerate of personal space needs and special needs
- Equipped with age, size, and ability-appropriate equipment, furniture and materials
- Welcoming of diverse races, cultures, and ability

B. Activties must:
- Allow for a combination of self-directed and staff-directed activities with plenty of choice
- Reflect both assessed and expressed needs
- Provide opportunities for active participation and passive reflection

- Encourage imaginative play, inquistiveness, and thoughtfulness
- Provide leadership opportunities when possible
- Incorporate the varied learning styles and developmental stages
- Value and incorporate cultural, racial, and linguistic diversity

C. Staff must:
  - Ensure that all children are treated with respect, honesty, and trust
  - Recognize and accept children's individual needs and circumstances
  - Use positive behaviour management methods
  - Assist children with valuing and celebrating diversity in the community
  - Continually and consistently model appropriate behaviour
  - Continually evaluate to ensure improvements and reflect changing needs

D. Connections to home must:
  - Ensure clear and on-going communication with parents and families with regard to their children's experience and safety
  - Be developed to encourage participation and input from parents and families

Objectives for Healthy Development of Children in Recreation Settings

Recreational play provides a vehicle by which the outcomes of physical, cognitive, emotional, and social development are achieved. The competencies acquired through participation in recreation programs provide a strong foundation to prepare children for future life experiences. The goal of recreation and sport programs is to provide child-centered activities and environments where children feel safe, welcome, competent, connected, empowered, and special.

The design of children's recreation and sport programs must take into consideration the following broader objectives:

1. To enable children to develop as considerate, cooperative, and caring individuals who demonstrate concern and respect for themselves, others, and their communities

2. To develop competencies in chosen skill areas by providing high-quality leadership and ensuring stage appropriateness and opportunities for self-direction and experiential learning

3. To provide opportunities for self expression and creativity through imaginative play, experimentation, and exploration

4. To provide positive role models and, in turn, opportunities for role modeling

5. To enhance competencies and learning through child-centered activities in both group settings and on an individual basis, focusing on fun and enjoyment

6. To build self-esteem and confidence by providing stage-appropriate, challenging opportunities, achievement of competencies, and growth through success

7. To provide opportunities for the development of both peer and nonparent relationships in a safe environment

8. To learn and experience responsibility, decision-making, independence, problem solving, team building, and self-management in a progressive manner

9. To assist children with the development of a lifelong commitment to physical fitness, health, and the positive use of leisure time

10. To provide an opportunity to gain an understanding and appreciation of the natural world through hands-on experience

11. To enrich children's lives through exposure to differences and to diverse and stimulating activities, leading to the acquisition of new skills and interests

Appendix B:
Child Maltreatment Guidelines

You have a legal obligation to report alleged maltreatment. It may take place in the workplace, or a child may tell you about his or her experience with maltreatment. You should follow these procedures for reporting child maltreatment.*

Handling a Suspected Case of Child/Youth Maltreatment

1. **Know your provincial legislation that defines duty to report.**
2. **Check with your employer for specific workplace policies and guidelines.**
3. Document all statements, conversations, and observations as soon as you are able. Describe the incident, situation, statement, or physical symptoms: include dates and times that these were evident. Keep these documents strictly confidential.
4. Check your impressions with colleagues who also observe or work with the child.
5. Report child maltreatment by dialing 0 for the operator and asking the operator to connect you with the organization responsible for dealing with child welfare in your province. Give the social worker the following information:

- Child's name, address, date of birth and gender
- Language spoken
- Special needs, if any (e.g., hearing impairment, mentally challenged)
- Siblings' names and ages
- Name(s) of parents, guardians
- Address and phone number of parents, guardians
- Language spoken by parents, guardians
- Time child usually arrives at the facility
- Time child usually leaves the facility
- Description of incident, situation, statement, behaviour, and/or physical symptoms that lead you to suspect abuse
- Times and dates of your observations

Seek social worker's advice on the next steps to take.

*Check with your employer for specific workplace or provincial guidelines.

6. If necessary, keep the child safe and in a supportive environment. **Do not interview the child.** The matter may go to court, so questioning should only be carried out by social workers, police, and/or lawyers familiar with the law.

7. Do not inform parents or guardians of the alleged maltreatment. That is the responsibility of the social worker assigned to the case.

8. Keep confidential all information about the child who discovered the alleged abuse, who reported it, and who has been accused. Make sure other instructors and your employer respect the confidentiality of the maltreatment allegation. This protects the child and the child's family, plus the person who reported.

9. Be aware that you may experience trauma after child maltreatment is revealed. Speak to your employer if you believe you require support.

Handling A Spoken Disclosure From A Child/Youth

1. Listen calmly and openly.
   - As the child speaks, you may be overwhelmed with your own feelings of anger, pain, and perhaps fear.
   - At the time of the disclosure, put your own feelings aside.
   - Be emotionally available to the child and listen.
   - Do not ask questions: do not interview.
   - Do not make judgments about the child or the possible abuser.
   - Give full attention to the child and nod understandingly as the story comes out.
   - To ensure the child's message is not overheard by others, move away from onlookers.
   - If you are inside, find a room where you have privacy, but always leave the door slightly open.

2. Reassure.
   - As a responsible adult in a position of trust, you must believe that this child has come to you with something to tell because of powerful, hurtful feelings.
   - Understand that your relationship with the child has allowed him or her to open up to you.

- Trust the child is speaking from a great need and open your heart to hear.
- Children who speak about sexual, physical, or emotional abuse often struggle with the desire to protect the abuser.
- Victims of all ages often believe—mistakenly—that they are responsible for the abuse they receive, and they hope the violence will just go away.
- Reassure the child that "It is not your fault."
- Explain that you are going to do your best to help.

3. Affirm.
   - Children often delay the disclosure and endure maltreatment for a long time before telling.
   - Let the child know that it is a courageous act for him or her to talk to you about maltreatment.
   - Tell the child that you are sorry he or she had to experience this.

4. Make a decision.
   - You should establish the immediacy of the danger to the child; you must not allow the child to return to a situation where his or her life would be in immediate danger.
   - Be honest with the child and let him or her know that you cannot keep this secret and that there are other people who need to know.
   - Decide whether this disclosure is reportable. If so, let the child know that you are going to report the disclosure—you do not want surprises for the child.
   - Call 0 and ask the operator to connect you with the organization responsible for dealing with child welfare in your province. Give the social worker the information listed under No. 3. Depending on the age of the child or youth, give as many choices as possible in the decision-making process (e.g., Does the child want to listen to you making the phone call?).

5. Document.
   - Record all statements, observations, conversations within the context of the disclosure; include time, date, place, and what was said by each person.
   - Keep all records in a confidential locked file, they may become necessary for a legal case.

6. Follow-up.
   - Consult your provincial legislation and, if the disclosure is reportable, talk to the social worker about how you can support the ongoing needs of the child.
   - If the disclosure is not reportable, develop a plan with other Water Safety staff on how the instructors can best meet the needs of the child.
   - Take care of yourself—it is difficult to know that children are being hurt.
   - Find someone you can trust to share your feelings.

Handling A Disclosure About A Staff Person

The following are suggestions on how to handle a complaint or disclosure about an instructor:
   - Listen to the disclosure.
   - Do not jump to conclusions.
   - Ensure that the disclosure is voiced in a private area.
   - Do not judge or question the disclosure.
   - Validate the person with the complaint.
   - Document the name, address, phone number of the person who voiced the disclosure and his or her complaint.
   - Record the name, address, and phone number of the child suspected of being maltreated.
   - Advise your aquatic supervisor/manager of the complaint.
   - Your aquatic supervisor/manager should file complaint with the organization responsible for child welfare in your province.
   - Your aquatic supervisor/manager will need to establish if the person is a risk to other children and, if so, suspend his or her contract until the investigation is completed.
   - Your aquatic supervisor should request the final report of the investigation (if available) to review.
   - Maintain confidentiality.

REFERENCES

Put the child first, National Youth Serving Organization, Ontario, 1989.

Help stop child abuse: a handbook for employers and volunteer coordinators, Ministry of Attorney General, Ministry of Social Services, Province of British Columbia, June 1994.

Child abuse policy handbook, Victoria YM/YWCA, June 1993.

Fairholm J: *Adolescent maltreatment: overview and response*, The Canadian Red Cross Society, B.C./Yukon Division, 1990.

Inter-ministry child abuse handbook: an integrated approach to child abuse and neglect, B.C., 1988.

APPENDIX C:
Water Safety Instructor Course Evaluation Criteria

This appendix provides an overview of the criteria on which *you* will be evaluated during the core of your course and your teaching experience. In *both*, you must have demonstrated *every single item* at least once. Continually check with your Instructor Trainer throughout the core of the course and your teaching experience evaluator to identify criteria that you have demonstrated and those that you need to work on to demonstrate.

Ultimately, it is YOUR responsibility to demonstrate each criteria to your evaluator. *Plan* to demonstrate specific items. *Plan* with your evaluator for opportunities to work on and demonstrate each criteria. With *planning*, *effort*, and *responsibility* you will successfuly complete your Water Safety Instructor course.

Core of the Course

EXPERIENCE

1. **Participates actively in all activities**
   Ask yourself, are you—
   - Taking part in all water activities including drills, games, and progressions?
   - Participating without a need for prompting?
   - Participating in dryland activities?
2. **Notes behaviours of instructor trainer**
   Ask yourself, are you—
   - Listening attentively?
   - Following directions?
   - Noting how you move, communicate and supervise?
3. **Demonstrates an interest in learning**
   Ask yourself, are you—
   - Volunteering for activities?
   - Becoming involved both in the water and out of the water?
   - Completing assignments on time?
   - Attending 100% of the course?

4. Asks questions

Ask yourself, are you—
- Asking knowledge questions?
- Asking information anaylsis questions?
- Asking judgment questions?

5. Demonstrates knowledge and skills of the Water Safety program

Ask yourself, are you—
- Performing the strokes to Level 12 standard?
- Performing all the skills in the AquaQuest program (e.g., front dive, treading water, etc.)?
- Demonstrating Prepare! Stay Safe! and Survive! water safety knowledge for all themes?

ANALYZE

6. Describes the progression steps for all swimming skills

Ask yourself, are you—
- Describing the progressions for developing swimmers, front crawl, back crawl, elementary backstroke, breaststroke, sidestroke, butterfly, and sculling to a level 12 standard?

7. Demonstrates knowledge of all Water Safety themes

Ask yourself, are you—
- Demonstrating knowledge of how to Prepare! Stay Safe! Survive! for Boat Smart!, Stay Warm!, Rescues!, Stop! Look! Listen!, Stop! Look! Go Slow!, and PFD and Me activities?

8. Identifies the importance of teaching water safety and swimming actively and in the water

Ask yourself, are you—
- Using examples of in-the-water activities for water safety and swimming?
- Choosing an in-the-water activity when given the choice?
- Analyzing how to make activities wet and active?

9. Identifies how to incorporate the injury prevention model within lessons

Ask yourself, are you—
- Identifying where to use the slogans effectively?
- Identifying activities that do or do not promote the importance of prevention?

- Identifying activities that have students discovering why we Prepare! Stay Safe! Survive!?
- Identifying activities in which students experience wise and unwise choices in a safe environment?
- Analyzing activities to determine which attitudes are being reinforced.

10. **Describes the safety supervision concerns when teaching any part of the Water Safety program**

Ask yourself, are you—
- Identifying safety supervision concerns and how to avoid them and solutions for water safety and swimming activities?
- Analyzing how safety supervision concerns could occur and how to avoid them and developing solutions for drills and activities?
- Identifying how to move around a formation to ensure that all students are in view at all times?
- Identifying importance of having an aid and whistle at all times while instructing?

11. **Describes all items in the Water Safety program**

Ask yourself, are you—
- Describing all knowledge and skills required for the AquaTots, AquaQuest, and AquaAdults program?

12. **Identifies how physical principles affect the performance and teaching of a physical skill**

Ask yourself, are you—
- Identifying how to use buoyancy, propulsion, and resistance factors to correct physical skills?

13. **Demonstrates development and use of teaching methods for both water safety and swimming skills**

Ask yourself, are you—
- Demonstrating planning and use of the direct, discovery, and games method for both water safety and swimming skills?
- Planning and using teaching methods to introduce a skill and to practice a skill?
- Demonstrating knowledge of the difference between introducing and practicing a skill?

14. **Demonstrates knowledge of the individualized approach to instructing**
Ask yourself, are you—
- Identifying methods to determine students needs, abilities, and interests?
- Identifying how to do an effective screening?
- Identifying methods to alter a method or plan based on each student's changing needs, abilities, and interests?

15. **Reflects on how their behaviour affects others**
Ask yourself, are you—
- Reflecting on previous water safety or instructing situations in which they have been involved and identifying how their behaviour impacted on those around them?
- Identifying their own personal learning and instructing style?

16. **Identifies how to incorporate inclusion within lessons**
Ask yourself, are you—
- Identifying how the individualized approach to instructing is in part based on inclusion?
- Identifying where to find information on meeting individual student's needs in their class?

17. **Identifies how to incorporate progressive learning within lessons**
Ask yourself, are you—
- Identifying the importance of using evaluation to give continuous feedback?
- Identifying how to use evaluation as a basis for giving feedback?
- Identifying how progressive learning can help students learn?

APPLY

18. **Demonstrates use of a variety of teaching methods, including direct, discovery, and games**
Ask yourself, are you—
- Demonstrating using all components of the direct method for both water safety and swimming skills?
- Demonstrating using discovery method for both water safety and swimming skills?
- Demonstrating using games method for both water safety and swimming skills?

19. **Demonstrates effective problem solving skills**

Ask yourself, are you—

- Identifying where communication problems exist when instructing both water safety and swimming skills?
- Identifying where progression problems exist when instructing both water safety and swimming skills?
- Identifying a variety of ways of solving each problem?

20. **Develops long-term lesson plans that ensure that each skill is covered a minimum of three times**

Ask yourself, are you—

- Developing a long-term lesson plan that begins with the skills reviewed from the previous lesson?
- Developing a long-term lesson plan that has like items grouped together?
- Developing a long-term lesson plan that covers all skills a minimum of three times?

21. **Develops short-term lesson plans that contain skill progressions, back-up plans, formations, equipment, and estimated amount of time**

Ask yourself, are you—

- Developing short-term lesson plans for a variety of levels?
- Developing short-term lesson plans that contain skill progressions, back-up plans, formations, equipment, and estimated amount of time?
- Developing short-term lesson plans that another instructor could use to instruct that lesson?
- Developing short-term lesson plans that are safe?

22. **Represents the Canadian Red Cross in a professional manner**

Ask yourself, are you—

- Demonstrating the seven Fundamental Priniciples of Humanity, Universality, Neutrality, Voluntary Service, Independence, Impartiality, and Unity?
- Using appropriate language, dress, and conduct throughout the course?

24. **Demonstrates initiative to lead peer activities**

Ask yourself, are you—

- Volunteering to take on extra tasks?
- Volunteering to lead presentations or group work?

25. **Accesses resources effectively and maintains an up-to-date knowledge of current research findings**

Ask yourself, are you—

- Using their Instructor Manual, strategy cards, and additional resources to prepare for lessons and presentations?

Teaching Experience

BEFORE

1. **Develops short-term lesson plans that reflect the individuals in their class**
   Ask yourself, are you—
   - Developing short-term lesson plans that contain skill progressions, back-up plans, formations, equipment, and estimated amount of time?
   - Developing short-term lesson plans that identify the opportunities for individual students?

2. **Plans for a variety of activities that will meet the needs of their class**
   Ask yourself, are you—
   - Planning most activities to take place in the water?
   - Planning to use a variety of instructional methods?
   - Planning activities that are ability level appropriate?

3. **Identifies site safety concerns and emergency procedures**
   Ask yourself, are you—
   - Identifying unsafe areas around the site?
   - Identifying your role during an emergency?
   - Identifying how to present unsafe situations?

4. **Gathers equipment before the start of class**
   Ask yourself, are you—
   - Gathering all the equipment needed for the lesson?
   - Placing the lesson equipment in a safe and easy-to-reach location?
   - Making sure you carry a buoyant aid and whistle at all times?

5. **Demonstrates a professional appearance throughout class**
   Ask yourself, are you—
   - Dressing to get wet and ensuring that students are easily identifiable?
   - Removing jewelery and other dangling objects?

DURING

6. **Screens all new classes in shallow water**

   Ask yourself, are you—
   - Reviewing the previous levels' skills and identifying key skills to screen?
   - Asking students about their skills?
   - Screening the skills of every student in shallow water (where appropriate)?

7. **Assigns area for the start of class and takes attendance**

   Ask yourself, are you—
   - Identifying specific areas as the meeting place for your students?
   - Informing students of the meeting place?
   - Reviewing where students need to meet for the next lesson?
   - Taking attendance quickly at the beginning of each lesson?

8. **Keeps ALL students in view at at ALL times**

   Ask yourself, are you—
   - Keeping your eyes on your class for the entire lesson?
   - Keeping yourself on the outside of each formation throughout the entire lesson and between the deep water and your class?
   - Keeping all students in front of you at all times?
   - Providing corrective feedback to one student and keeping the rest of the students in view?

9. **Uses formations that ensure optimum activity level and safe practice of skills**

   Ask yourself, are you—
   - Using a variety of formations?
   - Keeping all students moving in safe formations?
   - Recognizing when a formation is not appropriate or active for all students and altering the formation?

10. **Ensures that students are never left on their own**

    Ask yourself, are you—
    - Remaining with your class at all times?
    - Knowing where each student is at all times?

11. Enforces site rules throughout lesson

Ask yourself, are you—

- Modelling site rules at all times?
- Informing students of rules at the beginning of the session?
- Ensuring that all students follow the site rules at all times?

12. Keeps an aid within reach throughout entire class

Ask yourself, are you—

- Keeping a buoyand aid within arm's reach throughout entire class?
- Demonstrating an awareness of where your aid is at all times?

13. Maintains control of class at all times

Ask yourself, are you—

- Maintaining control of students during all activities?
- Identifying problems in class management and developing solutions?

COMMUNICATION

14. Keeps directions short and simple

Ask yourself, are you—

- Giving short, concise directions?
- Keeping your language understandable for your students?

15. Uses key points and perception checks

Ask yourself, are you—

- Using specific points to identify specific directions for tasks?
- Checking back with students on their understanding of a task?

16. Communicates respect to each student

Ask yourself, are you—

- Giving equal time and feedback to each student?
- Listening to each student throughout the class?
- Using each student's name throughout class?

17. Uses an effective tone to which students listen and react

Ask yourself, are you—

- Using a variety of tones and voice inflections to maintain the interest of your class?
- Ensuring that all students can hear you all the time?
- Ensuring students are listening before giving important directions?

18. Uses a nonthreatening body position at level of students

Ask yourself, are you—

- Keeping yourself at the eye level of your students?
- Keeping your arms open rather than closed?

19. Speaks assertively

Ask yourself, are you—

- Using a voice that students can hear?
- Using a voice that students listen to?
- Speaking with confidence?

20. Instructs with enthusiasm and empathy

Ask yourself, are you—

- Maintaining a high energy level throughout the entire class?
- Demonstrating enthusiasm?
- Noting when students are in difficulty and quickly correcting the situation?

21. Minimizes conflict between voice and body language

Ask yourself, are you—

- Ensuring that your body language mirrors your verbal message?
- Using both verbal and nonverbal means of communication?

ACTIVE AND WET

22. Keeps students active and in the water

Ask yourself, are you—

- Starting water activities almost immediately?
- Keeping all students moving, using a variety of structured activities?
- Remaining in the water with their students when appropriate?

23. Uses accurate demonstrations

Ask yourself, are you—

- Demonstrating skills before having students perform?
- Demonstrating skills exactly as you want your students to perform them?

24. Uses logical progressions that promote success
Ask yourself, are you—
- Reviewing known skills and knowledge as the first step?
- Using progressions that move from gross motor movement to fine motor movement?
- Using progressions that gradually increase the complexity/difficulty of each skill?
- Ensuring student success before moving to the next progression?

25. Varies methods and progressions for individual student's needs and abilities
Ask yourself, are you—
- Planning and using a variety of methods and progressions to meet different needs?
- Trying new methods and progressions to meet different needs?

26. Creates a learner friendly environment
Ask yourself, are you—
- Using activities that promote success?
- Using a variety of equipment to create interest?
- Maintaining an open and encouraging atmosphere?

27. Uses games with aims
Ask yourself, are you—
- Using games during the lesson?
- Ensuring that each game meet a specific learning objective?
- Not using games as simple time-fillers?

28. Uses a variety of teaching methods
Ask yourself, are you—
- Using the discovery method correctly?
- Using the direct method effectively?
- Using the games with aims method appropriately?
- Using all three methods in one lesson?

29. Provides and uses effective practice time
Ask yourself, are you—
- Keeping all students moving while practicing?
- Ensuring that students are practicing their drills correctly?
- Using shorter distances when students are first introduced to a drill or skill?
- Varying the drills that are used?

30. Using teaching equipment safely
Ask yourself, are you—
- Using a variety of equipment, but not using designated site safety equipment?
- Modelling safe use of equipment?
- Explaining how to use equipment safely?
- Ensuring that students use equipment safely?

31. Uses an appropriate activity level
Ask yourself, are you—
- Keeping students active at all times?
- Monitoring students endurance level during activities?

32. Provides individual attention that is balanced throughout the class
Ask yourself, are you—
- Providing each student with individual attention?
- Maintaining group activity level while giving individual feedback?
- Maintaining class safety while giving individual feedback?

33. Uses proper supports and holds
Ask yourself, are you—
- Using holds to maximize student's safety and success?

FEEDBACK

34. Provides specific feedback
Ask yourself, are you—
- Providing feedback based on the performance criteria of each skill?

35. Provides feedback directed at a changeable behaviour
Ask yourself, are you—
- Identifying the behaviour/skill to be maintained?
- Identifying the behaviour/skill that requires changes and taking steps to communicate the required change?

36. Provides feedback that is short and simple
Ask yourself, are you—
- Keeping your language understandable for your students and only communicating one change at a time?

37. Provides feedback that is immediate

Ask yourself, are you—

- Providing feedback immediately after skill is completed?
- Stopping a student from performing a skill incorrectly to provide feedback and correcting when appropriate?

38. Identifies which skill error needs to be corrected first

Ask yourself, are you—

- Identifying the most fundamental error in a skill when there is more than one?

39. Uses a variety of corrective techniques, including physical manipulation, overcorrection, and shaping

Ask yourself, are you—

- Using physical manipulation, overcorrection, and shaping?
- Using all three methods in one lesson?
- Providing a correction until success is achieved?

40. Breaks down a skill when correcting

Ask yourself, are you—

- Recognizing when using correctives is not improving a skill?
- Recognizing fundamental cause of an error to the skill (e.g., body position or coordination)?
- Breaking down a skill into an earlier progression to isolate practice?

41. Recognizes progress or lack of progress and adjusts approach

Ask yourself, are you—

- Recognizing when a student is not experiencing success or improvement?
- Identifying an alternative method of instruction to promote success?
- Working with a student to promote success?

42. Evaluates individual performance levels according to the established standards in the Water Safety program

Ask yourself, are you—

- Instructing skills to the performance criteria in the Water Safety program?
- Working through progressions and individual activities to achieve success?

AFTER

43. Completes all administrative work

Ask yourself, are you—
- Providing written feedback for each candidate?
- Completing worksheets?
- Identifying how the administration process is completed?

44. Evaluates the completion rate of students accurately

Ask yourself, are you—
- Identifying the skills that each student has demonstrated to standard a minimum of three times?
- Identifying the skills for which students require more practice to reach the standard?
- Identifying the skills that students were unable to do, but would not benefit by more practice?
- Identifying whether being able to complete a skill would result in safety concerns for the student or future classmates in the next level?

45. Communicates each student's success and continued needs with students and parents (if applicable)

Ask yourself, are you—
- Completing the progress memo for each student?
- Providing a written record of each student's success and future needs on the basis of observable skills?
- Reviewing the evaluation with students and parents if applicable?

Appendix D
Water Safety Instructor
Code of Conduct

The Canadian Red Cross Society

The Canadian Red Cross Society is a volunteer-based organization that provides emergency relief and humanitarian service to the public in time of disaster or conflict in Canada and around the world. The Canadian Red Cross Society operates a national blood service and numerous community-based health and social programs. These programs are offered in accordance with the seven Fundamental Principles of The International Red Cross and Red Crescent Movement: Humanity, Impartiality, Neutrality, Independence, Voluntary Service, Unity and Universality.

The Water Safety Services

The aim of the Water Safety Services is to prevent water-related injuries and fatalities by providing Canadians with:
- Awareness and knowledge to recognize and avoid dangerous water-related situations
- Knowledge and skills required to save their own lives
- Basic rescue skills to enable them to save others
- The knowledge and awareness to recognize hazardous aquatic environments and equipment in their communities and to provide solutions

Responsibilities of Water Safety Instructors

As an aquatic instructor, representative of The Canadian Red Cross Society, you will interact, on a professional basis, with fellow instructors, program sponsors, parents, participants, and your community at large. As you interact, your behaviour reflects back on The Canadian Red Cross Society as a whole. This Code of Conduct has been established as the standard by which your behaviour is measured.

1. Observe and promote the seven Fundamental Principles of The International Red Cross and Red Crescent Movement.
2. Treat everyone fairly within the context of their activity, regardless of race, gender, ethnicity, financial ability, sexual orientation, religion, disability, or age and within applicable provincial and federal legislation.
3. Consistently display high professional standards to project a favourable image of the Canadian Red Cross Water Safety Services.
   a. Refrain from public criticism of fellow instructors, program sponsors, parents, or participants.
   b. Abstain from any personal behaviours that may adversely influence or harm a participant.
   c. Refrain from the use of profane, insulting, harassing, or otherwise offensive language in the conduct of duties.
4. Ensure that the activity being undertaken is suitable for the age, experience, ability, and fitness level of the student.
5. Comply with registered medical practitioners' recommendations as they are communicated.
6. Ensure the personal safety of every student.
7. Maintain the Water Safety Instructor performance standards found in the Water Safety Instructor course teaching experience evaluation criteria.
8. Behaviours that constitute harassment or abuse are unacceptable. The Society's definition of harassment follows.

The Canadian Red Cross Society Harassment Policy

POLICY

The Canadian Red Cross Society is committed to providing a work environment that is supportive for productivity and the personal goals, dignity, and self-esteem of every person within the Society. This policy applies to all persons, regardless of age. The references to employees in this policy shall be deemed to include volunteers who shall be entitled to lodge a complaint following the procedures herein and against whom complaints may be filed.

To be successful in attaining this objective, it is essential to secure the mutual respect, cooperation and understanding of all employees. It is incumbent on both the Society and the employees not to condone or tolerate behaviour that constitutes harassment in the workplace, and the Society is committed to affording every employee a work environment free of harassment.

As the Society employs and deals with minors, express reference is made to the fact that this policy will apply to the described conduct in relation to minors. A minor or a minor's parent or guardian may file a complaint in accordance with this policy. In such an event, the complaint shall be forthwith reported to the Director of Human Resources, National Office, who in consultation with legal counsel will review the necessity for reporting the complaint to the child welfare authorities or the police of the jurisdiction within which the complaint arises.

POLICY REQUIREMENTS

National Office and Zone shall:
1. Provide a work environment free of harassment.
2. Inform all employees of this policy, including their rights and responsibilities.
3. Establish a procedure for receiving and investigating complaints of harassment with reference to the procedures outlined in The Canadian Red Cross Society Water Safety Leadership Program Revocation Policy.

4. Ensure that the procedure established provides (a) that the Director of Human Resources, National Office will be advised of any complaint received and the disposition thereof, and (b) for a final appeal by the complainant or any employee who has been disciplined to the Secretary General of The Canadian Red Cross Society.

DEFINITIONS

1. Harassment

Harassment means any improper behaviour by an employee of the Society directed at and offensive to any employee of the Society and which a person knew or ought reasonably to have known would be unwelcome. It comprises objectionable conduct, comment, or display made on a one-time or continuous basis that demeans, belittles, or causes personal humiliation or embarrassment to an employee.

2. Sexual Harassment

Sexual Harassment means any conduct, comment, gesture or contact of a sexual nature, whether on a one-time basis or in a continuous series of incidents,

a. That might reasonably be expected to cause offence, embarrassment, or humiliation to any employee; or

b. That might reasonably be expected to be perceived by the employee as placing a condition of a sexual nature on employment or on any opportunity for training or advancement.

Sexual harassment may be directed at members of the same or opposite sex and also includes any contravention of the human rights legislation applicable to the place of employment.

Appendix E
Leadership Program
Revocation Policy

All Canadian Red Cross Water Safety Instructors/Instructor Trainers may have their Instructor/Instructor Trainer designations revoked with justification by the application of The Canadian Red Cross Society Water Safety Leadership Program Revocation Policy.

The purpose of the revocation policy for Instructor/Instructor Trainer designations is to ensure the highest level of quality in Canadian Red Cross Society instruction of the Water Safety Program.

The revocation of an Instructor/Instructor Trainer designation will normally occur with justification when an Instructor/Instructor Trainer does not or will not abide by Canadian Red Cross Society standards, policies or procedures, in some way abuses the position of Red Cross Water Safety Instructor/Instructor Trainer or fails to abide by the standards outlined in The Canadian Red Cross Water Safety Leadership Program Code of Conduct. The Instructor/Instructor Trainer designation will automatically be suspended pending an investigation where the Instructor/Instructor Trainer has been accused or convicted of a serious crime, such as sexual molestation, embezzlement, assault, or any conduct unbecoming or offensive to The Fundamental Principles of the International Red Cross and Red Crescent Movement and which is directly related to his or her duties as an Instructor/Instructor Trainer. The process and procedures for dealing with such a situation are detailed below.

1. The Society has the obligation to document and investigate all complaints through the procedures established in accordance with this policy. A complaint must be filed in writing either by the complainant or documented by a Society representative. It is the Society's responsibility to keep each complaint on file.

2. The Instructor/Instructor Trainer against whom a complaint has been filed has the right to be immediately informed that a complaint has been filed. The Society is obligated to provide, within 5 days, the accused Instructor/Instructor Trainer with written (a) documentation of the complaint; (b) notification that an investigation will be held; (c) notification that the accused Instructor/Instructor Trainer has the right to respond; and (d) notification that it is the accused Instructor/Instructor Trainer's responsibility to co-operate throughout the investigation.

3. Once a complaint has been filed, the Society is obligated to investigate with a view to resolving the complaint to the satisfaction of all parties without the necessity of conducting a formal hearing. This includes interviewing the parties involved and any witnesses concerned. Each party has the right to be represented and accompanied by a person of his or her choice during the interviews related to the complaint. If the investigator is unable to resolve the complaint, a written report outlining the allegations of the complainant, the response of the accused Instructor/Instructor Trainer, the evidence of any witnesses, and the conclusions reached must be completed.

4. Once the written report has been completed, both parties are to be informed, in writing, of the decision reached and the reasons justifying it.

5. If the written report concludes that an Instructor/Instructor Trainer has not abided by Canadian Red Cross Society standards, policies, or procedures; abused the position of Red Cross Water Safety Instructor/Instructor Trainer; or failed to abide by the standards outlined in The Canadian Red Cross Water Safety Leadership Program Code of Conduct; his or her certification is to be revoked, and the terms of that revocation are to be communicated to the Instructor/ Instructor Trainer immediately.

All parties involved, including the Society, the accused, and the complainant, are to keep confidential the identity of the parties and the nature of the allegations as best as can be done consistent with the duty to fully and fairly investigate the complaint, unless there is a legal obligation to disclose the nature of the allegations.

While a complaint is being investigated, the accused Instructor/Instructor Trainer will have his or her certification suspended until the complaint has been resolved. Names of revoked Instructor/Instructor Trainers are to be forwarded to National Office for circulation among the Zones.

Appendix F: Learner Characteristics for Children

Item	Tots 12-24 months	Tots 2 to 4 years	Ages 4-7	Ages 6-9	Ages 8-13	Ages 12-16
Major feature	12-18 months, enjoys individual activity; 18-24 months, responds to adult guidance, plays beside peers	Well-developed language and mobility; still clings to an adult at ages 2-3; at ages 3-4 becomes more confident and independent, but still prefers individual activities	Enjoys individual activity; needs much attention; therefore should be with an adult or in a small group; Fear of unknown	Highly imaginative; activity is important; enjoys working, learning, and accomplishing; follows the instructor as a leader	Interested in developing skills and looking good	Peer group opinion becomes more important than the instructor; self-conscious in front of peers; wants to "look good"
Social characteristics	12-18 months, becoming independent; 18-24 months, will not yet cooperative with others	Often clings to parent at age 2-3 and has a favourite toy; tolerance of short separations and waiting appear at ages 3-4; begins to share	Very self-centred; will work with other children but considers self first	Individualistic but becoming interested in the group	Interested in the group; best pals with only a few friends; challenges authority.	Develops more personal relationships; enjoys more independence and responsibility
Physical characteristics	12-18 months, independent walking develops, much practice of eye-hand coordination; 18-24 months, attempts kicking and throwing, shows better judgment of size and position of objects	Very mobile and interested in exploring; at ages 3-4, becomes even more skillful; modifies movement speed	Coordination for refining skills is poor; little endurance; gets cold quickly	Coordination of large muscle activity (such as kicking) improving; endurance improving; primarily short distance swimmers	Growth spurts may affect coordination and endurance; generally good coordination; stronger endurance	Interested in perfecting each skill; growth spurts may be continuing; excellent coordination and endurance
Learning emphasis	12-18 months, Likes jingles, small objects; 18-24 months, will carry out requests and likes to mimic actions	Often questions and uses language to direct actions; at age 3-4 begins to understand good and bad	Learn best by watching and experimenting; very short attention span; usually fears unknown.	Ready to follow instructions to learn basic skills; reacts well to praise	Can think more abstractly, but can benefit more from concrete examples; greater attention span	Adult-like thinking
Teaching water safety knowledge	Directed at parent/caregiver	Directed at parent/caregiver primarily; some interest by child in stories; imaginative play as he or she gets older	Needs training to follow specific rules	Needs rules but requires reasons and examples	Requires reasons and is interested in exceptions	Challenges authority and must see that rules are reasonable
Preferred games	12 to 18 months, plays alone but needs an adult near by; 18-24 months, plays independently	Likes climbing into and out of; repeats rhymes and sings; as child gets older likes imaginitive play, mimicking everyday actions	Prefers individual activity (such as searching for rings) with some group interaction (e.g., as circle games such as "Motorboat")	Enjoys whole group games (such as frozen tag)	Enjoys more competitive games (such as relays)	Prefers individual challenges and stunts (such as head-first surface dives and scavenger hunts)

Appendix G:
Learner Characteristics of Adults

Item	Young adult (15-25)	Adult (21-60)	Older Adult (50+)
Major feature	Well motivated and independent; usually prepared to take a leadership role	Often motivated by watching their children learn to swim or fitness	Often interested in fitness; many have deep-rooted fears
Social characteristics	Self-reliant; adjusts to groups readily	Initially may be uncomfortable joining in a group; often participates for social benefits	Often self-conscious; may be motivated by social interest
Physical characteristics	Growth tapers off; endurance increases quickly; coordination depends on previous experiences, resulting in a great variety of abilities and speeds of learning	Endurance is slowly declining; flexibility is also declining, but through practice can be developed	Endurance diminishing; coordination and flexibility may be deteriorating; reaction time may slow
Learning emphasis	Motivation and attention span tend to be high	May be hesitant to attempt new skills and strokes; prefers private feedback	Requires a great deal of reassurance and positive feedback
Teaching water safety knowledge	Adventuresome and active; emphasize precautions in water sports	For students who are parents, emphasize the safety of children and preventing injuries	Common sense approach is appropriate
Preferred games	Enjoys stunts, challenges, and friendly competitions (such as water polo or underwater hockey)	Prefers individual stunts and challenges (such as learning competitive starts and turns); great interest in water fitness and master swimming	Prefers individual stunts, rhythmic swimming (such as synchronized swimming), and water fitness

Appendix H
Physical Principles

Understanding some basic physical principles will help you instruct your students to move through the water more efficiently:

- Buoyancy, or why things float in water
- Resistance and Propulsion, or why things move in the water

Buoyancy

First, the principle ...

Archimedes Principle states that a body in water is buoyed up by a force equal to the weight of the water displaced.

What does this mean? You float because your body displaces water. You can see this most easily when you lower yourself into a bathtub and the water level goes up. That's Archimedes' Principle at work.

When the weight of the water that you push up is more than your weight, you float.

How can you increase your buoyancy? There are several ways:

1. Change your *body type*. Granted, not easily done. Buoyancy depends a lot on how much muscle, fat, and bone you have. People with lots of muscle and heavy bone structure or those with little body fat do not float as easily as those with more body fat and less muscle. Bone and muscle *sink* in water. Fat *floats*.

    Your body composition does change with age, though. Very young children have little muscle and light bones, so they tend to float very easily. Young adults tend to have more muscle and less fat, and in general they do not float very well. Older people often have more fat and less muscle and tend to float more easily.

2. Change your *lung capacity*. This is easily done. Simply take a deep breath and hold it. This increases your volume without increasing your weight.

THE BUOYANCY FACTOR

A Water Safety Instructor will:

1. Emphasize appropriate body positions to maximize water displacement—Archimedes' Principle.

2. Encourage students to stabilize their centre of buoyancy and centre of gravity.

3. Emphasize the importance of relaxation: muscles are less dense when they are not tense and constricted.

4. Emphasize breath control: lungs filled with air increase volume without increasing weight.

5. Teach students how to scull: slight downward movements on the water will assist students in staying afloat.

6. Emphasize the importance of effective movement: the more efficiently we move forward, the better chance the water has of holding us up!

3. Change your *body position*. Also, very easily done. Simply "spread" your weight out across the water surface. Remember people float *in* water, somewhat like an iceberg, not on top of it like a beach ball. Keep your weight low in the water.

4. Change your centre of mass (gravity) and centre of buoyancy.

Centre of Mass is the point around which the weight of the body is evenly distributed.

Centre of Buoyancy is the point around which the buoyant properties of the body are evenly distributed.

Every time you move in the water your centre of mass, usually located in your hips, and your centre of buoyancy, usually found in your chest area, move. When you float, your centre of mass is below your centre of buoyancy.

If your centre of mass moves above your centre of buoyancy, you will still float, but will be unstable.

Your body will naturally roll and adjust until your centres are aligned. You can help your students with this by:

Assuring them the "tippy" sensation is natural.

Assisting them physically until they find their balance.

Encouraging them to experiment with different body positions to find the most stable.

Telling them to remain relaxed and take a deep breath; this moves your centre of buoyancy down.

Resistance and Proplusion

Put most simply, proplusion drives you through the water, resistance holds you back.

RESISTANCE

Resistance in water is often referred to as drag. There are three types of water resistance: form drag, wave drag, and frictional drag. All work to slow you down while swimming, but you can do things to lessen their effect.

> THE RESISTANCE FACTOR
>
> A Water Safety Instructor will:
> 1. Instruct students to swim straight to avoid eddy resistance.
> 2. Emphasize streamlining.
> 3. Encourage students to make all recovery movements gently, slowly, and close to the body.

Form drag relates to your body's shape and profile in the water. Think of the difference between a sleek, narrow boat slicing through the water and a wide tugboat pushing through it. To reduce form drag, emphasize streamlining.

Wave drag is caused by water turbulence, including the turbulence you generate as you swim. The faster you swim, the more wave drag you create. To reduce wave drag, use a smooth, even stroke; avoid splashing with your arms; and reduce side-to-side and up-and-down body motion.

Frictional drag comes from the surface of your body as you move through the water. To reduce frictional drag, you can wear a bathing cap and smooth, tight-fitting bathing suits. Some competitive swimmers even go so far as to shave their body hair to reduce friction!

PROPULSION

Proplusion is best summed up by stating Newton's three laws of motion:

- The Law of Inertia
- The Law of Acceleration
- The Law of Action and Reaction

and,

- The Law of Levers

The Law of Inertia is the tendency of a body at rest to stay at rest (static) and of a body in motion to stay in motion (dynamic).

What does this tell us about swimming?

- First, you need more energy to start a stroke than to keep it moving
- Second, the more streamlined your body, the more you benefit from dynamic inertia.

Thus, it's better to keep moving when swimming than repeatedly stopping and starting. Dynamic inertia allows you to rest briefly—think of the glides in breaststroke, sidestroke and elementary backstroke. Use that rest to your advantage but remember not to rest too long because you may end up having to overcome static inertia with your next stroke!

The Law of Acceleration is the principle by which a body's speed depends on how much force is applied to it and the direction of that force.

Simply put, this means that if you push off from a wall with twice as much force as someone else, you will go twice as far.

THE PROPULSION FACTOR

A Water Safety Instructor will:

1. Instruct students to move arms and legs so that propulsive forces are applied in a direction *opposite* to their desired line of travel—Newton's Law of Action and Reaction.
2. Encourge students to keep an even pace and not glide too long—Newton's Law of Inertia.
3. Instruct students to conserve energy through the application of force in an efficient manner—Law of Levers—bent arm pulls assist the student in bringing the workload closer to the muscles doing the work.
4. Instruct students to think *long and strong* in all propulsive movements—Newton's Law of Acceleration.

All these will keep your student UP and will cut down on resistance to forward movement.

Again, this tells you two simple things about swimming:

First, the more force you use in the direction of your stroke, the faster you will swim, and second, your swimming is more efficient when you stay in your chosen direction and when all your proplusive force is in that direction. In other words, avoid turns as you use energy to correct your direction instead of moving forward!

The Law of Action and Reaction is the principle that for every action there is an equal and opposite reaction.

What Newton was trying to say in regard to swimming was this: as your arm pushes (acts) against the water, the water pushes back (reacts), providing resistance to let you move forward.

The Law of Levers states that the product of the force and the force arm is equal to the product of the resistance and resistance arm.

In practical terms, what this is trying to say is "do a bent arm pull." By bending your elbow, you reduce the length of your resistance arm and thus improve your leverage; more leverage equals more proplusion.

Appendix I: Stroke Chart

FRONT CRAWL

AquaQuest levels	Arms		Body position and motion	Kick	Breathing and timing	Distance
	Recovery	Power				
Level 4	Recovers arms above water in a controlled, alternating manner		Maintains near horizontal body position, face in the water, keeping head straight	Flutter kick is at or near surface, with toes pointed	Breathes to the side, IF needed, exhaling under water	3 × 5 metres (in one lesson)
Level 5	Recovers arms above water in a controlled, alternating manner		Maintains horizontal body position, keeping head straight	Flutter kicks from the hips, toes pointed	Exhales under water, breathes to side as needed (may pause in side-glide position for up to 2 seconds)	3 × 10 metres (in one lesson)
Level 6	Extends hand entry forward of head.	Extends pull past hips.	Maintains horizontal body position, keeping head straight	Flutter kicks from the hips, toes pointed	Exhales under water, breathes to side as needed (no pause); coordinates relaxed breathing with alternating relaxed arm recovery above water	3 × 15 metres (in one lesson)
Level 7	Extends hand entry forward of head and in line with the shoulders.	Extends pull past hips	Rolls body on long axis, no hip sway; Maintains horizontal body position, keeping head straight	Flutter kicks from hips, toes pointed	Exhales under water, breathes to side as needed (no pause); coordinates relaxed breathing with alternating relaxed arm recovery above water	3 × 25 metres (in one lesson)

Continued.

FRONT CRAWL, _cont'd._

Level 8	See level 7	See level 7	See level 7	See level 7	See level 7	50 metres
Level 9	Extends hand entry forward of head and in line with the shoulders	Executes _bent-arm pull, in_ **S** _pattern_; extends pull past hips	Rolls body on long axis; with no hip sway; Maintains horizontal body position, keeping head straight	Flutter kicks from the hips, toes pointed	Exhales under water, breathes to side as needed (no pause); coordinates relaxed breathing _with_ alternating relaxed arm recovery above water	75 metres
Level 10	See level 9	See level 9	See level 9	See level 9	See level 9	100 metres
Level 11	Extends hand entry forward of head and in line with the shoulders	_Accelerates hands through the pull_; Executes bent-arm pull, in **S** pattern; extends pull past hips	Rolls body on long axis, with no hip sway; maintains horizontal body position, keeping head straight	Flutter kicks from the hips, toes pointed	Exhales under water, breathes to side as needed (no pause); coordinates relaxed breathing wiht alternating relaxed arm recovery above water	100 metres
Level 12	_Keep elbows high during recovery_; extends hand entry forward of head and in line with the shoulders	_Keep elbows high during pull_; accelerates hand through the pull; Executes bent-arm pull, in **S** pattern; extends pull past hips	Rolls body on long axis, with no hip sway; maintains horizontal body position, keeping head straight	Flutter kicks from the hips, toes pointed.	Exhales under water, breathes to side as needed (no pause); coordinates relaxed breathing with alternating relaxed arm recovery above water	100 metres

New performance criteria for each level is shown in italics.

BACK CRAWL

AquaQuest levels	Arms		Body position and motion	Kick	Breathing and timing	Distance
	Recovery	Power				
Level 4	No arm action required	No arm action required	Maintains body in stretched-out position	Flutter kicks in continuous manner, with toes pointed	Breathes in a relaxed manner	3 × 10 metres (in one lesson)
Level 5	No arm action required	No arm action required	Rolls body from side to side, leading with shoulders and keeping head stationary; maintains near horizontal body position with neck in line with spine	Flutter kicks in continuous manner, with toes pointed; kicks from kips, knees below surface	Breathes in a relaxed manner	3 × 15 metres (in one lesson)
Level 6	Recovers arms above water, in opposition to one another; Arms may pause for up to 2 seconds (one arm above head, one beside body)		Rolls body from side to side, leading with shoulders and keeping head stationary; maintains near horizontal body position with neck in line with spine	Flutter kicks in continuous manner, with toes pointed; kicks from the hips, knees below surface	Breathes in a relaxed manner; coordinates body roll with arm recovery	3 × 15 metres (in one lesson)
Level 7	Recovers arms in a straight and relaxed manner, no pause; recovers arms above water, in opposition	Extends pull past the hips	Rolls body from side to side, leading with shoulders and keeping head stationary; maintains near horizontal body position with neck in line with spine	Flutter kicks in continuous manner, with toes pointed; kicks from the hips, knees below surface	Breathes in a relaxed manner; coordinates body roll with arm recovery	3 × 25 metres (in one lesson)

Continued.

BACK CRAWL, *cont'd.*

Level					
Level 8	*Enters hands and catches the water at 11:00 and 1:00 positions; recovers arms in a straight and relaxed manner, no pause; recovers arms above water, in opposition*	Extends pull past the hips	Rolls body from side to side, leading with shoulders and keeping head stationary; maintains near horizontal body position with neck in line with spine	Flutter kicks in continuous manner, with toes pointed; kicks from the hips, knees below surface	Breathes in a relaxed manner; coordinates body roll with arm recovery	*50 metres*
Level 9	Enters hands and catches the water at 11:00 and 1:00 positions; recovers arms in a straight and relaxed manner, no pause; recovers arms above water, in opposition	Extends pull past the hips	Rolls body from side to side, leading with shoulders and keeping head stationary; maintains near horizontal body position with neck in line with spine	Flutter kicks in continuous manner, with toes pointed; kicks from the hips, knees below surface	Breathes in a relaxed manner; coordinates body roll with arm recovery	*75 metres*
Level 10	See level 9	See level 9	See level 9	See level 9	See level 9	*100 metres*
Level 11	Enters hands and catches the water at 11:00 and 1:00 positions; recovers arms in a straight and relaxed manner, no pause; recovers arms above water, in opposition	*Uses bent-arm pull in an **S** question mark pattern, keeping elbows high; extends pull past the hips*	Rolls body from side to side, leading with shoulders and keeping head stationary; maintains near horizontal body position with neck in line with spine	Flutter kicks in continuous manner, with toes pointed; kicks from the hips, knees below surface	Breathes in a relaxed manner; coordinates body roll with arm recovery	100 metres

Continued.

BACK CRAWL, *cont'd.*

Level 12	Enters hands and catches the water at 11:00 and 1:00 positions. Recovers arms in a straight and relaxed manner, no pause. Recovers arms above water, in opposition and coordination with body roll.	*Accelerates arms/ hands through the pull;* uses bent-arm pull in an S question mark pattern, keeping elbows high; extends pull past the hips	Rolls body from side to side, leading with shoulders and keeping head stationary; maintains near horizontal body position with neck in line with spine	Flutter kicks in continuous manner, with toes pointed; kicks from the hips, knees below surface	Breathes in a relaxed manner; coordinates body roll with arm recovery	100 metres

New performance criteria for each level is shown in *italics*.

ELEMENTARY BACKSTROKE

AquaQuest levels	Arms		Body position and motion	Kick	Breathing and timing	Distance
	Recovery	Power				
Level 7	No arm action required	No arm action required	Body is in horizontal back glide position; keeps the back, hips, and thigh nearly straight, just below the surface	Recovers legs symmetrically by bending and separating knees slightly wider than the hips; pulls heels beneath and just wider than the knees; flexes ankles and rotates feet outward (dorsi-flexed); whips feet out and around (power phase) to glide position with toes pointed (plantar-flexed)	Glides until forward momentum slows	3 × 10 metres (in one lesson)
Whip kick on back						
Level 8	Slides palms slowly up the sides of the body and extends arms slowly out to the side	Presses hands toward feet as legs kick	Body is in horizontal back glide position; keeps the back, hips, and thigh nearly straight, just below the surface	See level 7 Kick	Coordinates symmetric arm pull with kick, inhaling during recovery and exhaling during power phase; glides until forward momentum slows	3 × 15 metres (in one lesson)
Level 9	Slides palms slowly up the sides of the body and extends arms slowly out to the side	Arms accelerate through power phase; presses hands toward feet as legs kick	Body is in horizontal back glide position; keeps the back, hips, and thigh nearly straight, just below the surface	Legs accelerate through power phase; See level 7 kick	Coordinates symmetric arm pull with kick, inhaling during recovery and exhaling during power phase; glides until forward momentum slows	3 × 25 metres (in one lesson)

ELEMENTARY BACKSTROKE, *cont'd.*

Level 10	Slides palms slowly up the sides of the body and extends arms slowly out to the side	See level 9	See level 9	See level 9	50 metres
Level 11	See level 9	See level 9	See level 9	See level 9	50 metres
Level 12	See level 9	See level 9	See level 9	See level 9	75 metres

New performance criteria for each level is shown in *italics*.

AquaQuest Levels	Arms		Body position and motion	Kick	Breathing and timing	Distance
	Recovery	Power				
Level 7 Whip kick on front	No arm action required	No arm action required	Body is in horizontal glide position, face in or out	Recovers legs symmetrically by bending hips and knees; pulls heels toward the buttocks while separating knees slightly wider than the hips; flexes ankles and rotates feet outward; whips feet out and back around (power phase) to glide position with toes pointed	Glides until forward momentum slows	3 × 10 metres (in one lesson)
Level 8	Hands sweep together under the chin, keeping the elbows forward of the shoulders; arms recover forward to full extension	Presses extended arms/palms apart slightly wider than the shoulders; bends elbows and sweeps the forearms and hands downward and toward the chest	Body/head remains at or near surface	See level 7 kick	Coordinates symmetric arm pull and whip kick, inhaling during pull, exhaling during kick (i.e., pull and breathe, kick and glide); glides until forward momentum slows	3 × 15 metres (in one lesson)
Level 9	Hands sweep together under the chin, keeping the elbows forward of the shoulders; arms recover forward to full extension	Presses extended arms/palms apart slightly wider than the shoulders; bends elbows and sweeps the forearms and hands downward and toward the chest	Body/head remains at or near surface	Legs accelerate through power phase; see level 7 kick	Coordinates symmetric arm pull and whip kick, inhaling during pull, exhaling during kick (i.e., pull and breathe, kick and glide); glides until forward momentum slows	3 × 25 metres (in one lesson)

BREASTSTROKE, *cont'd.*

	Arms accelerate through power phase; Presses extended arms/palms apart slightly wider than the shoulders; bends elbows and sweeps the forearms and hands downward and toward the chest	Body/head remains at or near surface	*Legs accelerate through power phase;* see level 7 kick	Coordinates symmetric arm pull and whip kick, inhaling during pull, exhaling during kick (i.e., pull and breathe, kick and glide); glides until forward momentum slows	*50 metres*
Level 10	Hands sweep together under the chin, keeping the elbows forward of the shoulders; arms recover forward to full extension.				
Level 11	See level 10	See level 10	See level 10	See level 10	50 metres
Level 12	See level 10	See level 10	See level 10	See level 10	75 metres

New performance criteria for each level is shown in *italics*.

SIDESTROKE

AquaQuest Levels	Arms	Body position and motion	Kick	Breathing and timing	Distance
Level 10	Pulls leading arm (above head) to the chin to meet recovering trailing arm; extends arms into side-glide position, with trailing arm pushing toward feet (power phase)	Body and head are aligned in horizontal side-glide position	Recovers legs slowly by bending at hips and knees; extends one leg forward/one back, then scissors them together (power phase)	Recovers trailing arm and legs together, while leading arm pulls; inhales during recovery and exhales during the power phase	3 × 15 metres (one lesson)
Level 11	Trailing arm accelerates through power phase; pulls leading arm (above head) while recovering trailing arm, to the chin; extends arms into side-glide position, with trailing arm pushing toward feet (power phase)	Body and head are aligned in horizontal side-glide position	Kick accelerates through power phase; recovers legs slowly by bending at the hips and knees; extends one leg forward/one back, then scissors them together (power phase)	Recovers trailing arm and legs together, while leading arm pulls; inhales during recovery and exhales during the power phase	50 metres
Level 12	See level 11	See level 11	See level 11	See level 11	50 metres

New performance criteria for each level is shown in italics.

BUTTERFLY

| AquaQuest Levels | Arms | | Body position and motion | Kick | Breathing and timing | Distance |
	Recovery	Power				
Level 10 Dolphin kick	Arms are extended above the head or along the sides	No arm action required	Body moves in a continuous wavelike motion on the front, with hips remaining near the surface	Legs kick together (symmetric), originating from the hips; knees lead the legs during the downbeat of the kick (power phase), with toes pointed		3 × 10 metres (in one lesson)
Level 11 Evaluation is ONLY based on a willingness to attempt/practice the full stroke	Relaxes arms during recovery, extending arms/hands in front of the head as they enter	Pulls in a keyhole pattern, accelerating through the power phase, and pulling past hips	Body moves in a continuous wavelike motion on the front, with hips remaining near the surface	See level 10	Coordinates two dolphin kicks with one symmetric arm stroke; performs first downkick as arms enter water and second downkick as hands exit water; breathes, in any comfortable pattern, as the arms finish the pull, tilting the head up with the chin out	3 × 10 metres (in one lesson)
Level 12	See level 11	See level 11	See level 11	See level 11	See level 11	20 metres

New performance criteria for each level is shown in italics.

Appendix J
Safety Scenes

AquaTots 1

SKILLS

- Entry and exit with child
- Movement in water
- Basic kick and arm action

SAFETY SCENE

- Parent/caregiver and child enter backyard pool. They experience different types of movement in the water. They practice basic kick and arm action across the pool. Older children are playing in the pool. As the parent/caregiver exits the pool, the phone starts to ring. The parent/caregiver has the older children get out of the pool and takes the child with her as she goes to answer the phone.

WISE CHOICES

Parent/caregiver retains responsibility for child after exiting water

Parent/caregiver provides direct adult supervision of children when they are in the water.

SAFETY SUPERVISION/EQUIPMENT

Supervise the group carefully during entries and exits.

AquaTots 2

SKILLS

- Parent/caregiver and child put on PFD
- Parent/caregiver and child enter and exit wearing a PFD
- Parent/caregiver and child explore movement wearing PFD
- Parent/caregiver and child kick wearing PFD

SAFETY SCENE

- Parent/caregiver and child are visiting a waterfront. They put on PFDs and enter the water. They explore movement and practice basic kick to a designated point and return. Parent/caregiver and child exit from the water. The parent/caregiver remains close to supervise and leaves the PFD on the child, while the child plays at the water's edge. The parent/caregiver can relate that the PFD does not replace direct supervision.

WISE CHOICES

Parent/caregiver keeps the PFD on the child while he/she plays at the water's edge.
Parent/caregiver remains close to supervise.

SAFETY SUPERVISION/EQUIPMENT:

PFDs, toys

AquaTots 3

SKILLS

- Enters and exits water
- Identifies that a ball floats
- Practices floats with a ball
- Practices kicking holding the ball

SAFETY SCENE

- The child and parent/caregiver are playing with a ball at the water's edge. The ball is "accidentally" thrown in the water. Both child and parent/caregiver demonstrate Stop! Look! Go Slow! before entering the water to get the ball. Child and parent/caregiver practice floating and kicking with the ball once they are in the water.

WISE CHOICES

- Parent/caregiver and child demonstrate Stop! Look! Go Slow!
- Child understands that he or she must wait for the parent/caregiver before entering the water.

SAFETY SUPERVISION/EQUIPMENT

- Balls

AquaQuest 1

SKILLS

- Stop! Look! Listen!
- Shallow water entry
- Moves through water
- Exhales with face in water

SAFETY SCENE

- You are on a treasure hunt. Students enter the water, then they move through the water two different ways, as they put their faces in to find the treasure. When they find the treasure, they blow bubbles. Then they safely exit the water.

WISE CHOICES

- Examples: Wait for permission to enter water; choose a safe way to enter; stay with the class.

SAFETY SUPERVISION/EQUIPMENT

- Keep all students in view (semi-circle formation); ensure they can touch the bottom at all times; assist students when needed.
- Use an object that sinks for the treasure—with a safety message attached!

AquaQuest 2

SKILLS

- Stop! Look! Listen!
- PFD & Me
- Shallow water entry
- Roll-over floats

SAFETY SCENE

- You are at North Rustico beach (insert local name) with Mom, Dad, and a buddy, trying out your own new PFD! Students put on an appropriate PFD, describe two safety rules to their buddy while entering the water, and show Mom and Dad how to do roll-over floats in their PFD.

WISE CHOICES

- Examples: Wait for permission to enter water; Stop! Look! Go Slow!; follow the rules; fasten PFD properly.

SAFETY SUPERVISION/EQUIPMENT

- Assist students who need help; ensure PFD's are fastened properly; pair students with a buddy.
- The appropriate size PFDs (whistles, optional).

AquaQuest 3

SKILLS

- Change direction
- Front/back float relaxed
- Rhythmic breathing

SAFETY SCENE

- In shallow water, students push away from "edge" in glide position (e.g., deck, dock, you) and perform a relaxed front or back float for 5 seconds; then return to "edge" and do 10 slow bobs.

WISE CHOICES

- Examples: Only swim with supervision; swim with buddy; swim in depth of water for appropriate for ability; practice changing direction.

SAFETY SUPERVISION/EQUIPMENT

- Ensure that students can stand up if needed.

AquaQuest 4

SKILLS

- Safe boating equipment
- Side glides with flutter kick
- Front crawl

SAFETY SCENE

- You are completing an equipment checklist. Students are in two teams performing a relay. First student performs side glide with kick from point A to point B, picks out an appropriate boating equipment item, and then swims front crawl back to point B. Other team members repeat, until minimum safety equipment (by law) is identified by each team.

WISE CHOICES:

- Example: Choose right equipment, etc.

SAFETY SUPERVISION/EQUIPMENT

- Ensure that students don't get into each other's way.
- Use equipment required by law, mixed with other types of equipment (actual equipment or pictures of equipment.

AquaQuest 5

SKILLS

- Front/side roll entries
- Head-first sculling
- Back glide with flutter kick

SAFETY SCENE

- You are on the deck (or dock) helping the lifeguard clean up after public swim and slip while at the edge. Students perform a front or side roll entry, flutter kick on their back (10 metres), then sculls head-first (5 metres), before getting out.

WISE CHOICES

- Examples: Be careful walking or playing near the water; stay calm.

SAFETY SUPERVISION/EQUIPMENT

- Ensure safe depth and technique during roll entries; spot entries as needed.

AquaQuest 6

SKILLS

- Front stride dive
- Back crawl
- Partial blockage rescue

SAFETY SCENE

- You are swimming at the local pool, doing your last length before going home. Students do a front stride dive to enter the water, then do back crawl (15 metres) toward the shallow end. As they get out, someone on deck is coughing heavily. They simulate a partial blockage rescue (in partners).

WISE CHOICES

- Examples: Stop! Look! Go Slow!; dive only if safe; stay with person who is choking; tell someone else to get lifeguard.

SAFETY SUPERVISION/EQUIPMENT

- Dive only if and where site permits; staggered line formation.

AquaQuest 7

SKILLS

- Exposure to cold
- Stride entry
- Tread water
- Endurance swim (75 metres)

SAFETY SCENE

- You are at Lake Bonavista (insert local name), swimming with friends on a somewhat cloudy summer day; the water is cold. Students perform stride entry into water and then tread for 1.5 minutes. While treading, they describe signs/symptoms of hypothermia. Then they swim for 75 metres (including front and/or back crawl *and* whip kick). Then they get out because they're cold.

WISE CHOICES

- Examples: Stop! Look! Go Slow!; enter feet first, first time; swim close to shore; recognize signs of getting too cold; get out of the water and get warm.

SAFETY SUPERVISION/EQUIPMENT

- Ensure adequate space for stride entries; watch that students don't land on each other.
- Cards that show signs/symptoms of hypothermia.

AquaQuest 8

SKILLS

- Throwing assist with a line
- Front crawl
- Breaststroke (or elementary backstroke)

SAFETY SCENE

- You are swimming at Cultus Lake (insert local name) on a busy warm summer day. Students swim out to the end of the dock (breaststroke:10 metres, front crawl: 15 metres). As they are climbing onto the dock, they see an adult nonswimmer get pushed into the water. Students perform a throwing assist (in partners) and rescue the person.

WISE CHOICES

- Examples: Act quickly, choose an effective throwing aid; stay out of the water.

SAFETY SUPERVISION/EQUIPMENT

- Ensure adequate space for throwing assists.
- Use throwing aid with a line.

AquaQuest 9

SKILLS

- Preparing for safe ice activities
- Self-rescue from fall through ice
- Tread water

SAFETY SCENE

- You are ice skating at Pike Pond (insert local name). Students "fall" through the ice and demonstrate a self-rescue. Then the students tread water together while identifying all the ways to prepare for safe ice activities in order to prevent an ice incident.

WISE CHOICES

- Examples: Prepare *before*, and decide *if* ice is safe to go on; know ice safety zones.

SAFETY SUPERVISION/EQUIPMENT

- Ensure safe entries and adequate space during simulated "fall".
- Use flutterboards and/or mats, to simulate ice.

AquaQuest 10

SKILLS

- Controlled capsize survival skills
- Cold water HELP

SAFETY SCENE

- You are canoeing on Okanagon Lake (insert local name) on a sunny hot day. Someone forgets not to stand up while boating, and the canoe capsizes. Students demonstrate their survival skills, which may include HELP.

WISE CHOICES

- Examples: Prepare for the canoe trip (e.g., equipment, float plan); put on sunscreen and hat, stay safe while boating (eg., don't stand up, wear PFD); stay with the boat and stay calm, reduce heat loss, use whistle to get help, identify other causes of boating incidents.

SAFETY SUPERVISION/EQUIPMENT

- Ensure adequate space and safe entries during capsize (check with other instructors); don't overload the boat; do a head count after the capsize.
- Use simulated small craft; safety equipment (PFDs fit properly); float plan card or form.

AquaQuest 11

SKILLS

- Head-first surface dive
- Rescue breathing, with complications
- Tread water
- Choice of stroke

SAFETY SCENE

- You are doing a safety circuit with three groups (e.g., pairs), moving through three stations; each group starts at a different station. Station 1: students perform rescue breathing for an adult with distended stomach complication and then swim 20 metres (choice) to station 2. Station 2: students perform rescue breathing for child with vomiting complication and then swim 20 metres (choice) to station 3. Station 3: students perform a head-first surface dive, tread water (2.5 minutes), and then swim back to their start point.

WISE CHOICES

- Examples: Ensure no further danger before rescue breathing; enters the water safely.
- Safety Supervision/Equipment
- Watch each group; ensure that entries are safe; ensure adequate space (check with other instructors).
- Use dolls for rescue breathing (optional).
- Use cue cards for steps of rescue breathing and/or complications.

AquaQuest 12

SKILLS

- Throwing/reaching assists
- Choice strokes

SAFETY SCENE

- Students swim 50 metres (choice) followed by a throwing assist. Then they swim another 50 metres (choice) and demonstrate a reaching assist. They swim another 50 metres (choice) and finish by saying how they will apply Prepare! Stay Safe! and Survive! to a situation in which they see themselves.

WISE CHOICES

- Get trained (e.g., first aid, instructor, life saving)

SAFETY SUPERVISION/EQUIPMENT

- Ensure adequate space (check with other instructors); ensure safe entries into water.
- Use throwing and reaching assists.

AquaAdults 1-3

SKILLS

- Stop! Look! Go Slow!—entry
- Change directions
- Surface support
- PFDs/Life jackets

SAFETY SCENE

- You are at a friend's pool party showing off your new swimming skills! Students explain Stop! Look! Go Slow! and perform a safe entry of their choice, show how they can change direction while kicking on their front or back, and do a surface support for 15 seconds in deep water. As a bonus, the friends are given a quick tip about the differences between PFDs and life jackets!

WISE CHOICES

- Examples: Choose a safe entry based on site safety and personal abilities; respect your limits.

SAFETY SUPERVISION/EQUIPMENT

- Ensure that entries are appropriate to site; assistance may be needed.
- Wear PFD/life jacket (optional).

AquaAdults 1-3

SKILLS

- Causes of boating incidents
- Demonstrates how to enter/exit boat safely
- Demonstrates safe boating behaviour

SAFETY SCENE

- You are on a canoeing trip. Students demonstrate safe entry into canoe, show how to stay safe in boat, and identify primary causes of boating incidents.

WISE CHOICES

- Examples Choose to wear your PFD; choose to stay sober (it's the law); don't stand up; set a good example for kids.

SAFETY SUPERVISION/EQUIPMENT

- Don't overload boat; ensure that each student is comfortable with activity; ensure adequate space (check with other instructors).
- Use simulated (or actual) small craft, required safety equipment, PFDs that fit.

Appendix K
Common Equipment and Uses

Buoyant Rescue Equipment

Buoyant rescue equipment includes torpedo floats, ring-buoys, PFDs, and life jackets. These aids can be used in simulating rescues and in games and practices. For example, they can be used to support nonswimmers, for one student to pass to another in relays, and to pull students through the water to promote streamlined and proper body positioning.

Fins/Flippers

Used primarily during SCUBA and snorkeling, fins and flippers do have benefits for students. They enable students to develop proper leg kicks for front and back crawl. Their weight eliminates "bicycle" kick and adds confidence to many swimmers. Like all aids, do not overuse.

Goggles

Goggles increase underwater visibility and protect the eyes from chemicals in the water. These benefits may be overshadowed by how much time it takes to use them. Make sure that goggles fit snugly and that the strap fits around the top of the back of the head. Goggles should not be so tight that they leave red circles around the eyes. Such skin marks indicate that goggles are either too tight or are the wrong type. Many adults and some children have sensitive eyes and develop more confidence in their swimming when using goggles.

Hand Paddles

Hand paddles are sometimes worn during fitness or training workouts. Paddles help strengthen the shoulders, chest, and arms by increasing the resistance of strokes through the water. They are excellent for developing more power in a high bent-arm pull. Choose paddles that extend up to 2.5 centimetres around the hand and have a comfortable shape.

Do not overuse, since the increased resistance can strain shoulder muscles. "Aquafit gloves" are great, too, and tend to be more comfortable than paddles.

Hula Hoops

Hula hoops are large, thin hoops made of plastic. They are buoyant enough to float but cannot support any weight. Have participants swim through these hoops in games and drills.

Inner Tubes

Inner tubes are made from rubber and are very buoyant. They are excellent for practicing bent-arm pulls, especially with breaststroke. Larger tubes can support more than one student at a time.

Kickboards

A kickboard is usually made of a heavy styrofoam and is about 0.5 metre long. It is buoyant and can be used as a reaching assist. You can use a kickboard to support students when they're learning new strokes and drills, especially new kicks.

Don't let students rely on kickboards, however. As soon as students can float and glide on their own, they should be moving about without the aid of a buoyant object so that they develop their own strength and independence. When students do use a kickboard while moving, have them hold onto it with their hands only; they should NOT support their arms on the board or try to sit on it.

Mats

Mats made from styrofoam are very buoyant. Larger mats can support more than one student. Mats are excellent for simulating ice and water and for towing groups of students who are practicing their kicking. Parents also enjoy using mats when working with their infants.

Pace Clock

A pace clock is a large stopwatch used on the pool deck for timing swimming activities. The pace clock is not used to time students' swims because speed is not the goal of the Red Cross Water Safety program.

The pace clock can be used for organizing students for swimming in a loop. YOU can have your swimmers take off one at a time every 10 seconds. Students separate themselves enough in this way so that they don't run into one another. The clock frees you from having to tell each student when to start swimming.

Personal Flotation Devices (PFDs) or Life Jackets

All PFDs or life jackets must be approved. They must be a bright colour: red, orange, or yellow.

The benefit of the life jacket is its ability to turn an unconscious person from a face-down position in the water, allowing the person to breathe. To put a standard life jacket on, place the head through the keyhole, tie the neck ties, encircle the waist with the strap, and tie it at the front against the stomach (not against the life jacket itself).

PFDs are designed to keep a conscious person afloat but have less buoyancy and turning ability than life jackets. PFDs are designed for constant wear and help protect against hypothermia.

Both life jackets and PFDs can be used as simple support devices without being worn. However, when using them for simulated boat trips, be sure students wear them properly, and put them on before going into the simulated boat.

Pull Buoys

A pull buoy is usually made of two cylinders of styrofoam joined with a nylon cord or strap. Students can hold the buoy between the thighs or lower legs to keep the legs buoyant; this allows them to work on arm strokes without having to kick. With this support, students can learn new strokes, improve their arm action, and build upper body strength.

Sinking Toys

Sinking toys are usually made of rubber and may include certain toys and rubber rings. Sinking toys are excellent for experimenting with weight transfer and are useful for scavenger hunts. Sinking toys are good for games, but use them in a way that encourages students to practice skills, not just to fill time or have fun.

Water Safety Posters

This set of posters details information on diving, all six strokes, and water safety. They should be accurate pictures of "perfect" strokes and skills and are ideal for reinforcing your in-water demonstrations.

Swim Bars

Swim bars are like buoyant barbells. They are usually held in both hands for flotation and for keeping a student's balance during water walking or jogging. Students may also use them instead of holding onto the wall when kicking. Students should *not* sit on them.

Swimming Skills Video

This video gives a detailed analysis of all six strokes and proper diving. At sites where access to a VCR/TV is possible, the video is a nice accompanyment to in-water demonstrations and practice.

Appendix L
Cross-Contamination Guidelines

Policy Statement—
Rescue Breathing

As a result of the January 1986 decision of the Red Cross's Board of Director's meeting, the following statements related to Rescue Breathing are Society policy:

1. Direct contact, (human to human), is not required for participants practicing rescue breathing.
2. In all Canadian Red Cross Society courses (i) where Rescue Breathing is taught, it may be practiced using a mannequin, suitable device (ii) and/or a partner of the candidate's choice to demonstrate that the proper performance standard is met.

   The use of mannequins must be in accordance with acceptable medical procedures (iii).
3. In Red Cross Non-Certification courses candidates are required to demonstrate rescue breathing only up to but excluding contact and be able to describe how to make an effective seal and inflations.
4. In Red Cross Certification courses participants must demonstrate the complete rescue breathing sequence using a mannequin, a suitable device, or partner of the candidate's choice.
5. In all Red Cross courses in which participants maybe in direct contact with a mannequin, suitable device, or partner, instructors are required to inform participants in advance of the possibility of their contracting an infectius condition and that Red Cross is taking steps to reduce the possibility of a participant being infected.

January 1986

The Canadian Red Cross Society

Acquired Immunodeficiency Syndrome (AIDS)

July 14, 1989
Guidelines for First Aiders

1. FORWARD

   AIDS has caused concern for first aiders in two areas:

   a. when giving mouth-to-mouth resuscitation

   b. when dealing with someone who is bleeding

2. MOUTH-TO-MOUTH RESUSCIATION

   a. Mouth-to-mouth resuscitation has not been shown to transmit the AIDS virus. From a theoretical point of view, the only significant risk that could arise is when the casualty is bleeding from the mouth and the first aider has open mouth sores. In reality, however, the AIDS virus has not been shown to be transmitted when this is known to have occurred. Excessive concentration on the theoretical risks of AIDS transmission by mouth-to-mouth resuscitation may cause needless panic and lead to denial of care, both of which need to be prevented.

   b. Special devices for mouth-to-mouth resuscitation are not recommended for people who have taken an elementary first aid course. Use of rigid airways by untrained or inexperienced persons can cause bleeding to the casualty and actually increase the risk of contamination by the AIDS virus. Furthermore, people who have undertaken elementary first aid training rarely carry rigid airways and/or mouth guards at all times on the remote chance that they may need to resuscitate someone.

   c. Use of rigid airways, mouth guards, or similar equipment is only recommended for specialists who receive periodic training on their use as a job requirement and who carry these items with them at all times.

3. DEALING WITH SOMEONE WHO IS BLEEDING

   a. Blood should always be treated with respect. A number of infections, such as hepatitis B, may be passed on if blood is not handled carefully. AIDS does not require new procedures, but merely re-emphasizes the need for observing the good hygiene practices you have been taught.

b. Safe handling of blood in a first aid situation does not require special protective equipment or excessively high levels of protection. What is required is basic hygiene, a few precautions, and good common sense.

c. First aiders should realize that the AIDS virus is fragile. Once outside the body, it will not survive for long and is easily and quickly killed by heat, household soaps, bleach, or alcohol.

d. Unbroken skin provides a good barrier to prevent the AIDS virus from entering the body. The chance that the AIDS virus will enter the body through broken skin or through mucous membranes is slight. Studies of a large number of health-care workers indicate that even serious accidental exposure to infected blood rarely leads to transmission of the virus.

4. SPECIFIC RECOMMENDATIONS

a. Avoid direct contact. If possible, casualties who are bleeding should be encouraged to stop the bleeding themselves. Using the casualty's own hand, the first aider should show him or her how to apply direct pressure to the wound, using a clean cloth if available. If bleeding casualties are unable to help themselves (e.g., children, the elderly, the severely injured), etc., the first aider should stop the bleeding. If possible, use vinyl or latex gloves or some other barrier to avoid coming into direct contact with the blood.

b. As a matter of routine hygiene, cover your exposed cuts and grazes with a dressing, preferably one that is impervious to water. It is highly recommended that first aiders with open sores on their hands wear clean vinyl or latex gloves when treating casualties who are bleeding or have open wounds. If gloves are not available, try to avoid direct contact with blood. Be sure to change into clean gloves after treating each casualty and, if conditions permit, to wash your hands before and after using gloves.

c. Clean yourself and the casualty. After first aid care, wash yourself and affected areas on the casualty thoroughly with hot, soapy water. If blood splashes in the eyes or mouth, rinse immediately with lots of water. WASH YOUR HANDS.

d. Avoid cutting yourself when giving care. If you do get a cut, encourage the wound to bleed freely for a little while, then wash with soap (except around the eyes) and warm water. Apply antiseptic or alcohol and a dressing if possible.

e. Mop up pools of blood carefully. If blood spills occur, mop up the blood and dispose of the materials safely (i.e., in plastic bags or by burning or burying them). Avoid direct contact with the blood. Afterwards, treat the spill area with disinfectant or a bleach/water solution (i.e., mix one (1) part Javex (5.25% sodium hypochlorite solution) with nine (9) parts of cold water).

f. Wash clothes, linens, and instruments with soap and the hottest water available (above 70 degrees C) if they are stained with blood. There is no need to dispose of clothes or instruments as long as they are well washed. You should wash materials stained with other body fluids in the same way for general hygiene, although significant concentrations of the AIDS virus are only found in blood, semen, and vaginal secretions.

g. Don't try to guess who might be infected. People infected with the AIDS virus may look and feel well. Treat everyone with the same high standards of care, practice, and respect. Consistently high standards will also protect you and the casualties in your care against a number of other diseases.

Mannequin Decontamination

Mannequins must be decontaminated during use, as described in the following sections. Some of the newer mannequins have disposable plastic bags that protrude from the mouth and cover the mannequin's face. Others have individual mannequin faces that can be applied for each person's practice and removed after the person has practiced a skill. Use only models of mannequins that can be decontaminated after use according to the recommendations below.

Mannequin Decontamination Supplies

To decontaminate mannequins during use, you need a decontaminating solution and a large number of gauze pads. The recommended solution is 60 millilitres of liquid chlorine bleach per 5 litres of tap water. This solution should be made before each class and discarded after use. Do not use scented bleach, which contains perfume, because it may give a taste to the plastic.

Since some people find bleach objectionable, a 70% alcohol solution (isoproponal or ethanol) can be used as an alternative. Although alcohol kills many bacteria and viruses, there are some that it will not kill. However, if the mannequin's face is scrubbed vigorously with 70% alcohol and a clean gauze pad, it is highly unlikely that any infectious disease will be transmitted.

Mannequin Decontamination Procedure

During practice sessions the mannequin's entire face and the inside of its mouth must be cleaned after use by each learner. Demonstrate the following procedure, telling learners that they should use this procedure to clean after they use the mannequin.

1. Dry the mannequin's face with a clean 4" × 4" gauze pad.
2. Wet a second clean gauze pad with decontaminating solution.
3. Squeeze excess solution from the pad. Scrub the mannequin's face and the inside of its mouth vigorously with the soaked pad (being careful not to tear the mouth).
4. Place the wet pad over the mannequin's mouth and nose and wait 30 seconds.
5. Discard the pad and dry the mannequin's face with a third clean gauze pad.

Mannequin Decontamination After Class

As soon as possible after the end of each class session, all mannequins should be properly cleaned. In addition to the decontamination solution and gauze pads, you need a baby bottle brush, soap and water, basins or buckets, non-sterile disposable gloves, and any other supplies recommended by the mannequin manufacturer. Follow the manufacturer's recommendations for correct disassembly. Scrub the parts with warm, soapy water, rinse them, and decontaminate them with a solution of liquid household chlorine bleach and water (60 millilitres of bleach to 5 litres of water). Vigorous scrubbing with soap and water is as important as scrubbing with bleach. Wear disposable gloves while decontaminating mannequins. The mannequin's body, hair, and clothes should also be washing periodically to ensure that the mannequins are clean and attractive.

From CRCS: First Aid—The Vital Link Instructor Manual, July 14, 1989.

Appendix M
Lesson Plan Form

Name: _____   Time: _____

Location: _____   Lesson No. _____

Level: _____   Date: _____

Equipment:		
Strategy Cards:		
Time	**Progression**	**Formation**
Back-Up:		
End of Lesson Notes:		

Appendix N
Task Analysis

The individualized approach to instruction involves identifying student needs, abilities, and interests; developing an approach and altering when needed. However, some students require a more in-depth breakdown to learn certain skills. This requires a *task analysis.*

Task analysis is a process of instructing and recording learning. There are *three steps* in a task analysis.

1. *Identifying the components of a skill and breaking them into a progression.* For example, the components for instructing submersion and breath control are:
   a. Student practices blowing an object on land.
   b. Student practices blowing an object across the water surface.
   c. Student practices exhaling with face 15 cm from the water.
   d. Student practices exhaling with chin touching water.
   e. Student practices exhaling with mouth just underneath the surface, next mouth and nose just under the surface, and finally submerging the whole face.
   f. Student practices with face under the water, lifting face for a breath several times in a row.
   g. Students practices exhalation routine several times in a row using an upright bobbing position. Student can incorporate holding onto a floating object or the edge while maintaining their body position.

2. *Assessing the skill.* This involves determining what your student *can* do. Where in the progression steps for submersion and breath control are they? If Mohammed can exhale above the water surface, he now needs activities that practice exhaling with just his mouth in the water.

   An additional part of assessing the skill involves creating an objective for the student. An objective involves three things: description of the performance, description of the conditions, and description of the performance criteria. For example, Dion will swim 25 metres of front crawl (*performance*) at a Level 5 level (*performance criteria*) beginning in chest deep water at the water's edge (*conditions*).

3. *Instructing the components of the skill.* When instructing each skill component, there is a sequence to follow: You prepare a student for a skill; the student responds and performs; you provide feedback and reinforcement on the student's performance.

When preparing a student for a skill, you need to use a variety of *prompts*. A prompt is an instructional cue that can be of a high or a low degree. The lower the degree, the more independent your student is. Utimately you are moving toward a student who can perform skills independently. There are three types of prompts.

PROMPT	DEFINITION	HIGH DEGREE	LOW DEGREE
Physical prompts	You physically touch your student.	Manipulating student's arms through a full front crawl motion	Touching shoulder to remind students to roll to breathe
Visual prompts	You encourage your student to visually focus on a movement or sequence.	Demonstrating blowing bubbles	Using an exaggerated open mouth to remind student to blow bubbles
Verbal prompt	You use any kind of sound, word, or instruction	"1–2 Breathe, 1–2 Breathe"	"Breathe"

As you move down through the prompts, ensure that you always combine a verbal prompt with your physical and visual prompts. This will enable you to gradually reduce the physical and visual prompts, yet still have your student respond to a verbal prompt.

An example of how to structure a progression plan for your student would be...

| Student's Name: _____ | Date: _____ |

Instructor's Name: _____

Task Sequence	Phy.	Vis.	Verb.	None	Comments

Appendix O
Adult Learning Inventory Form

This questionnaire will help you and your Red Cross instructor tailor the AquaAdults program to meet your needs and interests. Please take a few moments to answer the questions and then give the completed form to your instructor. Be sure to talk to your instructor if you have any questions.

Motivation

Why did you register in the AquaAdults program? (Check all that apply.)

To learn to swim	( )	To overcome fear	( )
To swim better	( )	I/neighbours have a pool	( )
For exercise/fitness	( )	To be able to swim with my kids	( )
For water safety tips	( )	To learn how to react in a water emergency	( )

Other reasons/comments:

_____

_____

_____

Previous Water-Related Experience

Have you ever taken swimming lessons?   Yes ( )   No ( )

When? _____

Have you ever been involved in a water-related emergency? Please explain:

_____

_____

Do you have any first aid training (e.g., CPR)? _____

Please indicate the following:

Activity	I've done it!	I'd like to do it!
Canoeing	( )	( )
Kayaking	( )	( )
Sailing	( )	( )
Power Boating	( )	( )
Triathlons	( )	( )
Water Aerobics	( )	( )
Fishing (Ice fishing)	( )	( )
Snowmobiling	( )	( )
Skating	( )	( )

Other: _____

Swimming

Do you feel comfortable in deep water? Yes ( )   No ( )
Do you swim regularly? Yes ( )   No ( )
How often?_____
Which swimming strokes, if any, do you already know how to do? _____

Which swimming strokes would you like to learn/improve? Rate the strokes you have chosen so that your instructor will know where to start!

Front crawl	( )	Breaststroke	( )
Back crawl	( )	Sidestroke	( )
Elementary backstroke	( )	Butterfly	( )

Specific swimming goals/comments: _____

_____

_____

Water Safety

Learn how to PREPARE! STAY SAFE! & SURVIVE! in and around the water. Your instructor will teach you some basic water safety knowledge and skills. With the water safety modules you can learn more; ask your instructor or read the AquaAdults booklet for more information on these modules. Which of the four modules are you interested in (please rank your choices 1 to 4):

Boating Safety   ( )   Home Pool Safety   ( )
Ice Safety   ( )   Waterfront Safety   ( )
Specific safety information needs/interests:_____

_____

Comments and Questions

_____
_____
_____
_____

WELCOME TO AQUAADULTS!

NOTE: Do you have any medical conditions? Talk to your instructor. Your program site may ask you to complete a health information form.

Appendix P

Next Steps...
Becoming an Instructor Trainer

An Instructor Trainer is responsible for training, evaluating and supporting Water Safety Instructors. To become an Instructor Trainer, you must have the following *prerequisites:*

1. 18 years of age
2. A current Water Safety Instructor certification
3. A minimum of 2 years experience teaching the Red Cross Water Safety program
4. Completion of an application that includes:
   - Proof of prerequisites
   - Letter of interest explaining why you wish to advance to this level
   - Two references, with at least one from an employer

Candidates who meet the prerequisites will then go through a two-step training process. This involves a course and a practice teaching experience.

The Instructor Trainer Course

Successful applicants attend a *20 hour training course* that is run in two modules. There is a specific evaluation done throughout each module.

1. Facilitating: (12 hours) This module details the specifics of how to teach adults and older adolescents how to teach. This module is very generic and can apply to any program.
2. Water Safety Program: (8 hours) This module details the specifics of how to teach and evaluate the Red Cross Water Safety Instructor course.

The Practice Teaching Experience

Those who are successful in the training course will then take part in a practice teaching experience. The Instructor Trainer candidate assists an Instructor Trainer for one complete course.

- Candidate must teach at least half of wet and dry content sessions
- Candidate must participate in the evaluation of the candidates
- Candidate must attend one complete Water Safety Instructor course.

Using a given set of observable, performance criteria, the Instructor Trainer evaluates the Instructor Trainer candidate. The candidate has a maximum of two evaluated practice teaching opportunities over a two year period to demonstrate the required performance criteria.

A Master Instructor Trainer will monitor the candidate and, in consultation with the supervising Instructor Trainer, is responsible for recommending the candidate for certification.

The Red Cross Society is responsible for certification.

References

Adapted aquatics: promoting aquatic opportunities for all, 1989, The Canadian Red Cross Society.

Aquatic instructor manual for teaching parents and young children, 1987, The Canadian Red Cross Society.

British Columbia elementary school presentation on water safety manual, 1993, The Canadian Red Cross Society.

Drowning among recreational boaters in Canada, 1994, The Canadian Red Cross Society.

Drowning among 1 to 4 year-old children in Canada, 1994, The Canadian Red Cross Society.

Langendorfer SJ, Bruya LD: *Aquatic readiness: developing water competence in young children*, Champaign, 1995, Human Kinectics.

National drowning report, 1994, The Canadian Red Cross Society.

Safe boating guide, 1991, The Canadian Coast Guard.

Small craft safety instructor guide and reference, 1987, The Canadian Red Cross Society.

Swimming and water safety, 1995, The Canadian Red Cross Society.

The Canadian lifesaving manual, 1995, The Lifesaving Society.

The inclusion action pack: increasing active living opportunities for persons with a disability, 1995, Active Living Alliance for Canadians with a Disability.

The vital link, 1994, The Canadian Red Cross Society.

Video: *All ways welcome*, 1993, Ontario Ministry of Culture, Tourism and Recreation.

Video: *Home pool safety: it only takes a minute*, Washington DC, 1994, The American Red Cross Society.

Video: *Sudden impact*, Toronto, Forevergreen Television & Film Production.

Video: *Swimming skills*, 1995, The Canadian Red Cross Society.

Glossary

ABCs. Airway, Breathing, Circulation.

Airway obstruction. The blockage of the airway that prevents air from reaching a person's lungs. See also **partial blockage** and **complete blockage**.

Breaking waves. Waves that result when the peak of the wave starts to splash and foam. If caught in breaking waves, duck under the water and swim just below the foaming white water, where it is calm.

Complete blockage. A blockage of the airway in which the person is conscious or unconscious; is unable to breathe, speak, or cough; may have a bluish face; and may clutch at the throat with one or both hands (universal distress signal for choking).

Corrective method. A process of positive reinforcement designed to improve the skills and abilities of the participant.

Drift. A current that flows parallel to the beach between the shore and the sandbar. It is caused by the waves pushing water across the sandbar and onto the beach at an angle. Sometimes drifts are very strong. When swimming in surf, always glance at the shore, and be careful not to let the current drift you away from your point of entry. The drift could easily carry you into an obstruction such as a rock, protruding post, or even into a **rip**. If you are caught in a drift, don't swim against the current. Swim toward shore. You will eventually reach safety farther down the beach.

Emergency. A situation requiring immediate action (e.g., a sudden injury or illness).

Exhaustion. No longer having the energy to keep swimming or floating; can be prevented by resting often while you're swimming. Exhaustion can occur from cold water, from lying in the sun too long, from swimming when you're tired, or from swimming too long and too hard. Know your endurance limits. Stay safe by swimming distances parallel to the shore and in shallow water. If tired, perform a resting stroke.

Formation. How you and your class are positioned in the pool area. Using effective formations makes your classes safer and easier to control. They also allow you and participants to see and hear one another *all the time*.

Hollow waves. Waves that result from the peaks of a steep wave curling forward in advance of the main body of the wave. The tremendous force of water falling on you can drive your head and body into the sand, and the turbulent water will be full of air bubbles that will *not* support your body. Swimmers have broken their necks by diving into such waves.

Hydraulics. Whirlpools that happen as water flows over an object, causing a strong downward force that may trap a swimmer. The water surface may look calm and fool you because the hydraulic does not show from the surface. To avoid this hazard, don't swim near areas where the water drops off. If you are caught in hydraulic, don't fight it; instead, swim to the bottom, swim out with the current, and then reach the surface.

Hyperventilation. A dangerous technique some swimmers use to try to stay under water longer. By taking a series of deep breaths and forcefully exhaling, the level of carbon dioxide is reduced. This delays the time when the carbon dioxide level triggers the demand for the body to take a breath. This practice is risky because the level of carbon dioxide in the blood is what signals the body to take each breath. If students hyperventilate and then swim under water, they could pass out before their body knows it is time to breathe.

Hypothermia. A life-threatening condition in which the body's warming mechanism cannot maintain normal body temperature and the body cools. Exposure to cold (in water or air) causes the body to lose heat faster than it can produce It. Hypothermia is a lowered core body temperature, below 35 C. Signs of hypothermia are mild-to-severe shivering, bluish lip colour, sluggish speech, abnormal behaviour, poor coordination, slow breathing, stiff muscles, and unconsciousness. Death can occur.

Life jacket. A type of approved flotation device that can turn an unconscious victim onto the back from a front-float position.

Panic. A sudden and overwhelming terror. It occurs in most water accidents and can keep you from helping yourself or someone else. The more skilled you are and the more you know about water safety, the less likely you are to panic or react helplessly. Having a personal emergency plan is the best way to prevent panic.

Partial blockage. People with a partial airway blockage can often get enough air into the lungs to try to dislodge the object by coughing. They may also be able to speak. People with a partial blockage may emit high-pitched or wheezing sounds when trying to breathe in, may cough, or may clutch at their throat with one or both hands (universal distress signal for choking).

Rips. Currents that may be present whenever there are sandbars just off shore or slight depressions on the shoreline extending into the water. Rips are caused by large volumes of water, trapped between the shore and the sandbar, returning to sea through a channel between the sandbars. The higher the waves, the stronger the current. A strong rip can carry you away from the shore toward the channel. It starts very close to the beach and picks up speed as it approaches the channel but will disappear beyond the sandbars, depending on the height of the waves. Signs of rips include a streak of murky or dark water extending out to sea, a place outside sandbars where the waves don't form breakers of white caps and foam, and bits of wood or straw moving seaward toward the sandbar. If you get caught in this kind of current, swim parallel to shore until out of the current. Many people have become panicked, frightened, or exhausted trying to swim against the current toward shore. When you are out of the current, swim toward shore over the sandbars with the waves and away from the area in which the rip has formed.

River currents. These currents are often unpredictable and fast moving. They may change direction abruptly because of bottom changes. You might not see the current on the water surface, even though it may be strong below the surface. A current can slam you into an unseen object such as a rock. If you are being carried by a river current, roll over onto your back and go downstream feet first to avoid crashing headfirst into a rock or other obstacle. When you are out of the strongest part of the current, swim straight toward shore. Because of the current, you will actually move downstream at an angle toward the shore.

Rolling waves. Appear to be swells or steep waves, without white caps or foam at their peaks. If they are steep, you are advised to duck through the top.

Surf. The water's edge combination of ocean, waves, and currents. Surf conditions can change in minutes with changes in tide, wind, or the ocean bottom. Each affects the other, and they may combine to form drifts, undertows, or rips.

Tides. A rise and fall in the water level. Tides change about every 6 hours, and the rise and fall of the water level varies considerably from area to area. With a change of tides, there may be a radical change in surf and beach condition. A shirt in wind direction and speed will also cause changes. You may observe the following changes. A sandbar may appear, disappear, or change; rips may start, stop, or change their strength or positions; waves may change in size, strength, or direction.

Undertow (or runback). The return flow of water that has been thrown on the beach by waves. If the beach is short and steep, the undertow will be very strong. Sometimes a step-off or crevice will be present, which increases the undertow force. An undertow is intermittent: absent when the wave is rushing up the beach, strong after the wave breaks and flows back down to water. It does not pull you down under the water, but it may pull you toward deeper water. It often washes the sand or pebbles from beneath your feet, causing you to lose your balance and fall into the water. If you feel the force of the water tugging at your lower legs and feet, keep well balanced and work your way toward shore with the next incoming wave. If you have fallen into the water, paddle with your hands and kick your feet slowly, stay in a swimming position, and let the next incoming wave help you toward shore.

Waves. See **rolling waves**, **breaking waves**, and **hollow waves**. If you get caught in the turbulence of a large wave, relax in a curled or fetal position, hold your breath, and wait until the wave passes over you, releasing you to the surface. Don't panic! Conserve your breath! Wait!

Red Cross Zone Addresses and Telephone Numbers

Atlantic Zone
70 Lansdowne Avenue
Saint John, New Brunswick
E2L 3X3
Telephone: (506) 674-6132

Ontario Zone
5700 Cancross Court
Mississauga, Ontario
L5R 3E9
Telephone: 1-888-890-1997

Quebec Zone
6, Place du Commerce
Ile-des-Soeurs
Verdun, Quebec H3E 1P4
Telephone: 1-800-592-7649

Western Zone
1305-11 Avenue S.W.
Calgary, Alberta
T3C 3P6
Telephone: 1-888-307-7997

Canadian Red Cross
National Office
170 Metcalfe St. Suite 300
Ottawa, ON
K2P 2P2
Telephone: (613) 740-1900

VISIT OUR WEBSITE
www.redcross.ca